W9-DGS-528

Our Days Dwindle
Memories of My Childhood Days in Asante

T. E. Kyei

Edited with an introduction by Jean Allman

HEINEMANN
Portsmouth, NH

CABRINI COLLEGE LIBRARY
610 KING OF PRUSSIA ROAD
RADNOR, PA 19087

#44969106

Heinemann
A division of Reed Elsevier Inc.
361 Hanover Street
Portsmouth, NH 03801-3912
www.heinemann.com

©2001 by T. E. Kyei

All rights reserved. No part of this book may be reproduced in any form or by
any electronic or mechanical means, including information storage and retrieval systems,
without permission in writing from the publisher, except by a reviewer, who may quote brief
passages in a review.

ISBN 0–325–07042–3 (Heinemann cloth)
ISBN 0–325–00251–7 (Heinemann paper)

Library of Congress Cataloging in Publication Data

Kyei, T. E. (Thomas E.)
    Our days dwindle : memories of my childhood days in Asante / T.E. Kyei ; edited with
an introduction by Jean Allman.
        p.   cm.
    Includes bibliographical references and index.
    ISBN 0–325–07042–3 (alk. paper)— ISBN 0–325–00251–7 (pbk. : alk. paper)
    1. Kyei, T. E. (Thomas E.)—Childhood and youth.   2. Ashanti Region
(Ghana)—Biography.   3. Ashanti Region (Ghana)—Social life and customs.   I. Allman,
Jean Marie.   II. Title.
CT2508.K94 A3 2001
    966.7—dc21   00–063248
    [B]

British Library Cataloguing in Publication Data is available.

Paperback cover photo: Photo of T.E. Kyei courtesy of the author.

Printed in the United States of America on acid-free paper.

04 03 02 01 00 SB 1 2 3 4 5 6 7 8 9

To my children
and
my children's children

When I was a child, I used to talk like a child,
and think like a child, and argue like a child.

— St. Paul, 1 Corinthians 13:11

CONTENTS

A LIST OF MAPS AND FIGURES

EDITOR'S INTRODUCTION

Nyansa nyɛ sika na wɔakyekyere asie.
(Wisdom is not gold dust that it
should be tied up and put away.)

Nearly a decade ago, as part of a research project on gender and colonialism in the Asante region of Ghana, I was working through the papers of the eminent British anthropologist, Meyer Fortes, at Cambridge's Centre for African Studies. Fortes had been the leader of the three-person research team which undertook the "Ashanti Social Survey" in 1945-1946 under the auspices of the West African Institute. The bulk of the material collected by Fortes was then on deposit at the Centre. Because of Fortes' interest in marriage and family, the data seemed especially relevant to my own work.

As I shuffled through box after box of original material — questionnaires, household surveys, interviews — I kept coming across the name "Kyei." I was consistently struck by both the richness and the sheer volume of material this "T.E. Kyei" contributed, and yet his was not a name I could readily connect to published results of the Survey.[1] Thomas E. Kyei, I later learned, served as the "Principal Research Assistant" on the project. Yet the copious pages of field notes packed in those Cambridge boxes, as well as Kyei's lengthy typescript, "Some Notes on Marriage and Divorce among the Ashanti," attested to a central role not only in the collection of data, but

---

[1] See, for example, M. Fortes, "The Ashanti Social Survey: A Preliminary Report," *Rhodes-Livingstone Journal* 6 (1948), 1-37; "A Demographic Field Study in Ashanti," in F. Lorimer, ed., *Culture and Human Fertility* (Paris: UNESCO, 1954); and M. Fortes, R.W. Steel and P. Ady, "Ashanti Survey, 1945-1946: An Experiment in Social Research," *Geographical Journal* CX (1947), 149-79.

also in its intepretation. It was a role, it seemed to me, not particularly well-captured by the designation "field assistant."[2]

As a "research assistant," Kyei remained largely invisible to those scholars, like myself, only familiar with the published results of the "Ashanti Social Survey," despite the fact that much of what western scholars know of family, marriage and kinship in colonial Asante comes, directly or indirectly, from the painstaking, behind-the-published-scenes work of Kyei in the 1940s. Indeed, only recently has that invisibility begun to give way. In the early 1980s, Kyei revised his original 1946 "Notes on Marriage and Divorce," and in 1989 Cambridge's Centre for African Studies made the important commitment to publish the manuscript in their African Monograph series.[3]

It was in discussing that manuscript with the staff at Cambridge in 1991 that I learned Mr. T.E. Kyei, then in his early eighties, was living in Kumasi, the regional capital of Asante. I promised the staff I would give Kyei an update on the status of his manuscript when I arrived in Kumasi early in 1992. Little did I know how important that chance encounter with a name — "T.E. Kyei" — in a Cambridge archival box would end up being. Over the course of 1992, I had the privilege of meeting regularly with Kyei and of benefitting, as many others have, from his keen insight into Asante's twentieth century past. As mentor and colleague, he was endlessly patient with my constant questions — about changes in family life, about subtle shifts in Twi language use and meaning, and, of course, about the intricacies of marriage and divorce. Kyei was a teacher, colleague, mentor and friend. Thanks to his patience and generosity, I left Kumasi that year a much more learned student of Asante history, but also increasingly wary of the language with which western-trained scholars have come to describe their "field research

---

[2] See, for example, M. Fortes, *Kinship and the Social Order* (London: Routledge & Kegan Paul, 1970), 208. See, also, Fortes, "Kinship and Marriage among the Ashanti," in A.R. Radcliffe-Brown and Daryll Forde, *African Systems of Kinship and Marriage* (Oxford: International African Institute, 1970), 262.

[3] This rich, detailed monograph appeared in 1992. See T. E. Kyei, *Marriage and Divorce among the Asante: Study Undertaken in the Course of the Ashanti Social Survey (1945),* (Cambridge: African Studies Centre, Cambridge African Monographs 14, 1992).

experiences"[4] — a language through which teachers and mentors too often become "informants," and local historians — "oral sources."

Toward the end of my 1992 stay in Kumasi, Kyei shared with me his autobiographical work-in-progress, *Our Days Dwindle* — a four-volume, unpublished memoir which traces his life from early childhood (1910s) through Ghana's independence in 1957. He asked if I could offer any advice on getting some or all of the volumes published. My answer came quickly. Once I picked up the manuscript, I could not put it down. Having studied Asante history for nearly twenty years, I had read nothing that could rival Kyei's detailed and compelling account of daily life in rural Asante in the early decades of this century. I thus left Kumasi in 1992 intent on seeing *Our Days Dwindle* to print.

The process of preparing the manuscript for publication took much longer than either of us anticipated, and we had to adjust the final format based on concerns about length and marketability. *Our Days Dwindle: Memories of My Childhood Days in Asante* is thus a lightly edited version of the first volume of Kyei's original memoirs.[5] To have included all four volumes would have resulted in a rather unwieldly seven hundred page book. That said, my task as editor was extremely easy in some regards, and exceedingly difficult in others. On the one hand, the manuscript did not require extensive annotation, as is often the case with personal memoirs. On the other hand, if we were to get the manuscript down to a length that would make it accessible and affordable to as broad an audience as possible, then some cuts had to be made, and those editorial decisions were extremely difficult. I did not want to disturb the manuscript's integrity or make any changes that would shift the intended audience of the original manuscript. While some sections of the typescript have been cut and there has been copyediting throughout, the book is

---

[4] For recent, critical reflections on fieldwork and "field experiences," see the collection of essays in C.K. Adenaike and J. Vansina, eds., *In Pursuit of History: Fieldwork in Africa* (Portsmouth, NH: Heinemann, 1996).

[5] My hope is to publish a second book, based on volumes two and three of the original manuscript, in the near future.

faithful, in content and spirit, I believe, to the first volume of the memoir that was originally completed in 1983.[6]

Kyei put his reminiscences to paper over a decade ago for his children and his grandchildren. In much the same way that his mother and father and aunts and uncles imparted their life stories to him, Kyei wanted to share his life history with the younger generations of his family. And yet any reader of *Our Days Dwindle* will feel immediately and warmly welcomed to listen in to this wonderful telling of family life stories. Kyei vividly recaptures for his children and for the rest of us the world of early colonial Asante through a child's innocent and inquisitive eyes — a child born only a few years after Asante came under formal British colonial rule in 1901. His are everyday stories of people in his home town of Agogo: how they lived, what they ate, what they sang, what they wore, where they travelled and what they believed. The detail on social and material life in Kyei's memoirs is unparalleled in the scholarly literature on early colonial Asante, and the central narrative — Kyei's early life story — is as compelling as some of the very best Ghanaian historical fiction. That Kyei is able to accomplish this, while embracing such a diverse audience, may be, in no small part, due to his long experience as a teacher and to his background in ethnography, which not only included work on the "Ashanti Social Survey" but also training in social anthropology at Oxford. Though he writes from the position of a "cultural insider," he is, at the same time, able to look at his world through the eyes of an ethnographer, to intuit the questions of an outsider, and then weave answers seamlessly into his narrative. T.E. Kyei, in short, is a consummate cultural translator.

Recently, social and religious historians have begun to recognize and to write extensively on the important role of African catechists and "cultural middlemen" in the expansion of Christianity on the continent.[7] They have convincingly

---

[6] I owe special debts of gratitude to Anna Vinegrad and Lynn Zelem for extensive assistance with copyediting and preparation of the camera-ready copy.

[7] The examples are too many to list here, but most recently, see L. Sanneh, *Encountering the West: Christianity and the Global Cultural Process: The African Dimension* (Maryknoll, NY: Orbis, 1993); P. Landau, *The Realm of the Word: Language, Gender, and Christianity in a Southern African Kingdom* (Portsmouth, NH: Heinemann, 1996); J.D.Y. Peel, "For Who Hath Despised the Day of Small Things:

demonstrated that Christianity was spread through African initiative, largely on African terms. Very few scholars, however, have reflected on the similar roles played by cultural translators like Kyei and the ways in which they have actively shaped the contours and content of the ethnographic and historiographical record on Africa, particularly as it has developed in Europe and North America. Yet whether his name appears in indexes to secondary sources or not, Kyei's work on marriage and divorce has been absolutely critical to scholarly understandings of kinship in twentieth century Asante. His memoirs should have a similar impact on the social history of colonial Asante. They should also challenge scholars, particularly western-trained scholars, to rethink the ways in which they have categorized "sources." For example, the emphasis social historians have placed on African voices and oral traditions/histories and the concommitant categorization of historical sources into "primary" and "secondary" renders African autobiographical texts, like Kyei's, invisible: they slip through the crack between primary (oral "voices") and secondary (historical scholarship in the western tradition). Kyei's autobiography should force scholars to rethink the rigidity, if not the very existence, of these categories.

T.E. Kyei joined his ancestors in *Asamando* on the 5th of December 1999, shortly after his ninety-first birthday. He remained active — physically and intellectually — throughout those last months. Indeed, his close proofreading of the second-to-last draft of this manuscript caught elusive typos I had missed on several rereadings. With *Our Days Dwindle*, T.E. Kyei has given to his children, grandchildren, great-grandchildren, and those yet unborn, one of the most precious gifts one can give in Asante — a family history, a remembered past. For the rest of us, he has opened a private window onto Asante's rich and complex history and allowed us the privilege of looking and listening and understanding.

Missionary Narratives and Historical Anthopology," *Comparative Studies in Society and History* 37 (1995), 581-607; D. Peterson and J. Allman, "Africans Meeting Missionaries: Special Issue," *Journal of Religious History* 23:1 (1999), especially contributions by D. Peterson, P. Landau and B. Moss; and T. Spear and I.N. Kimambo, ed., *East African Expressions of Christianity* (Oxford: James Currey, 1999).

PROLOGUE

The Seven Ages of Man

All the world's a stage
And all the men and women merely players:
They have their exits and their entrances;
And one man in his time plays many parts,
His acts being seven ages. At first the infant,
Mewling and puking in the nurse's arms.
And then the whining school-boy, with his satchel,
And shining morning face, creeping like snail
Unwillingly to school. And then the lover,
Sighing like furnace, with a woeful ballad
Made to his mistress' eyebrow. Then a soldier,
Full of strange oaths, and bearded like a pard,
Jealous in honour, sudden and quick in quarrel,
Seeking the bubble reputation
Even in the cannon's mouth. And then the justice,
In fair round belly with good capon lin'd,
With eyes severe, and beard of formal cut,
Full of wise saws and modern instances;
And so he plays his part. The sixth age shifts
Into the lean and slipper'd pantaloon,
With spectacles on nose and pouch on side,
His youthful hose well sav'd, a work too wide
For his shrunk shank; and his big manly voice,
Turning again toward childish treble, pipes
And whistles in his sound. Last scene of all
That ends this strange eventful history,
Is second childishness and mere oblivion,
Sans teeth, sans eyes, sans taste, sans everything.

— William Shakespeare
As You Like It, Act 2, Scene 7

PREFACE

Our days dwindle under your wrath
our lives are in a breath
— our life lasts for seventy year,
eighty with good health
but they add up to anxiety and trouble
ever in a trice, and then we are gone
—*Jerusalem Bible, Psalm 90*

The proverbial life span of three score years and ten has been reached and passed. Much water, as they say, has run under the bridge. The flow, many a time, has been slow, smooth and pleasant. On several occasions it has been fast, boisterous, whirl-pooling and near-dangerous. In sum, it has been a worthwhile existence and I should have every reason to be thankful to my Maker for my being sent to the world and born in Asante in the unique period covering nearly three-quarters of the eventful twentieth century. I should be thankful too for the opportunity offered me to make some humble contribution to the education and other social development and progress in the country, particularly during the exciting forties, fifties and sixties of this century.

The divine injunction on procreation has been fully and faithfully discharged. I have played my part in the perpetuation of the human species. To my children and all who come into being through my genes I leave in the pages that follow a sketchy account of my life. Hereditary flaws traceable in their lives may be blamed on me, their progenitor. If my struggles and endeavors, on the other hand, could be a source of inspiration or encouragement to any of them to better life, a purpose of my sojourn on this earth would have been happily fulfilled. Serenely would I then, on my exit, bow in the words of Lord Alfred Tennyson's King Arthur:

I have lived my life,
And that which I have done,
May He within Himself make pure.

I owe to some dear people a great debt of gratitude for their inspiration, guidance, encouragement and help given in several ways. To my own parents in particular, I am grateful for the heavy all-round sacrifice they made toward my up-keep and up-bringing. To Mother, Hannah Akua Agyei, for her industry and resourcefulness, her "no-nonsense" way of dealing with my childhood and manhood lapses, and, above all, for her deep motherly love, care and affection. To Father, Papa Kwabena Nkɛtea (Kwabena Yamoa), for his inimitable matter-of-fact approach to problems, his perseverance, tolerance, complete self-respect and clear sense of perception which blended to build around him an aura of gentle, amiable disposition.

I have to thank the late Fred Irvine (later, Professor Irvine) of Edinburgh University, my College tutor who, as far back as 1928, the last year of my teacher-training course, when I accompanied him in one of his early field and plant collecting trips to places in the Agogo section of the Afram Plains, put into my mind, through earnest exhortation, the idea of writing at some appropriate time of my life, an account of my reminiscences. To the late Professor Meyer Fortes of Cambridge University, I am indebted for widening the vista of the memory of my rich Asante heritage, during my secondment, as Principal Research Assistant, to the 1945/46 Ashanti Social Survey of which he was the Director. The encouragement received from the eminent Social Anthropologist in the course of our friendship which lasted until his demise in 1982, inspired the effort to put into print some of the essential information concerning my lineage, the Agogo Asona *Abusua*, which hitherto, has been passed from generation to generation from memory. I am grateful to the elderly members of my *Abusua* (lineage) men and women, now dead or living, particularly to my "Uncle" Kofi Donko (Thomas Bonsu), the Akyeamehene of Agogo, for their open-heartedness, their patience and tolerance in telling me candidly all that I asked about my ancestry.

Among several other helpers, I have to thank my friend, M.M. McLeod of the Ethnography Department of the British Museum in particular, for the invaluable assistance given in solving some of the many intricate and time-consuming problems involved in the publication of the Memoir. My greatest thanks go to Professor Jean Allman for her untiring efforts to have this memoir published

Here and there in the text, week-day birth-names and the initial letters only of proper names of some persons have been given. This is on the grounds of expediency. I plead that no statement, remark, observation or comment has been made in the Memoir with malice. My sincere apology therefore goes to those to whom anything unwittingly said might be considered hurtful or harmful.

T.E. Kyei
Kumasi, 1995

Map 1

A Map of the Gold Coast, 1927

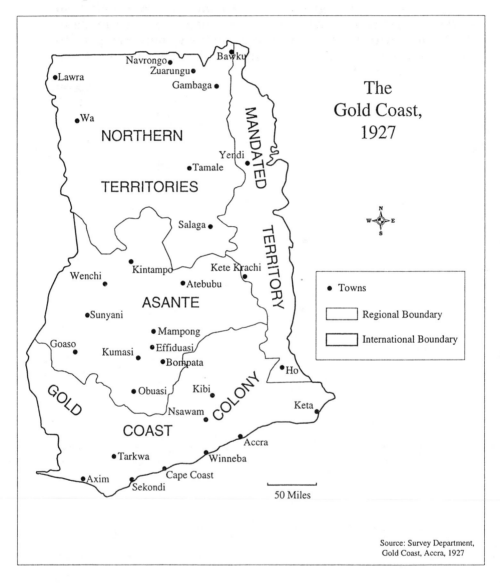

Map 2

A Map of Asante, 1927

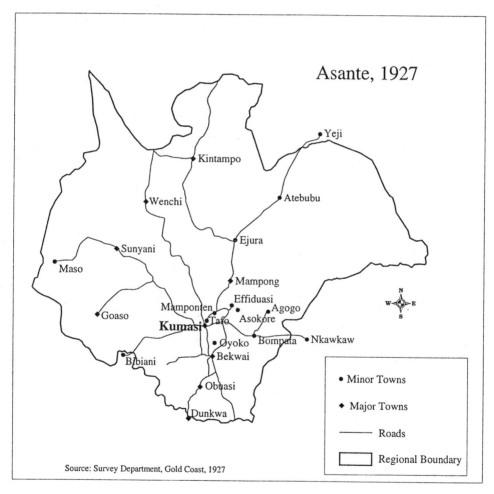

Asante, 1927

Yeji

Kintampo

Wenchi

Atebubu

Ejura

Sunyani

Maso

Mampong

Effiduasi

Mamponten

Agogo

Goaso

Tafo

Asokore

Kumasi

Oyoko

Bompata

Nkawkaw

Bibiani

Bekwai

Obuasi

Dunkwa

- • Minor Towns
- ◆ Major Towns
- ——— Roads
- ☐ Regional Boundary

Source: Survey Department, Gold Coast, 1927

—1—

A STRANGER HOME FROM SEKYERE-KWAAMAN

It was a bright sunny day in a dry season of the year. This is the farthest my memory can go in the vivid recollection of some of my childhood days' events. I was sitting on the bank of a stream. By my side, my infant brother, Kwabena, was lying on a mat spread in the shade of a big tree. The stream ran close by the town and it was in it that the women of Sekyere-Kwaaman did their washing. Among a group of them there that day was my mother. In the stream itself were children of my age playing. Some of them were diving; others were running and chasing or throwing splashes of water one against the other. I could not join them in the stream as I was confined on the bank to keep watch over my little sleeping brother and to drive away *tse-tse* flies (*ahuruhɛ*) which attempted to steal a bite at him. When little Kwabena awoke and started to cry, Mother came and took him on her lap to feed him. Thus released, I ran to join some of my mates at butterfly catching. The prized ones among the swarm whose habitat was the neighbourhood of the stream, were large, brilliant poly-coloured flies such as the glorious and magnificent Swallow Tails (*Drurya antimachus*).

Washed cloths, clothes and blankets were spread to dry on the open spaces on both banks of the stream. Washing dry, Mother collected all her pieces and folded them into two bundles. I was given the lighter one to carry and walked in front of her back home. My father was busy packing our belongings when we reached home. All day the next day was occupied in packing and on some preparation for what betrayed an imminent long journey. Utensils were scrubbed clean; the almost bare room was swept neatly and some take-away food was prepared. In the evening Parents were away on a round of good-bye saying to their friends.

Early the following morning familiar faces — friends of my parents — men and women, called at the house. Some came with pots of palm-wine which were consumed in a sad mood after a libation for a safe-journey had been poured by an eloquent elder. We left Kwaaman, the town of my first childhood recollections, and, with it, the playmates of my early years. Quite a number of the friends followed to see us off on the bank of the stream where three days earlier Mother had done her last washing. After repeated rounds of hand shakes when several eyes were filled with uncontrollable tears, we parted — they, back to Kwaaman, and we, forward to Agogo, a town whose name I had often heard in parents' conversations as yɛ'kurom (our home town). Our journey was by foot and along a narrow path overgrown in places with weeds. I walked between Mother who was leading and Father who followed, both carrying on their heads a load each of our belongings. Mother, in addition, carried Kwabena on her back. Our destination that day, I was told, was another town called Kumawu.

I recollect that after covering some long distance we arrived at a river whose name was given as Onwam. We unloaded on its bank for a short rest and a quick meal. Before we continued the journey, Father sought and cut from a nearby bush a stick the length of which he measured to his own height. A notch was marked on it at a point exactly the same distance from the ground to his navel. With the stick held ahead in his fully stretched right hand, he proceeded cautiously, step by step, to take a sounding of the river at the point of crossing. Standing gazing at Father's exploits I saw him cross to the other bank, the depth at the deepest part having been thus ascertained as below his navel level. He re-crossed and came back to us, telling Mother assuringly, "Yɛbetumi atwa" ("We can safely cross it").

A shuttle of crossings followed, altogether six more journeys from bank to bank were made by him. I was the first to be ferried. Sitting astride on his shoulders, I clutched firmly at his head and was carried to the other bank where I was lowered gently to the firm ground. He waded back to the other bank, carried Mother's load on his head, took hold of her right hand and led. She followed rather tremulously. With Kwabena on her back and a supporting stick held in the left hand, they joined me at my side of the bank. The fourth and last shuttle was completed when he crossed to us bringing his own head load.

We reached Kumawu. Our hostess was a matrilineal kinswoman of Father's, married to a Kumawu man. Both she and her husband received us warmly. It was in their house that evening that I had the first taste of deep affection to be manifested to me at Agogo. My *Sewaa* (Father's "sister") arranged for a big cockerel to be killed to prepare a nice meal in my honour: "*Munkum akɔkɔ nyɛ akoko-nkwan maa Yaw.*" ("Kill a chicken to prepare a nice soup for Yaw.")

After an early morning breakfast we continued our journey the following day to Bɔdɔmase where we stopped for the second night. Tired and travel-worn, I slept soundly soon after our arrival and, except for a short break in my sleep for a bath and a bite, saw or heard not much of what took place that evening at Kumawu Bɔdɔmase. The third day of our journey was a day of great expectation. We were reaching Agogo, my home-town, the place I had so often heard mentioned as "*yɛ'kurom*" that evening.

The first few miles from Bɔdɔmase took us to Abedimsabi, the last Kumawu village on our way. Luck was with us that last day of our journey home. A young couple, also natives of Agogo returning home, became our travelling companions. The wife's head load was light and the husband carried nothing (*ɔnam nsansa*). They were therefore both in a position to give us needed help. She relieved Mother all the way of the burden of carrying Kwabena, except when he had to be fed. The young husband took full charge of me. Where the footpath went through a stretch of boggy mire and on difficult patches, he carried me straddled on his strong, muscular shoulders. The path to Agogo cut through a dense forest. Starting from the very outskirts of that removed Abedimsabi village, competing foliage of tall trees formed a thick canopy through which the sun's rays pierced in places, throwing silvery grey lights on giant trunks.

As the physical body entered the impenetrable forest, the mind roamed wildly in the realms of fantasy and the many stories I had heard told at our *anansesɛm* (story) telling nights at Kwaaman became realities. I imagined things. The small Abedimsabi village we had just passed was Ananse-kurom wherein dwelt the wily, guileful, worldly-wise Kwaku Ananse and his family:

- Aso Adwoa, the beloved middle-aged wife, comforter and confidante,
- Ntikuma, the eldest son and a "chip off the old block,"
- Afu-Dotwe-Dotwe, the second son and the blue-eyed boy of the family,
- Nyiwa-Nkronhywea, the third son and a problem child,
- Ti-Konon-konon, *kaa-kyire*, the last born, and precocious child of Eno Aso Adwoa.

The shade tree (*gyedua*) I saw standing in the village centre was no other than the particular one which the wiseacre Kwaku attempted to climb to hide on its top a calabash in which he had stored all the wisdom painstakingly gathered from every corner of the world. In my imagination I could clearly see Kwaku, bathed thick in sweat, struggling in vain to climb the tree with the Calabash of Wisdom fastened securely on his generously large abdomen. I could see with my mind's eye his son, Ntikuma, standing arms akimbo and looking on askance and in strange surprise at the silliness of his father's undertaking. I could hear him suggesting to his Old Man if it would not have been wiser had the calabash been carried on his back for a quicker and unimpeded climb. I imagined I saw the crestfallen Father Kwaku acting half-heartedly on the youngster's advice as I was leaving behind the small village. And there it was! That big hole in a mound on my right was the very one which Agya-a Ananse, the compassionate Father Kwaku, one day in a long period of acute food shortage plaguing all in the land, braced himself to enter in desperation.

"Come, what may," he grimly determined, "Life or Death (*Owue a, ewu . . . nkwa a, nkwa*), through thick and thin, high above and down below, food must be got to feed the famishing family." I followed Ananse to that somber Nether-township wherein dwelt not a soul but a sole, decrepit, ugly old woman. I imagined I heard Kwaku's bold challenge: "*Kuro Mumu, Mumu, Mumu, anomaa nni mu?*" ("Hideous, horrible, desolate city, is no one, not even a bird in here?"). I could hear the faint response from the weak, feeble voice of the lone Granny who lived in the place, "*Anomaa wo mu a, na εyε O-O!*" ("Befitting ought it be, had a bird herein been!"). Still roaming in imagination, I could see Sasabonsam, the Forest Monster, sitting gleefully on the top of a tall tree doing legs tricks: Shortening and lengthening them alternately, simultaneously and telescopically. Yes, there they were, I could surely see them! The stout twines around the big tree trunks not far away were those bewitching legs. And there was no doubt about it. I could hear this eerie heart-scourging laugh: "*Hee-e-e-e-e-e-e-Ha-ha, ha-ha, ha-ha!*" A shrill cry was heard breaking the depressing silence of the dim forest: "*Koko, koko, koko, kyin-kyin-kyin-kyin-kyin-kyin-koko!*"

"Kokokyinaka," said Father abruptly, laconically, as if in anticipation of a question from me. "Aha! Yes, THAT is Kokokyinaka, the She-Bird!" I said to myself delightedly. I had not forgotten that nice story our jovial story-teller once told us at Kwaaman about Kokokyinaka, the Bird. I liked it. It said:

Once upon a time (*da bi*), a devastating, "white" famine (*ɔkom fufuo*) raged throughout the whole of Animal Land (*mmoadoma-kurom*), killing a large number, almost all, of its inhabitants. Colonies of beasts were exterminated; flocks of birds succumbed; shoals of fish perished; congregations of reptiles were wiped out; flies and insects, fleas and bugs, worms and crustaceans vanished in swarms, and clusters of crabs died on dry sands of river beds.

The She-bird had not a thing to give to her fledgling young ones to eat, not even a morsel of grain. They were all going to die, too. She had to think hard. She worked out a clever plan fast. She hopped from house to house to undertake *kokonte* meal-kneading jobs for a reward of wee-bit portions which she carried swiftly to feed the dying children. And because she was so frequently away from home whoever called to see her was told, "*Ɔkokyin aka.*"("She's gone round a-kneading.") Hence Kokokyinaka replaced the provident Mother-bird's proper name which was not completely forgotten.

That cry of the caring *Kokokyinaka* Mother-bird was to me a summons to all Birds and Beasts of the Kingdom of the Wild to meet their King at a Durbar to be held under the big tree standing yonder. I anticipated meeting any moment the King of the Deep Silent Forest (*Kwae Bibirem Hene*), sitting majestically in his palanquin with a large retinue, preceded by dwarfs (*mmoatia*) whose heels pointed forward and toes backward, as they rambled, duck-like, in the forest. I started to ponder the response I should give if His Majesty greeted me when I met him. Should I address him "Papa Ɔsebɔ" (Leopard), or should it be "Agya Etwie?" Then I remembered. When the Kwaamanhene once passed by our house and greeted Mother she responded politely: "*Ya-a-a Nana!*" So it must be, the proper address for the King of the Forest must be "*Ya-a-a, Nana Kurotwiamansa!*" (Much obliged, Grandfather Leopard).

"But, wouldn't the King eat me up?" I wondered, puzzled. Physical ears strained to hear from afar the deep frightening cry of the King: "*Kuro...wim! Kuro...wim!! Kuro...wim!!!*" to strike terror into the hearts of his subjects and to silence all living things in his silent domain. I turned my head here and there, to the left and to the right. Mother, following closely behind my benefactor on whose shoulders I then sat astride, saw my head movements and, wondering what the matter might be with me, asked worriedly: "*Yaw, wotwitwa woani kru, kru, kru, apɛ deɛbɛn?*" ("Yaw, what are you looking for turning your head here and there?") The interruption brought my mind back from the deep state of imagination to the realm of realities — into the land of the Humans. We plodded on to Agogo.

Soon we saw a colony of monkeys on top of some trees quite close to the footpath. They were in their element: swinging freely from bough to bough; eating fruits or peering inquisitively down to steal a look at the wayfarers walking erect on their two feet on their bushy track on land below them. Father, anticipating a question, said, "*ɔkwakuo,*" pointing to a big one shouting mockingly, "*Woahu! Woahu?*" ("Have you seen it?"). Another one of the species hanging on the nearest branch, he called "*boapeawa.*" "That one far away there is ɛfoɔ," he said as he halted to give me a clear view of a jet-black monkey sitting at ease on top of a very high branch, suckling her baby. I was delighted to see ɛfoɔ in the flesh and alive, for I had taken a fancy to an *ɛfoɔ*-skin (ɛ*fo-nwoma*) which Father placed at the foot of his bed.

We plodded on to Agogo and reached an *asoɛ-yɛ* (rest-stop) which was a clearing near a spring equipped with propped sticks for unloading, and with some wood logs on which to sit and rest. We stopped there for a while and had a meal. "One more stop, Yaw, and we should be in Agogo," said Father to me soothingly. Refreshed, we resumed our journey, passed through Amoakonsuo hunting camp, crossed the Asɔ Stream and reached Ɔboakyi, the first Agogo village at the other end of the Kumawu-Agogo forest. We entered Nana Ampoma's cottage and unloaded. Our host was Mother's father's younger brother and so she, of course, called him simply *Agya*, without adding any other name. He was away plucking cocoa on his farm which was not far but was quite close to the cottage. Mother followed him there to greet him.

Nana Ampoma's cottage at Ɔboakyi contained three separately placed mud and wattle built huts, roofed with raffia palm leaves (*daha*). Floors were hard switch-beaten, dressed neatly with reddish-brown ochre clay (*ntwoma*). An unroofed *wawa* tree-bark enclosure served as a bath-place. A small pit latrine, some fifty yards away and screened by a growth of some stunted thicket, completed the bare structural needs of the humble farm dwelling place.

In no time Nana Ampoma had returned home bringing with him a pot of foaming fresh palm-wine to welcome his son-in-law(*ase*). A little shorter than my father, Nana Ampoma was a small-built, hardy, smart man with greying hair. Father was served with a drinking calabash (*sa-koraa*) after Nana had taken the first helping of the drink. I was allowed a sip after a few drops had been poured on the ground for the Departed Souls of the relatives of the two men. I enjoyed the sip and licked my mouth dry. Father did full justice to the welcome drink and drained two calabashes leisurely. Splashing the dredges of the last one to the ground, he exclaimed jovially, "*Kuse!*" *Amaneɛ* (the purpose/reason for a call/visit) followed.

After a meal which was hurriedly prepared for us by Nana Abunyawa, Nana Ampoma's industrious wife, we left on the last lap of our journey to Agogo. The road from Ɔboakyi to Agogo followed a gradual incline terminating on the Pemfen stream. From there it ran along the watershed of Aboabo, one of the two sources of Agogo town water supply, and a tributary of Pemfen. A short distance from Pemfen we saw three young women (*mmabaawa*) running excitedly to meet us. News of our arrival had reached home and those happy-looking, comely maidens had been sent to meet us and help relieve us of our head loads. We reached home — Agogo.

Our house[1] was in Salem, the then Basel Mission quarter of the town. It was symmetrically designed and simply constructed almost wholly with local materials. The walls were built with swish (*ɔfapem*) about ten feet high, roofed with shingles (*nsenyerɛ*) prepared from the *ɔtweneboa* tree, plastered and lime-washed inside and outside and completed with a coating of coaltar about two feet high from the floor level. Rooms opened into a spacious, rectangular yard of about thirty feet wide and fifty long, partitioned with *odwuma* boards. Each section of the compound house had a roofed

---

[1] See Figure 2, p. 9.

Figure 1
A Ground Floor Plan of Our House in Salem, Agogo, in 1914

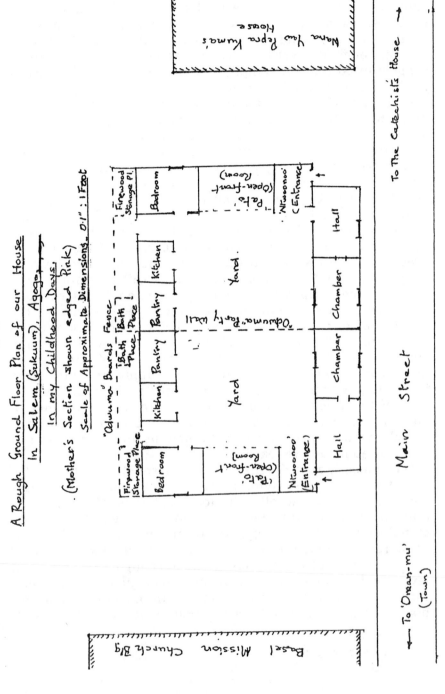

A Rough Ground Floor Plan of our House in Salem (Sukuum), Agogo, in my Childhood Days.

(Mother's Section shown edged Pink)

Scale of Approximate Dimensions, 0.1" : 1 Foot

Figure 2
A Sketch Plan of the Agogo Town Lay-out in about 1914, Showing *Aborɔnoo* (Quarters)

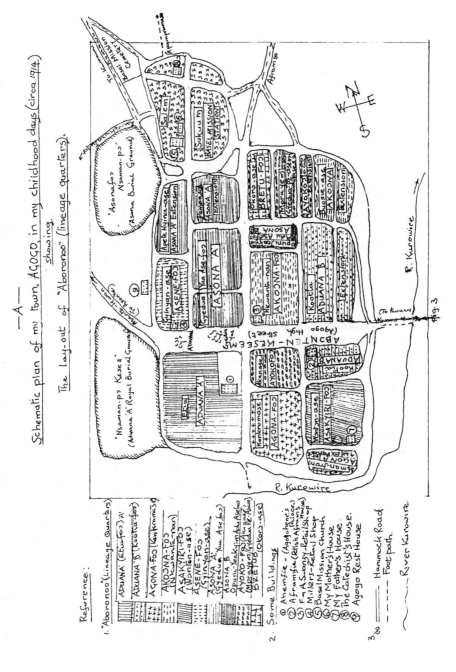

—A—

Schematic plan of my town, AGOGO in my childhood days (circa 1914)

showing

The lay-out of "Aborɔnoo" (lineage quarters).

Reference:

1. "Aborɔnoo"(Lineage Quarters)
   - ADUANA (Etuo-foɔ) A
   - ADUANA B (Koolta-fɔɔ)
   - AGONA-foɔ (Kontromɔɔ)
   - AKOONA-foɔ (Nkwanta-man)
   - ASAKYIRI-foɔ (Wonlan-ase)
   - ASENE-foɔ (Kyin-yan-ase)
   - ASONA A (Gyedua Yua Ase-fɔɔ)
   - ASONA B
   - Opuni-Jenkyima/Asaka
   - AYOKO-foɔ (Nkyean-kura)
   - BRETUO (Okɔrɔ-ase)

2. Some Buildings
   - ① Ahemfie – (Agogohyene's)
   - ② Aframfie (Kesh Afram's Palace)
   - ③ F. A Swanzy-Retail Shop
   - ④ Millers-Retail Shop
   - ⑤ Basel Mission Church
   - ⑥ My Mother's House
   - ⑦ My Father's House.
   - ⑧ The Catechist's House.
   - ⑨ Agogo Rest House.

3. ══ Hammock Road
   - - - - Footpath.
   ～～ River Kurowire

entrance (*ntwoonoo*), an apartment or a sitting-room and a bedroom along the main street from town (*ɔman-mu*), with a kitchen and a spacious store-room. Adjacent to the entrance was an all-purpose room (*pato*) with the sides to the yard open. Behind the kitchen and store-room wing was *atuntuma*, an open yard with a bath-place and space for firewood stacking and for other odds and ends.

The living rooms were reasonably spacious and sensibly ventilated. The bedroom had two wooden windows each of which was about three feet high and two feet wide, one opening into the main street and the other one, facing it, into the yard. The sitting-room had one window of the same size and it also opened into the main street with the entrance door opposite to it. I learned later that the house originally belonged to two brothers who were members of the first Christian community, but when they back-slid it was, in accordance with the then canon of the church, forfeited. One section of the house was assigned to my mother and the other to the wife of one of the brothers who persisted in her faith.

It was in the open-front room, the *pato*, that we were given our first round of welcome. Having been seated therein, my mother's mother, Nana Yaa Kwaane, offered Father a pot of the customary palm-wine (*akwanso-sa*). As part of the formalities. Nana enquired: "Aah, Kwabena, *ɛha deɛ,deɛ yegu ara ni, na ɔkwan so?*" ("Well, Kwabena, you have come to meet us as you see us now, but what is it that has brought you here?") Briefly my father replied and said something to this effect:

All the motherly messages you have been sending to me reached me. I wish, in the first place, to thank you for your kindness and concern for my welfare and well-being. Akua and I have come back home for good to undertake cocoa farming, as you have been consistently advising us to do. We have come prepared to work the land you have had reserved for us at Apampramasu. We are ready to start bush clearing as soon as I have settled one or two matters. I am in no doubt that you will help us establish ourselves at home. I have not much to say at the moment other than to express to you, my good Mother, my sincere thanks for your wise and motherly advice.

Nana's response was long and windy, She started narrating all that had taken place from the time the couple left Agogo some years back; relatives who had died since the time they departed and went abroad, and, in some cases, the causes of their death and funeral obsequies; relatives appointed to take their guns (in the case of men) or their hoes (in case of women) — *ad nauseam.*

Then she came to the point which, I could sense, interested Father keenly: the rush of able-bodied young men as well as women of Agogo to cultivate large cocoa farms resulting in a large-scale scramble for available virgin forest land in all localities. She gave some description of the land she had set aside for him: its approximate size, promising fertility, yield prospect as well as the neighbours with whom he would share common boundaries. She concluded by tactfully urging her son-in-law to end his long wanderings abroad so that he could stay at home and concentrate on cocoa farming which was, in her view, a sure way of safe-guarding his own future and the future of his wife and children. She assured Father that she would fulfill her promise to give him all possible assistance in his new venture. More handshakes with repetition of *Akwaaba* followed.

The innermost "family" gathering thus ended with the parents retiring for a brief period of preliminary unpacking. Meantime, my mother had arranged for messages to be sent ahead to advise a few of her elderly relatives of our arrival and a visit which was to be expected. I had by that time become fairly familiar with formalities followed on the occasion of visits and the pattern they took, namely:

Nkyia
> Visitors entering a house shook hands with all inmates they met there, both old and young. I noticed that only the right hand was used, never the left.

Adwa-too
> Hosts provided seats for visitors in a convenient part of the yard or in the open-front *pato* room.

Akwaaba
> Host/hostess and adult inmates of the house returned greeting with handshakes, after which they took their seats often in a semi-circular form, where convenient, facing the visitors.

Akwanso-sa
> Host/hostess offered a pot of palm-wine to the callers/visitors through the male leading member of the guests.

Ahataye-yie

First helping of the drink was served in a drinking calabash to the giver of the *akwanso-sa* (drink offered to welcome a visitor or visitors).

Nsa-hye

Serving of the drink, starting with the leading male visitor, the visitors, both men and women, and to all other persons present, except children, who might be allowed a sip or two from a kindly grown-up. *Asee*, the last pour, was served to the guest or the leader of the callers.

Aseda

"Thank You for the drink" by visitors, done often with handshakes.

Amaneɛ-bɔ

Reason/purpose for the visit, given by the leading member of the visitors or one of them asked to speak on behalf of the leader.

Efie-amaneɛ-bɔ

Response, narrating pertinent relevant news, comments or reply to points made in the *Amaneɛ-bɔ*.

Akwan-sre

Leave-taking by visitor, generally ending with final handshakes.

We were not long in getting ourselves properly prepared for our first formal visits to our closest relatives. They included Nana Kwaku Pepra Panin (Mother's father in Salem) and Nana Yaw Nkroma (Mother's grand-uncle, also in Salem). Then we crossed the boundary between Salem and the Town to the house of what I later came to know very well as that of our *Ofie-Panin*, (the Head of our "House"). It was situated in the *Apetenyinase Borɔnoo*,[2] which was accorded the most moving welcome. Already seated as we arrived were most of the elderly close relatives of Mother's.[3] Those I recollect present that evening included:

- Nana Kwadwo Bofoo (Nkansa), our *Ofie-Panin*, Mother's uncle.
- Nana Panin Afua Adem (Gyaa), Mother's mother's mother.

---

[2] See Figure 2, p. 9
[3] See Appendix 3.

- Nana Akua Adwapa, Mother's mother's mother's sister.
- Nana Yaa Kuma, Mother's mother's sister.
- Nana Adwoa Bruku, Mother's mother's sister.
- Nana Kwabena Atɔbra, Mother's mother's brother.
- Wɔfa Osei Yaw Panin, Mother's mother's sister's son.
- Eno Ama Ataa, Nana Yaa Kuma's daughter.

Present in the house were also some young men and women I cannot very well remember.

Formalities completed, Nana Panin Afua Adem (Gyaa) who, since our arrival at the house, had kept me seated on her lap even at my age, looked affectionately in my face making me feel not a little embarrassed. Moving her body in sharp turns to the left and then right, and in a mood of infectious delight, the old grandmother spoke with a drawl and addressed me:

Ee-e-e, Adanse Kyei Yeboa,
Wo ni!
Ɔkɔkɔɔ Nana Yaw,
Wo ni?
Akwaaba!
Akwaaba!!!
Akwaaba!!!"

(Hi, Kyei Yeboa of Adanse,
Nice to see you.
Grandson of "Gold," i.e. a wealthy man,
Glad to see you,
You are welcome.
You are welcome.)

Spitting little drops of saliva on top of my head, she continued:

Mihyira wo kosɛ, kosɛ, kosɛ!
Nyin fromfrom,
Nyin kyɛ, na bɛwo ba to me!

(I bless you from the depths of my heart
Grow in health,
Grow to full maturity to beget a child to be named after me.)

The formal meeting of my people to welcome me, in particular, ended when it was almost dark. Parents therefore decided to postpone their visit to Father's relatives to the following day. Father continued alone to greet his uncle,

Opanin Daatano. As we were leaving our family house, I overheard several complimentary remarks: "*Wankyɛre nyin. Akua, aye adeɛ.*" ("He has grown fast. Congratulations to Akua.")

As I held my mother's hand on our way back to Salem, I had a proud feeling. I was in my own place, among my *abusuafo* (lineage members) in my home-town. It was a moment of elation that might have been as lofty as, if not loftier than, the mood in which Sir Walter Scott was when he penned:

> Breathes there the man, with soul so dead,
> Who never to himself hath said,
> This is my own, my native land!
> Whose heart hath ne'er within him burned,
> As home his footsteps he hath turned
> From wandering on a foreign strand?
> If such there breathe, go, mark him well;
> For him no Minstrel raptures swell;
> High though his titles, proud his name,
> Boundless his wealth as wish can claim;
> Despite those titles, power, and pelf,
> The wretch, concentrated all in self,
> Living, shall forfeit fair renown,
> And, doubly dying, shall go down
> To the vile dust, from whence he sprung,
> Unwept, unhonour'd and unsung.

> — *The Lay of the Last Minstrel*, Canto vi, st. 1

Some time later on our way to the farm, Mother explained to me the reason for the rapturous reception I received from my *abusuafo*, and confided to me how and why it all happened. The gist of the story, as far as I can recollect, was as follows:

Papa Nkɛtea, as Mother affectionately called Father, was the only son of Enɔ Ama Nkoso[4] Agogo Ɔsakyirini (a member of the Agogo Asakyiri lineage). She died, a few months after the birth of her child, under some circumstance which, to the ears of the modern twentieth-century man, would sound strange. The infant boy was left in the charge of Nana Ya Akwiankwaa, his mother's younger and only sister.

When he grew into manhood, Papa Nkɛtea teamed up with a group of young men (*mmeranteɛ*) of his age and went rubber-tapping (*amae-mmɔ*) in Bono (Brong). When in Bono area far away from home, he heard of job opportunities opened nearer home at Obuasi in

---

[4]   See Appendix 2.

Asante in the mines of the Ashanti Gold Fields Corporation. Wasting no time, the young man went to Obuasi where, without any difficulty, he found work as a sub-contractor for the supply of firewood to the mines. Frugal, he was able to save some substantial amount with which he purchased a sewing-machine and learned to cut and sew dresses for both men and women.

Brass band playing was by then a craze in most towns in Asante, but particularly in the Sɛkyerɛ area. Groups of bandsmen in the area vied with each other, not only in the blowing of instruments, but also in the imaginativeness of their uniform. Good tailors were in great demand and their services were handsomely paid. It was in such a situation that Papa Nkɛtea returned to Agogo in search of a spouse.

She was an Ɔsonani, some of whose members she was closely related to (she reminded me) and we had met in her Uncle Kwadwo Bɔfoɔ's house the day we returned from Kwaaman. I had by then known that Nana Kwaane was my mother's mother and that Nana married Nana Kwaku Pepra, my mother's father, but I did not know that they had born six children of whom Mother was the second child.

Agya was one of the people from Agogo who went to Abetifi to negotiate with the Basel Missionaries there for a church to be established in Agogo. When they succeeded, he became one of the first presbyters and, eventually, the Senior Presbyter of the Agogo church at the time we returned from Kwaaman.

The first catechist to open the church and a school at Agogo was Tikya Owusu. She was one of the first children to be baptized in the Basel Mission church at Agogo and was given to Tikya Owusu as his housemaid (*abaawa*). On Tikya Owusu's transfer from Agogo, the maidservant went with him to Akropong where she remained till she came of age when she was brought home to Agogo to be married.

It was then that it happened. The *aberanteɛ* tapper-woodcutter-turned-tailor, Kwabena, chanced to spy Akua and found, "She can cook. She can bake. She can do all sorts of things." But unlike the lass of the song, Akua was not "too young to be taken for a Mammy." They agreed to marry and they did marry in the proper customary ways. She was an *ababaawa* (virgin) of charm and extraordinary femininity, and he, an *aberanteɛ* (young man), vigorous and with all manly attributes. With their meeting, pregnancy was taken as a matter of course, a natural development, and was expected instantaneously, as it often was the case. But alas, in the case of Kwabena and Akua, that was not to be! Despite trying as hard as they could, pregnancy delayed and delayed and delayed. Anxiety grew and suspicion became rife as to what might be wrong with one or the other of the couple.

"Was she barren, if not, was he impotent?" Tongues wagged. Insinuations went their fast rounds. A situation was being reached when some unpleasant decision was expected to be taken by the wife's "family" to force a dissolution of the marriage on the ground of childlessness. The husband and wife, under these circumstances, decided to seek help from someone somewhere. At Ɔboanim near Sɛkyerɛ Gyamaase, at that time, lived a herbalist reputed to be a specialist traditional gynaecologist-cum-paediatrician. Kwaku Boaten was his name. And so to Kwaku went Kwabena and Akua. They met Kwaku at home at Ɔboanim. That man, Mother described, was an ordinary middle-aged person. There was about him no pretension: no fetish, no juju, no talismans; no paraphernalia of a fetish priest and, above all, he was not a greedy cheat.

She and her husband were received in the herbalist's plain room. His wife sat by suckling her infant child. On hearing their *amaneɛ* (the purpose of the visit) Kwaku, without any fuss or bragging, put his left hand on the wife's bared stomach and the right hand on the husband's, waited for a while and told them in a most casual manner and quite confidently: "*Anuanom, biribiara nni mo mu biara ho.*" ("Brother and sister, there is nothing wrong with any one of you.") Turning to the husband he assured him suavely, "*Wo yere bɛwo.*" ("Your wife will bear a child.")

The herbalist undertook to handle their problem and promised to do all he could to help, provided the couple co-operated. The co-operation that he needed, he explained, was quite simple and so it might not be easy to give. All that he would instruct was to be followed strictly; every medicine he would give was to be prepared and applied as he would direct. Asked about his fee, the herbalist said he would charge nothing but an *ntoaseɛ* (down payment to a medicine-man before treatment was started), of *doma-fa* (3s. 6d.). Of his own volition the husband was to promise and keep to himself before he went to bed with his wife that night, the *aboadeɛ* (pledge upon successful treatment) he would wish to offer on the birth of the child. He stressed firmly, however, that whatever was voluntarily pledged was to be redeemed promptly and faithfully.

Finally, Kwaku Boaten requested that on the day that the child was born, he was to be formally informed with a cock, if it was a boy, or a hen, if a girl. Mother recollected that all she saw about the man, Kwaku Boaten, was too ordinary and all that she heard, too simple to believe. She wondered if they had not gone all the way to Oboanim to waste time. She however pulled herself up. They had given their word to co-operate and would do just that, the simplicity or the ordinariness of the situation as she saw it notwithstanding.

They went home. The course of treatment was started immediately. That evening their patron sent to them the two packets containing some herbs wrapped in *anwonomoo* leaves. Instructions for preparation and application were:

First Treatment: Contents in the smaller packet (leaves and some herbs) *posa* (grind the leaves) in the palms in cold water in a calabash. Strain. Add *hyire* (refined white clay) and drink before going to bed.

Second Treatment: Contents of the bigger packet, also some leaves *yam* (grind on a stone). Add pepper called *ntonkom*. Strain. *Fa kɔsa* (apply as enema) once daily in the morning before meals for seven days.

Third Treatment: On the eighth day the patron brought with him another packet containing some herbs and a piece of a bark of a tree. Preparation — *noa* (boil) together all the contents of the packet with seven palm nuts. Pound and prepare for *abɛ-duro* (medicinal palm soup). Add any meat except *ɔkɔtɔ* (crab), *nwa* (snail), *bɔmɔnee* (stinking salted fish). Eat the soup with *fufu* ball prepared with seven fingers of small size plantain (*apem*).

Mother recollected that she was assured that, after that third treatment, *ɔrenkɔ afikyire bio* (she would not go to the "backyard," meaning to menstruate again). It came true. To her unbelievable surprise, she continued her narration, her period which had, until then, been very regular, ceased. On the fortieth day she went to report to her patron as instructed. That same evening Boaten brought with him to her a wrapped packet containing three assorted herbs — two fresh and green, the third, dry.

Fourth Treatment: Preparation and application: *Noa* (boil) all the contents in the packet with *mmɛ-dwoa mmiensa ahoroo mmiensa* (three palm nuts times three). Pound the lot together and use the water in which they were boiled to make *abɛ-duro* (medicinal palm soup). The soup is to be eaten with *fufu* balls of *apem*. Use for the soup the head of *okusie* (a big type of rat) caught alive. *Mfa okusie a wawuo anase afidie ayi no nyɛ nkwan no.*" (Never use the head of an already dead or trapped *okusie* in the preparation of the soup).

Papa Nkɛtea organized a strong *okusie* hunting party the following morning and, in no time, an *adueku* (*okusie*) had been caught alive. It was a male. Its head was severed and used in the preparation of the soup.

Fifth Treatment: Also some herbs and leaves used for *abɛduro*, was a prophylactic against *asram* (a children's disease affecting the cranium, then endemic in parts of Ashanti).

Sixth Treatment: That was for safe delivery and was given in the ninth month of the pregnancy.

And the time came. Early on a Thursday morning the long wished-for child was born. It was a male. Labour, handled expertly by an elderly woman traditional midwifery specialist, was easy and delivery, safe. Kwaku Boaten was informed. He went at once to see the *ɔbaatan* (mother) and the new arrival, carrying under his armpit a small cloth bag from which he picked a small *dufa,* a dark-brown pill, the size of about the thumb, prepared from the bark of some trees, pounded and moulded into a conical shape and dried in the sun. The herbalist scraped the *dufa* in fresh juice of lime squeezed on a grinding stone. The stuff was cleared from the stone with his right index finger and rubbed gently on the tongue and throat of the newly born baby. The full course of treatment was completed on the third day after delivery with *nteteɛ* (vaccination of the child against convulsion) and was performed as follows: from his cloth bag Kwaku Boaten picked a *mmɔtɔ-toa,* a small calabash pot containing some black medicinal powder, called *mmɔtɔ.* A little of the *mmɔtɔ* was worked into fresh lime juice squeezed on a grinding stone. With a small, cleanly sharpened knife, Boaten made sets of three small light cuts on the forehead between the eyelashes, on the nape, and on all joints both left and right on the body, namely: the shoulders, the elbows, the wrists, the lower end of the vertebral column, the knee and the feet. The preparation of the black powder in lime juice was then pressed into each set of cuts with the index finger of the right hand, starting systematically from the head to the foot. At the end of the operation, Papa Nkɛtea inquired about *akyiwadeɛ* (avoidance). Kwaku Boaten thanked him for the reminder and said: "*Okyiri nkamfoɔ* [5] *okyiri odompo. Onni bi da.*" ("A species of yam called *nkamfoɔ* and the flesh of an animal called *dompo* are the child's taboo. He should never eat of any of them in his life.")

On Thursday that followed the arrival of the child the proud, jubilant father named him "Kyei," after his own father, Kyei Kofi,[6] one time *Kyidomhene* of Agogo and an influential member of the then Agogohene's Council of Elders. Nana Kyei Kofi's father, I was told, was the Chief of Ankaase, called Yamoa Pɔnkɔ,[7] a man of considerable influence and affluence in the Kwabre area of Asante in his time. Yamoa Pɔnkɔ was said to be so rich that he hung gold nuggets on the boughs of an orange tree standing in front of his palace. In consequence he had the following horn chant in his *abɔn* (appellation):

Afrifa Yamoa Pɔnkɔ,
Merebɛkɔ mekurom Ankaase
Daamerɛ ankaa gyedua so mpɔ

Asuo Kyirade fa nnipa
Yamoa Pɔnkɔ Baafoɔ karii sika
Mprendwan mmienu guu mu

---

[5] See Appendix 4.
[6] See Appendix 2.
[7] See Appendix 2.

Kakyereɛ asue no sɔ:
Ɔmfa n'aseni biara da.

(Afrifa Yamoa Pɔnkɔ,
I shall be going into my town, Ankaase,
Wherein citrus orange shade tree grows gold nuggets.
River Kyirade drowns men.
Yamoa Pɔnkɔ Baafoɔ, the Noble,
Weighed and dropped into it gold worth twice eight pounds,
Instructing the river not to drown any of his descendants.)

Mother at that stage drew my attention back to the meeting
of our family on the day we returned from Kwaaman. When
Nana Panin Afua Adem addressed me saying,"*Ɔkɔkɔɔ Nana
Yaw*" ("The grandson of Red, i.e. Gold"), she referred to the
riches of my great-grandfather, Yamoa Pɔnkɔ of Ankaase. The
narration on my coming into being, which I had listened to
with interest and rapt attention, ended just as we reached the
farm at Apampramasu. I was left to mind the fire just set at
ahyehyɛ-yɛ (a cleared area for packing foodstuffs and other
farm produce to be head-loaded home), while she engaged
herself in clearing a site to dig some cocoyams.

—2—

THE TOWN I GREW UP IN

As days went by, my circle of playmates widened. Through our own games, and while running errands, I got to know the principal places of my new surroundings. The town of Agogo, I recollect, had two major quarters. The small one, comprising only about thirty compound houses, was Salem or Sukuum, as it was popularly known. In that quarter dwelt members of the Basel Mission Christian community. By far the larger part of Agogo was the Ɔman-mu, the Town, where the bulk of the people lived who continued to observe their traditions and customs rigidly and upheld their religious beliefs faithfully. Houses in the town (Ɔman-mu) were built in contiguous quarters called aborɔnoo,[1] most of which were named after trees planted for a ritual purpose or, simply, as a shade tree. It was in the borɔnoo that members of a particular lineage (abusua) generally lived together in a community. The principle aborɔnoo, as I knew them, were:

Atowaa-ase
   In that borɔnoo dwelt the ruling Section "A" (Adehyeɛ) of the Aduanafoɔ. It was also known as "Etia" ("End of Town").

Gyedua-yaa-ase
   It was the original Asonafoɔ borɔnoo. In the course of time, it extended to Apetenyinase where, because it lay on a slightly elevated ground, it was also called "Pampaso".

---

[1] See Figure 2, p. 9.

Konkormase

The people who planted a *konkroma* shade tree and lived in the area were the Agonafoɔ.

Kurotia

("The other end of the town.") It was the *borɔnoo* of Section "B" of *Aduanafoɔ* who owned the Fetish Afram. The other name of the quarter was therefore, Afram-Tia.

Akan-ase

It was the *borɔnoo* of *Ayokofoɔ*. Later, a section of the people moved to a new site which earned two names: Gyedua-Pɛ-Asɛm and Mprayɛm.The new site of the extended *Ayokofoɔ* was called Mprayɛm because, it was said that one Ampoma who lived in the *borɔnoo* forced any person who fouled the place to sweep (*pra*) the whole area clean. Consequently, the place was referred to as "Mprayɛm" ("the Place of Sweeping"). In the same quarter stood a shade tree, *gyedua*. It was such a restful place that many a young man went to sit under it for an evening chat, but was enticed to do something wrong which always landed him in some trouble. The shade tree, therefore, earned the name "*Gyedua-Pɛ-Asɛm*" ("The Trouble-Monger Shade Tree").

Wɔntɔn-ase

The *Asakyirifoɔ* planted a *ɔwɔnton* tree for their *abusua* area. They were, therefore, referred to as "*Wɔntɔn-ase-foɔ*."

Gyinyaase-foɔ

The Asene people first settled under a *gyinyan* tree and were referred to as "*Gyinyan-ase-foɔ*."

Nkwanta-nan

The meeting place of four roads. That was the *borɔnoo* of the *Akoɔnafoɔ* of Agogo. As their numbers increased, a section of the *abusua* moved and settled at a new site under an *akɔnkɔreɛ* tree which had already been named after one Buosie. The new Akoɔna quarter was therefore called "Buosie-Asefoɔ."

Ɔkɔrase

The Bretuo people lived under an *okoro* tree and their quarter was therefore called "Okoro-Ase," and the people referred to as "*Okorase-foɔ*."

Abɔten-tia-ase

The land given to the Basel missionaries for their church in Agogo was full of palm-trees (*abɔten-tia*). The early Agogo Christians who were popularly called "*Sukuum-foɔ*," were at times referred to as "*Abɔtentia-ase-foɔ*."

A place name often heard in Agogo in those days, which has continued to be heard up to now, was "Dɛntɛ-boɔ," a cave lying roughly west of the town, with a rock-face forming a grey-brown background to the town. A legend about the cave has it that it was, for some time, the dwelling place of a fetish called "Dɛntɛ," who immigrated from somewhere in Akuapem to settle in Agogo as the guest of Akogya, the fetish of the Agogo town. It was said that both the host and his guest lived together very cordially. They played together, ate together and did a lot of things together in a very brotherly manner. They shaved one another, too. One day, in the process of shaving his host's head, beard and armpit, Dɛntɛ cut the tongue of his host, Akogya. That cruel action of Dɛntɛ so angered Akogya that he was compelled to eject his guest, who flew away to Krakye in the east, and settled there permanently. That, it was said, accounted for the impediment in Akogya's speech, making his talks, transmuted through his priest, sound like that of a shortened-tongue person.

For some time now the cave, Dɛntɛboɔ, has been a place of attraction to many interested visitors to Agogo. The pity is that most of the relics said to have been left behind by the fleeing Dɛntɛ have been filched away, leaving only the "immovable properties" of the ungrateful guest, such as, what was said to be, the wives' bath-place and the *ɔware* game-board carved on a flat stone where the august fetish played with his beloved wives.

Compared with the other places in those days, Agogo was a well laid-out town. A main street called "*Abɔnten-kɛseɛ*," ran through it, dividing it into two almost equal sections. Leading into the *Abɔnten-kesee*, roughly north-west, was the then footpath called "*Asante-kwan*," which led to Kumasi and other places in Asante. At the end of it, south-eastward, started the *Kwawu-kwan*, which led to Kwawu and other places on the coast. The footpath crossed the Kurowire stream, lying about a quarter of a mile from the last building of the town. On the left and right of the *Abɔnten-Kɛseɛ*, minor streets branched into all parts of the town. Those minor streets had no particular names.

The principal buildings in *Ɔman-mu* included the *Ahemfie* (the Chief's house) and the houses of the major fetishes

(*Abonsom-Fie*), such as *Afram-fie, Anɔkye-fie, Tanɔ-fie, Ɔdomankama-fie.* Of importance, too, were the various *abusua-fie* (houses of heads of the various lineages) in which were kept Black Stools (*Apunnwa* or *Nkonnwa Tuntum*). Then there was a small, solitary building called "*Kokoado*," which was the resthouse of *Komisa* (the Commissioner). Its other name was *Oburonii-fie.* In Salem (*Sukuum*) were, of course, the church building (asɔ*redan*) and the catechist's house (*tikya-fie*).

On the town's outskirts in various places were the burial grounds. As in life, where the *abusuafo* lived together in a *borɔnoo* (quarter), so in death, the members of a lineage were interred on common burial grounds called *Nsamam-pɔ* (Ghosts' grove). I have a vivid recollection of the grove of my lineage (*Asonafoɔ Nsamam-pɔ*). It was in a thick forest, a virgin forest, lying opposite an open space in front of the Basel Mission church building, and on the left of the footpath that led from the town to the Aboabo stream and thence to Kumawu.   Our *Nsamam-pɔ* was in close proximity to Apetenyinase, a part of the Asona quarter of the town (*Asonafoɔ borɔnoo*). *Nsamampɔ-kɛseɛ*, the burial ground for the deceased members of Section "A", the royal Aduana lineage, lay in proximity to the Etia *borɔnoo*, on the left along the Asantekwan. Burial grounds for the other lineages (*mmusua*) were similarly sited near their living quarters (*mmorɔnoo*). The Christian community also had a separate cemetery which they called *Amusie-yɛ.*

The town had two sources of water supply: Aboabo and Kurowire streams. Aboabo was a spring of clean, clear water, cool and refreshing. It never dried in the *harmattan* season, however severe it might rage. The water collected just at the entrance where it bubbled out from underneath a solid rock. Water at that point could, therefore, not be dipped, but had to be collected, calabash by calabash, into a receptacle which was then carried back home on the head a distance of about a mile away. Kurowire, on the other hand, was a running stream but not quite so pure. It swelled swiftly in the rainy season, but became very shallow and had stagnant pools in places during the dry season. It lay west of the town and ran in the south-easterly direction towards the Afram plains within which it became a tributary of the Onwam river It was not considered a source of pure water and was mainly used for laundry, washing and other household purposes rather than for drinking. A very small and quite insignificant spring ran south-east of the town into the Kurowire, a short distance away. It was rarely used except in times of acute water shortage. The spring was called *Siaw-akuraam*, after one Siaw, the founder of the cottage which stood on its bank.

The main occupation of the majority of the people of Agogo at the time of our return from Kwaaman was farming — food crop and cash crop farming. Food crop farming was a woman's occupation, but a husband had to assist the wife to clear (*dɔ*) the bush and fell (*bu*) big trees growing in the cleared area. Food crop farms were on secondary or fallow lands (*mfofoa*) which lay not far away from the town, hence the name *mfikyi-fuo* (a farm on the outskirts of the town). A woman generally farmed more than one *mfikyi-fuo*. My grandmother, Nana Kwaane, had four such farms situated in four different parts of the town. We, her grandchildren, used to accompany her to Nkwantam on the Agogo-Hwidiem road (then a footpath) to a site which is the present football field of the Presbyterian Training College; Atwomamanso, which was off the then Agogo-Kumawu footpath; and Kusibo and Ɔboase. In the latter *mfikyi-fuo*, Nana grew some upland rice, the first rice farm I saw.

Nana, in addition to popular crops such as plantains, cocoyams, beans, yams, maize and tomatoes, grew some other crops which are rare in Agogo, namely, pumpkins (*ɛferɛ*), *kooko*, and *atwibo*. The latter was a species of cocoyam whose stalk instead of tubers, was boiled and eaten. One other crop she grew up with but which is now very rare, is *akam*, a climber which bore aerial potato-like tubers. Crops in our grandmother's *mfikyi-fuo* were grown for the pot, not for sale. There were, however, occasions when some food items she could not grow were needed. Salt was one such item. When such a need arose, we, the children, were sent out to barter some of the produce she grew for the needed item. We went about the town carrying stuffs such as garden-eggs, pepper or plantains in a large, flat wooden plate called *apampaa*, crying aloud, advertising: "*Kosua mua, mua, bɔrɔdee/nuadewa /amako, ni-e-e!*"("For barter, an egg-a-lot plantain/garden-eggs/pepper.")

Cocoa was the main cash crop then, mostly grown by men in virgin forests some distance away from the town. Enterprising women, particularly those elderly and unattached ones, made their own cocoa farms alongside the men. My grandmother had her own farm at Apampramasu where an area adjacent to it was reserved for Father. Nana Pepra, my mother's father, had a cocoa farm at Bepɔso, fertile land lying in a valley at the other side of an escarpment behind the present-day Agogo Saviour Church quarter. I learned later that the farm was one of the first cocoa farms in Agogo. As my mother had already told me, Nana Pepra was one of the pioneers who negotiated with the Basel missionaries in Abetifi, Kwawu, for a church to be established at Agogo. Through that connection, a few cocoa seeds were obtained by the first elders of the Agogo church from the missionaries and were planted in the town. As prospects for the financial potential of the crop grew brighter, both Christians and non-Christians of Agogo embarked on the serious cultivation of cocoa as a cash crop.

It was then the practice that members of an *abusua* farmed separately on a particular locality. My *abusuafoɔ*, the *Asonafoɔ*, for instance, owned farmlands lying east of the town and, in the course of years, expanded eastward, deeper and deeper into the forest. And so it was that at the time my father returned from his wanderings and settled to farm, the *Asonafoɔ* farms were congregated on a locality about two miles away in the vicinity of a stream called Apampramasu, hence the name of all farms in the area.

The practice then, as now, was that a farmer constructed, in a convenient spot close to his/her farm, a cottage of one or two, sometimes three huts as the need required. It was there that he/she stayed for a duration to work full time, making a day return-trip to town, once in a while, to buy a few necessary items such as salt, kerosene, tobacco and occasionally, smoked herrings (*ɛman*). With cottages scattered about and in such close proximity, life in the Apampramasu farming area was not lonesome. On the contrary, it was kept lively with reciprocal visits after work and on days when no serious farming work was done. It was often the practice that all members of a cottage went a-visiting, moving from one cottage to the other, for a chat, for an indoor game, or, in the case of grown-ups, to discuss some important family matters. Such rounds were called *nkuraa-tɛpa*, which we, the children, enjoyed immensely. Reciprocal services were rendered between members of the cottage community. By some mutual agreement, one family might work one day on another's farm, say, on bush-clearing (*adɔ*), tree-felling (*abuo*) or seedling-planting (*atɔdwe*), such service to be reciprocated on another day. The system was called *nnɔ-boa*.

Cocoa pod splitting day (*kookoo-bɔ da*) was a grand occasion of reciprocal service, when almost all farmers in the neighbourhood went to help a fellow farmer to split his/her heaped cocoa pods for fermenting. Early in the morning of a kookoo-bɔ day, men, women and children — all in a cottage — proceeded to a specially prepared spot on the farm for the splitting of the beans (kookoo-abɔyɛ). There they met to work communally. All sat around the heaped mountain of cocoa pods. The men folk did the splitting of the pods with cutlasses (machetes) while women and children did the scooping of the beans from pods into baskets. The contents of filled baskets were emptied into a shallow pit lined with fresh plantain or banana leaves. When all pods had been split, the heap was covered with more plantain/banana leaves and left for about five or six days to ferment.

Kookoo-bɔ day was a pleasurable occasion of work and eating. Palatable dishes were prepared to serve the visiting helpers, and all had enough to eat their fill. The food that I enjoyed most was boiled plantain served with nkontomire and corned beef stew. I recollect that about six days after our Apampramasu neighbours had helped split Nana's cocoa pods, the heap was uncovered and the steaming, fermented beans were carried in baskets to the cottage. They were spread to sun-dry on palm branch mats called asrɛnɛ which were supported by a long platform (apa), about three feet wide, raised about three feet from the ground. When satisfactorily dry, the beans were stored in some large baskets called nkɛntɛnku. A few days later, by some arrangement, someone I heard called Bruka (Broker) arrived at our cottage to buy the dry cocoa beans from my grandmother. Father worked with the broker on behalf of my grandmother. A portable weighing scale (nsɛnia), the broker's stock-in-trade, which he brought with him, was suspended on a stout beam of the hut. Into a cloth bag hung on the scale, basketfuls of the dry beans were poured. I stood by and watched the weighing operations. The thing called nsɛnia fascinated me most, particularly a small thing on it which moved down and down as the beans were poured into the bag held on it. As the pointer reached down to a marked point, I heard Father's sudden cry, "Piren! Aso! Aso!" ("One load! It's just right, just right!") The number of "loads" (sixty pound weight) weighed was recorded by putting aside a grain of corn to represent one load sold. From a "Ready Reckoner" which the broker brought with him the total amount to be paid for the purchase was ascertained. Father could read a Reckoner and so Nana was satisfied that the correct amount had been paid for the purchase.

Asokore, near Effiduasi, was at the time the nearest cocoa buying centre to Agogo. In that town were stationed agents and staff of the major European cocoa produce-buying firms. Established there were Cadbury & Fry, F & A Swanzy, Millers Ltd., C.F.A.O., S.C.O.A. and B.M.F. Each of the firms owned a big shed and other cocoa-buying paraphernalia. Cocoa bought in Agogo by brokers was conveyed to Asokore by hired carriers at a charge of six shillings a "load" (*piren siren nsia*). Mother teamed up with a group of hired carriers called *apaafoɔ* to convey the lot purchased from Nana to the Cadbury and Fry yard at Asokore, within an agreed period. She collected one load (*piren*) and told me that I would accompany her to Asokore. I was thrilled. A pack of a small quantity of beans taken off her one *piren* "load" was prepared for me.

In the afternoon of the following day, we left Agogo, on foot, in company of other *apaafoɔ* (hired carriers), passed through Hwediem, Amantra, Nyinanapɔnase, Akutuase to Wiawso, where we stopped for the night. Early in the morning of the following day, at the first crow of the cock (*akɔkɔnin-kan*), we left Wiawso, passed through the forest of River Anun (*Anun-kwayɛ*) and crossed Nsikawa-Nsikawa stream whose banks were strewn with some white mica-like crystals. River Anun was fordable, it being the dry season of the year. We reached Brepro, which was at that time a small Asokore village, stopped for a short rest, and continued our journey to Asokore, arriving there about midday. The stronger members of the carriers returned, upon off-loading, to Wiawso, for the second night. They were back in Agogo the third day. The industrious hired carriers (*apaafoɔ*), able-bodied young men and women, had each earned six shillings in three days for conveying on their heads a load (60 lbs.) of dry cocoa beans on a footpath to Asokore, a distance of about twenty-five miles.

Mother could not go back with the group that returned to Wiawso that day. My ankles were badly swollen (*mpensa akye me*) and she had to stay behind for a day to attend to me. Fortunately for us, a lineage sister of Mother's, Maame Dede, who was married to Opanin Kwame Kra, an Elder of Asokore Stool, was in town. She readily agreed to take care of me while Mother went back to Agogo on a second trip to bring another load of cocoa. When she returned to Asokore four days later, I was fit enough to travel with her back to Agogo.

When Mother had left me behind at Asokore, I hobbled around to see places in what was, at that time, a bustling commercial centre. From such rounds I learned that the cocoa bought and brought to Asokore was packed into big barrels by coopers, some of whom I saw at work in a yard of a produce-buying firm. The barrels were rolled along a wide road by some strong labourers of the firms to a bigger town called Kumasi, which was, I was told, about the same distance from Agogo to Asokore. From Kumasi the cocoa was put on to a vehicle called *oketekye* (train) which moved on rails, and conveyed it to the coast (*mpoano*) where there was a wide expanse of salty water called "*ɛpo*" (the sea). A bigger thing that moved on the sea, called "*ɛhyɛn*" or "*stima*" (ship) carried all the cocoa, including my grandmother's beans, to some land very, very far away, called *Aburokyire*. I overheard from the conversation of some of the employees of a buying firm that all the good things in the shops at Asokore, such as cloths, cutlasses, enamel basins, sardines, sewing machines, sugar, talc power, pomade, felt hats and others that could be obtained only in Kumasi, came from the place, *Aburokyire*, the country of the "White-man," some of whom I saw in the offices and yards of the buying firms at Asokore.

A greater part of my pre-school days in Agogo was spent with my parents in our Apampramasu farm cottage. Life in our "bush place" was a pleasant one of which I cherish a very happy memory. An atmosphere of serenity, emanating from the primeval forest where Father had started his first clearing (*odupirie*) for his new cocoa farm, animated me. There was a complete mutual understanding between husband and wife. Wife saw husband's point of view; tolerant husband appreciated the wife's assistance, and both parents worked together towards a common goal: that of striving to bring up all the children they produced fit, in every respect, to live in the world.

Our wants in our Apampramasu cottage were few and essential needs in those days, could be reasonably satisfied. Parents worked hard at a new farm by themselves without any hired labour. Father did the hardest work that needed to be done by a man, such as clearing of thick bush. Occasionally he received help, on a reciprocal basis, in the felling of trees and in the sowing of seeds directly on the farm (*atɔdwɛ*) without nursing them on beds. Mother did lighter, but by no means unessential jobs, such as roasting plantain, cocoyam or yam for us. She gathered dead pieces of wood around some particular trees such as *esa*, which were to be killed without felling with an axe, so that they could be left to stand for use as firewood.

When both parents were busy with their various farm work, I was often left to mind the fire. Alone, I watched birds fluttering above on trees, or some little creatures crawling on the ground, or other insects flying about in search of their food. The feeling which, at that time, filled my little mind was what Godfrey Thring has perfected in the following two verses:

Not a bird that doth not sing
Sweetest praises to Thy Name;
Not an insect on the wing
But Thy wonders doth proclaim.

Every blade and every tree
All in happy concert ring,
And in wondrous harmony
Join in praise to their King.

Our source of meat in our Apampramasu cottage was small fresh-water fish called *mmɔbɔnsɛ*, crabs and prawns trapped at the confluence of Ntɔn and Apampramasu streams, both of which ran close by our new farm and formed sides of the boundaries of Father's farmland. Some traps were also set in the uncleared forest bordering the farm clearing to catch small mammals, such as *ɔtwe*, *adowa*, *okusie*, *ɔkankane*, *aberɛbeɛ* and *apɛsɛ*. Occasionally an *odompo* was caught in his trap, but it was always given away to some of our neighbours. My parents always bore in mind the avoidance which the Ɔboanim herbalist, Kwaku Boaten, had imposed on me. *Odompo* was one, and the meat of the forbidden animal was never eaten by my mother or father till they died.

There were times when traps failed and Father had no luck with his gun. I recollect one such occasion when there was not a piece of meat left in Mother's covered calabash in which meat and other ingredients for the preparation of meals were stored (*adidi-pakyie*). We had to eat a meatless soup (*ntohuro*). But Mother excelled. She had no meat of any kind, not even crabs or *mmɔbɔnsɛ*, but there were some eggs, and there were some broad beans (*apatram*), some *mmirebia* (small species of mushroom), and there were, of course, abundant fresh cocoyam leaves (*nkontomire*). A soup prepared with boiled eggs, *mmirebia*, broad beans and fresh cocoyam leaves, flavoured with *prɛkɛsɛ* fruits, which was served with ample, supple balls of plantain *fufu*, was eaten with relish. It was, I still feel, one of the most enjoyable meals I have ever had, if not more so than some of the best repasts, served on an à la carte menu, that I have so far taken in some of the best restaurants in Europe.

AN HONOURED PROFESSION
THAT IS NO MORE

Aframso, that part of the Agogo Stool land lying roughly ten miles north, northeast and east of the town, was, in my childhood days, a grassland country of vast grazing grounds which afforded an ideal habitat for wild big game. In the forest belt fringing it, Agogo hunters had built hunting camps called *nnanso,* where they stayed temporarily for some time to carry out their hunting business. In those days, Aframso was a word synonymous with smoked fish and wild game meat (*adwene ne mpunam*). Men and women of the town went to hunting camps in the area and brought back home to sell head loads and head loads (*mpakan*) of fish and meat. People from other towns passed through Agogo to Aframso to buy meat and fish which they, too, carried away in packs to sell in far away places. Hunting was then not only lucrative, but also a highly honoured occupation

My mother's mother, Nana Yaa Kwaane, was the first born daughter of a big game hunter of his day. His name, I learned, was Kwasi Atwereε, a member of the Agogo Asakyiri lineage. That, I concluded silently in my head, accounted for her fastidiousness and disconcerting discrimination in her diet. To Nana, any soup not pot-full of choicest meat plus fish was *nkwan-foo* (worthless soup). From stories that she often proudly told us on hunting and about hunters, I gathered the following facts. Hunters in Agogo, in her day, were of three grades:

A **Grade 3 hunter,** who was, as it were, an amateur. He did not kill to sell, but to provide meat for the wife to prepare their meals. Farming was his full-time occupation, but he owned a flint-lock gun which he carried on his shoulder to farm. Father, I knew, was one such hunter. I recollect that at the end of the day's work on the farm, Mother and I went ahead home to prepare the evening meal while he tarried behind. Left alone, he went into a nearby bush to stalk small mammals such as *ɔtwee, apɛsɛ, akranteɛ,* or larger birds such as *kokokyinaka, akɔkɔhwedeɛ* and *ɔnwam.* If he succeeded, he brought home his kill, at times for a part to be used in the preparation of the day's main meal. I remember that one day he brought home a leaf-wrapped packet which contained a killed *ɔmampam!* The look of the thing horrified me. I was so taken aback by the shape and colour of that giant reptile, that I could not enjoy eating its meat. Father "went to bush" (*ɔkɔ wuram*) infrequently, because, as he so often remarked, hunting (i.e. amateur work) took much of the time he needed for work on the farm.

A **Grade 2 hunter,** Nana defined, was *ɔbɔfoɔ* — a full-time hunter. He lived in a hunting camp to kill to sell wild big game such as *ɔtrɔmoo, oburumuu, ɛkoɔ,* and medium-size game, such as *ɔwansan, ewuo, kɔkɔte.* He hunted and killed also monkeys, mainly *ɛfoɔ, anwenhema, ɔkwakuo* and *boapeawa.* The difference between a Grade 1 and Grade 2 hunter, I understood, was of a small degree. Nana explained that a Grade 2 hunter was one who hunted to kill for sale, but had not succeeded in killing an elephant (*ɛsono*).

It was only a **Grade 1 hunter,** *ɛsommɔfoɔ,* who had killed one or more elephants. Both Grade 1 and 2 hunters hunted with a flint-lock gun of larger calibre than that used by an amateur, Grade 3 hunter. In the case of a Grade 1 hunter, however, a single bullet called *akorabɔɔ,* was used to load a gun of still larger bore called *ɔnanta.*

We learned from Nana that in every *abusua* (lineage) in Agogo, there were big game hunters of fame and distinction who were the pride of all the members. It gladdened my heart to hear from her that our *abusua,* too, could boast of a long line of distinguished, professional Grade 1 Agogo hunters. Among those then living, she mentioned to us the names of the following illustrious ones: Kwasi Kuuwa, whose *nnanso* was at Asratoase; Kwabena Tatrota, whose *nnanso* was at Asuaafu; Osei Yaw Panin, Kwasi Sei, Osei Yaw Kuma, three brothers with one *nnanso* at Mpatampa; Kwaku Apau, whose *nnanso* was at Anwan-tifii.

From Nana's stories I gathered that most of the big game hunted, such as *ɛsono*, *ɔtromoo* and *oburumuu*, had *sasa* (evil spirits) and were therefore known as *asasa-mmoa* (evil spirit-possessing animals) whose hunting necessitated some ritual performance and observances before and after they were shot and killed. I had the good fortune of witnessing one day the excitement created in Agogo by the news of the killing of what must have been one of the last few elephants left in the area. I quite well remember that just about the time that farmers were returning home from their farms, the quiet afternoon of the town was disturbed abruptly by two earth-shaking sounds of *ɔnanta* (big caliber) gunshots. From the east and in the direction of the road to the Afram Plains (Aframkwanso) the sounds boomed, echoed and reverberated in the *Dentɛ-boɔ* (Dente Cave): "*B - U - U - U ... M - M - M ...! B - U - U - U ... M - M - M ...!!*" Then followed the plaintive voice of a big game hunter, singing *abɔfo-nnwom* (the hunter's dirge). Suddenly Agogo town went wild. The air was filled with excitement everywhere. People were seen rushing in a hurly-burly in the direction of the dirge singer. Mother, who had joined the crowd, returned to tell us, "*Wɔfa Kuuwa akum ɛsono.*" ("Uncle Kuuwa has killed an elephant.") In a hurry she started packing. She put into a net bag (*atena*) a few things for a journey to Asratoase the following morning. Before we woke up that morning she was gone.

Customary formalities connected with elephant-killing, I learned later, were that, immediately Nana Kuuwa shot and killed the beast, he cut off its tail (*ɛsono-dua*) which was to be presented to the Agogohene, to announce formally the kill to him. The Agogohene, on his part, presented the hunter with a "welcome drink" and some gunpowder as a formal expression of his appreciation of the hunter's daring deed, and to congratulate him on his success in killing the biggest of the big animals. Some ritual was performed (*yi mmusuo*) in the *ahem-fie* to sanctify the hunter's body and fortify his soul. That done, the Chief nominated a court servant (*ɔhene bɔfoɔ*) to accompany the hunter to his Asratoase *naanso*, and thence, to the spot where the carcass lay (*ɛson-nwa-yɛ*). The servant's duty was to supervise, as the Chief's representative, the dressing operation and collect the Chief's customary share of the meat. Whoever desired, I was told, could join the elephant carcass-dressing party. All who went assisted in one way or the other in the operation. Men cut meat, women and children carried pieces of dead wood (*egya*) to make fire for the smoking of chunks of meat, or they fetched water that was needed for general cleaning purposes. The Chief's share was the first to be cut and given to the court servant. Stool Elders and other prominent people of the town were all given their traditional shares of parts of the body. That done, everyone who took part in the operation had a generous share of the meat and the rest was sold to people who had travelled to the place purposely to purchase some of the meat. Mother and the rest of the dressing party returned home in a few days. During the week and the few days that followed, Agogo was a-go-go with smoked meat of elephant (*ɛson-nam*). Ɔbɔmmɔfoɔ Kuuwa's deed confirmed to me the obvious truth in the often quoted proverb, "*Ɔbaakafoɔ na okum ɛsono ma amansan di.*" ("It is an individual who kills an elephant for the consumption of a nation.")

As was natural, many stories were heard told about the animal and its killer — some true, some fantastic and others, frightening. We, the children, listened to all of them eagerly and only wished we had been there at Asratoase, the hunting camp. A story about the elephant that fascinated me most was the exaggerated size of the beast. The animal was said to be so gigantic that, to dress its carcass, openings the size of a door to a large room had to be cut from outside, through which the operators entered the body to remove the entrails. I should confess that it was some thirty years later, when I saw a live elephant in a London Zoo, that the erroneous image of the colossal size of the animal was corrected. According to Mother, a large portion of the part of the animal's body that was in direct contact with the ground became septic. Much time and effort therefore had to be spent on curing meat of that side to save as much of it as was possible from becoming putrid and to make it fit for eating. Part of the meat I enjoyed eating out of the share Mother brought home from Asratoase was cut from the trunk — the flexible snout of the large animal.

Grandmother told us that before she was married to Nana Pepra, her first husband, she stayed most of the time with her father, Nana Kwasi Atwereɛ, a Grade 1 hunter (*ɛsommɔfoɔ*) in his hunting camp at Onyinatokuro, now Anane-kurom. According to her, herds of elephants then roamed about freely quite close to the camp. The killing of elephants was, in consequence, frequent. As time went on, more and more of the animals were killed and the remaining ones moved farther and farther away to live in remote and inaccessible places on the plains. That, she affirmed, had resulted in making their tracking tedious and their killing a rare affair. It was for that reason, in her view, that there was so much ado and excitement generated by the killing of a single elephant in our day.

In the hierarchy of rank, Nana rated hunters as next to the Agogohene and fetish priests and priestesses. In times of war, she commented, hunters played a very important role. As men conversant with the terrain of particular areas, they became invaluable and trustworthy scouts for the Chief, the Commander of his army. In times of peace, they provided the people with meat. Hunters, such as her father, could earn what was regarded in those days as a substantial income from the sale of meat of animals they killed. A hunter's skill, his exploits, his resourcefulness in times of war, and his income-earning capability combined to make him an influential member of the community till his profession was superseded by the cocoa industry introduced into the town during the closing years of the nineteenth century.

A Hunter's Tail-End

A story was told of a Grade 1 Asona hunter. Yaw O. was his proper name, but he was popularly called Yaw Akwankwaa. The jocular Akwankwaa killed an elephant and earned from the sale of its meat an amount of £40 (*mpredwam num*). We were reminded that *mpredwan num* was, in those days, a substantial sum of money — a princely amount which made the earner feel noble. In his state of swollen-headedness, Akwankwaa, bragging about his windfall prosperity, swore by the Agogohene oath, Praso, and said, "*Meka Nana Praso sɛ, nneema nsi mapampam da.*" ("I swear by Nana's Praso, henceforth, never will I belittle myself by carrying any load whatsoever on my head.") Returning from his farm one afternoon, Akwankwaa obliged his wife by carrying home for her some sticks she needed for snail-skewering. A court servant who saw him carrying the sticks took him prisoner for breaking the Agogohene's oath. Payment of customary fee and fine was no problem to ɔbɔmmɔfoɔ Akwankwaa, but the amount so paid made a heavy inroad into his pride and purse and a dent in his self-proclaimed wealth.

Record of a Conversation with the Daughter of a Big Game Hunter

A recent conversation with ɔbaa-panin Abena Toaa, the eldest surviving daughter of Nana Osei Tatrota, one of the famed Agogo Asona big game hunters, has confirmed my childhood estimation of hunters and hunting. It has summed up for me clearly the factors that contributed to the high rating of a profession that is now no more.

Taking part in the conversation were: Q., Questioner, Yaw Kyei (T.E.); A., ɔbaa-panin Abena Toaa, daughter of Nana Osei Tatrota, the hunter; and N., Akwasi Aninakwaa, nephew and successor of Nana Tatrota and a lineage "uncle" to Questioner.

Q. ɔbaa-panin, I heard quite a lot in my childhood days about the hunting exploits of Nana Tatrota, your father, all of which fascinated me. As a daughter who, I understand, stayed with him for a long time, I am sure you will be able to tell me more about that distinguished hunter.

A. You are quite correct. Apart from my mother, I can say that I am the person who stayed closest together with Agya and longer than any of his relatives.

Q. Your mother, I am unable to recollect ever having had the opportunity of meeting the old grandmother. What was her name and her *abusua*?

A. Awo was ɔsakyiri-nii. Her name was Nyantakyiwaa.

Q. I understand that Aberewa Nyantakyiwaa and her children, including you, did live most of the time with Nana Tatrota at his hunting camp. What was the name of the place, Nana's *nnanso*?

A. Asuafu was the original name. Later, it was named Mankara, and is, today, Osei-kurom.

Q. Did Nana go hunting (*kɔ wuram*) every day of your stay at Asuafu?

A. Every day, except on *nna-bɔneɛ* (sacred days) such as *Akwasidɛɛ, Awukudɛɛ/Kuudopaakuo, Memeneda Dapaa, Fɔdwoɔ, Kwabena* and *Fofie*.

Q. Did it happen that Nana stayed overnight in the bush or did he always return home for the night?

A. Many a time he stayed overnight and alone in the bush, but, except on rare occasions of circumstances unforeseen, he always told us beforehand when we were not to expect him back home for a night or two.

Q. Did you, his children and your mother, remain alone at the camp when he was away hunting?

A. No, Agya had two domestic servants (*ofie-nnipa*), one or the other, or both of them at times, always remained with us at the camp.

Q. Two *ofie-nnipa*? Who were they?

A. Yaw Dab and Kwasi Don.

Q. How did Nana come by the two domestic servants?

N. The two servants, Yaw Dab and Kwasi Don, were both natives of Agogo. They were not bought-slaves, but were given as pawns against loans that their individual heads of family (*ofie-panin*) took from my uncle. (*Yɛdɛ wɔn sii awowa*). No interest was charged on the loans and there was no fixed time for repayment. The agreement was that each man who was given as security for the amount lent, was to stay with the creditor, serve him and be employed to do any reasonable work as might be desired or requested of the servant. He was redeemable when the amount lent had been repaid in full.

Q. Did you know the amount loaned in respect of each servant?

N. A *predwan* on each man pawned.

Q. A *predwan* ... £8—, you mean?

N. The amount, Yaw, may sound too small in your ears, but understand that in those days a *predwan* was a giddy amount, comparable, I should venture to say, to thousands of *Cedis* in the so-called modern Ghana of our day.

Q. Was the amount repaid?

N. Kwasi Don's people repaid to redeem him after a long time. Yaw Dab, on the other hand, died in servitude and was replaced with another servant.

Q. *Ɔbaa-panin*, I understand Asuafu was right in a deep forest. How did the family get its supply of foodstuffs when living in such a place?

A. We stayed many months continuously, sometimes a whole year, at Asuafu. There was no problem of food supply. A shortcut led from the camp to Onyemso village where we obtained our supply of all the food we needed, including plantains, and cassava, cocoyams, yams and *kokonte*. *Kokonte* could last very long and so did dry corn (maize) which we got in good quantity. We supplemented our Onyemso supply with wild yams (*aha-bayerɛ*), which grew in abundance in the forest during the rainy season.

Q. What animals did Nana kill?

A. Several of them. Except as a pastime or for the kitchen when he used his small calibre gun to kill antelopes and other smaller animals, Father spent most of his time at Asuafu killing for sale big animals such as *akoɔ, okoo, aburumuu* and *asono* (elephants).

Q. Elephants?

A. Yes, elephants. He killed three elephants at one spot one day.

N. Two of them fell quite close together, but the third animal fell about a quarter of a mile away from the other two. Uncle explained that something went wrong with the lock on his gun causing the bullet to deflect and missed a vital spot he had aimed at. Defect notwithstanding, the beast was killed.

Q. And, *Ɔbaa-panin*, where was that place?

A. Bobuso, it was.

Q. Bobuso — a place so close to Agogo. I reckon it is under ten miles from town.

A. Yes, that was the place. Elephants were common all round the place in those days and herds of them roamed to places still nearer to Agogo.

Q. *Ɔbaa-panin*, could you say roughly when the three elephants were killed at one spot one day at Bobuso?

A. It was the time of *Tikya* Saka. Kwadwo Saka, who was named after him, had just been born.

Q. Mr. W.G. Saka, Teacher/Catechist, Agogo Scottish Mission Church, between 1918 and 1920. What happened after the three elephants had been killed?

A. Father brought to the *nnanso* the tails of the three animals which were taken home the following day for presentation to the Agogohene.

N. The tail of an elephant had to be severed immediately it was killed for presentation to the Chief. That established the hunter as the bona fide killer of the animal. If that was not done, another hunter who happened to be at the scene, could cut the tail off, and his claim to the ownership of the carcass would be upheld indisputably.

Q. Was any ceremony performed by Nana in connection with the killing of an elephant?

A. Yes, there was a ceremonial hunting-dance (*yesi abɔfoɔ*).

Q. Did you take part in any of the ceremonial hunting-dances?

A. Yes, several times. On three such occasions I was the *asasaduro* (spirit purging medicine) carrier.

Q. *Asasa-duro*? What was it?

A. I am afraid I cannot tell you what the ingredients were. That was a secret known only to the *abɔmmɔfoɔ*. My part was to carry it. It was a medium-size brass basin containing water, some herbs and a few other things. The basin with its contents was gently placed on my head. It was a very light load at first, but it increased in heaviness in the course of the dance. On the third and last time that I carried the *asasa-duro* basin, it became increasingly heavier and heavier and the unbearable weight of the thing broke my neck and quite nearly made me collapse.

Q. I understand that women were also at the ceremonial hunting dance and that they sang in accompaniment to drums and gong-gong beating all the time. Could you, Ɔbaa-panin, sing to me some of the *abɔfo-nnwom* that you sang?

A. Easily, but I become intensely grief-stricken any time that I sing a*bɔfo-nnwom*. For your sake, however, I shall oblige, tolerate the grief and sing just one song, not more, I am afraid.

Q. I am much obliged, Ɔbaa-panin. One will be fine. I do not wish to cause you more grief than you are able to bear. Shall we hear it?

Ɔbaa-panin Toaa took out of her mouth a short *tweapea* stick she had been chewing all the time, cleared her throat thrice and, in a smooth, heart-piercing soprano voice, sang:

Akwasi Woraka a, otu o!
Otu a, osi he?
Otu a, osi mmɛn mu.
Adomse Ayɛboafo,
Mihunii a, anka ne ne Agya kɔɔe.
Anomaa ɔkɔdeɛ Brasiam,
Otu a, ne nsam' abogya-bum.

Tears that had filled the old woman's eyes streamed down the cheeks. She sighed; she heaved and sobbed.

N. Abena, I understand. It's *Akwasidɛɛ, Da-bɔneɛ* today. A sacred day. I can understand.

Q. "Uncle" Kwasi, I must confess, it all sounds Greek to me. I mean the meaning of the *abɔfo-dwom*.

N. It must, indeed be, Yaw. Any *abɔfo-dwom* has a hidden meaning expressed in classical Asante. Therefore, to the uninitiated such as you, some explanation of the words used in the verse is always necessary before its deep meaning can be intelligently comprehended and its beauty fully appreciated. In the verse of the song you've just heard sung, for instance, "*Woraka*" — in plain Asante, means "*ɔbarima kokɔɔdurufoo*" (a valiant, brave and courageous man); "*tu*" — to the ordinary ear, means "to fly" physically on wings. In the dirge, however, the work is used in a mystical sense, meaning, "to become invisible" (*yera*). Uncle had an *ayera* talisman, which, in the face of extreme danger, rendered him invisible. It was a sort of built-in thing which worked when, for instance, he had shot at a wild animal, such as *ɛkɔɔ*, and the enraged beast rushed and charged at him. At such a crucial moment the *ayera* talisman became potent automatically, and, by its power, mystical I mean, the physical body of the hunter was not only hurled up to hover above the horns of the wild, raving charger, it was also invisible. The sentence "*Otu a, osi mmɛn mu,*" therefore, described the condition of the hunter as he hovered, unseen, over the horns of his assailants. In addition to the *ayera* talisman, Uncle had stuck on the backside of his hunting-smock (*batakari*) an amulet which protected him against any sudden attack, such as a gunshot, from behind. He also wore into the bush a small anti-snake talisman which had the power of scattering from him venomous snakes and other poisonous creatures. "*Adomse*" means "father," begetter, font of generosity. "*Ayɛboafo*" is a gallant, chivalrous, brave man; protector of the weak; helper of the poor and needy and comforter of the oppressed. "*Ɔkɔdeɛ*" is, of course, the physical bird of prey, the eagle. "*Brasiam*" is an appellation portraying the attributes of the eagle, namely manliness, strength, purity and fearlessness. "*Abogya-bun*" means fresh warm blood, and it symbolized purity and straightforwardness in any dealing. You can, I am sure, now perceive that the *abɔfo-dwom* which Abena just sang, was metaphorical. It implied, but did not explicitly state, the similarity of the strong and fearless eagle which killed its prey clean, and the valiant, benevolent, courageous hunter who was prepared to face all dangers but abhorred meanness and underhand dealings.

Q. Thank you, "Uncle." May I attempt to translate the verse of the *abɔfo-dwom* that Ɔbaa-panin Abena has just sung? This is how I understand it:

> Akwasi, the brave and valiant (hunter) who flies (i.e. can become invisible when faced with danger)
> Where does he perch/settle when he flies?
> He perches (i.e. hovers invisibly) over horns (i.e. of the assailant)
> Font and begetter of generosity, helper of the distressed and the needy,
> Had I known, I would have gone with Father (i.e. to witness the exploits of the hunter on the field)

Eagle the Bird, strong, clean and fearless (i.e. referring to the hunter)
It flies as it holds in his hands, warm and fresh blood (i.e. kills in purity and gains without subterfuge).

N. You've got it right.

—4—

A MYTH . . . ? A MIRACLE . . . ? OR A MYSTERY?

There are more things in heaven and earth, Horatio,
Than are dreamt of in your philosophy.
— William Shakespeare
Hamlet, Act 1, Scene v

The above was a quotation with which our college Chaplain started a group discussion on Comparative Religion. It was from the Reverend Gentleman, too, that I heard for the first time the following familiar story. A sage strolling along the beach one afternoon came across a child. The sprightly little thing was very busy. He ran back and forth, dipping sea water from the mighty billowing ocean into a hollow scooped out of the sand on the beach. Asked what on earth he was doing, the smart little chap told the old man he was filling his hollow with all the water of the sea. Startled, the old man suggested to the child that he was surely wasting his time doing the impossible. The headstrong young fellow retorted by saying he knew what he was doing: he knew his hollow could contain all the water of the sea and told the sage slightingly that he was to be left alone to fill his hollow. The Chaplain likened the little child on the beach unto some arrogant humans who felt themselves so clever, so omniscient, they could unravel all the many mysteries of the world (deep sea) with their little minds (a hollow in the sand on the beach). Our discussion ended with the Chaplain's warning against inflexible dogmatism in matters of religious beliefs, and on a note of brief admonition: "Keep your minds open!"

Dogmatism in the Agogo Salem of our boyhood days kept our minds tightly closed against any belief other than what the missionary from Abetifi upheld and propounded. The first biblical command, "You shall have no gods except me" (Exodus 20, 3) was to be rigidly enforced and forcibly observed. In consequence, despising or showing downright contempt for all and every traditional belief was often a mark of good membership of the Salem community. Anything and everything about fetishes was regarded profane, ungodly, a sin, and was therefore to be shunned like a plague.

We, the children of the Christian community, were often obliquely encouraged to hold in extreme contempt, to the extent of challenging, some performances of the "people living in darkness" (*antifurae-foɔ*), as the non-Christians living in town (*oman-mu-foɔ*) were called. I recollect one particular thing that we, the young faithfuls, delighted in doing to sneer at the "servers of wood and stones" (*abosomsom-foɔ*) who used to make offerings of one, two or three uncooked eggs and mashed plantain mixed with palm oil (*ɛtɔ*), to the spirits of streams, rocks or some tree regarded as sacred. The offering was served on particular leaves, chiefly *ɛdwen* or *son-mmɛ*, and left at a point on the bank where a footpath crossed the stream; at the foot of a particular tree, or at the entrance of a cave. It was our wont — we children of Salem — to go about hunting for such offerings and removing the eggs which we took home to boil and eat.

There were two such spirit-placating (*mmusu-yie*) spots on the path to our farm. One, and the nearest to the town, was at the entrance of a rock-cave, *ɔbɔɔ-Abenaa*, the other spot, whose spirit was said to be a woman, was a little farther away in a small clearing on the bank of the Apampramasu stream. Parents of the Agogo Basel Mission church saw their children collect eggs for offerings to "heathen gods," but turned a blind eye; people in town knew the offerings were tampered with by the children of Salem, but ignored it and did not protest. We did all that to prove that our membership of the Salem community (*yɛyɛ sukuufoo*) had made us invulnerable to the power of Satan, the Devil. "*ɔbonsam tumi ntumi yɛn*" (the power of Satan cannot overcome us), we upheld and proclaimed boldly. And yet! And yet we saw on weekdays things contrary to what was preached and vehemently condemned on Sundays at church services. We heard things which were incomprehensible and difficult to explain rationally. Some incomprehension was about witches and their craft.

On clear moonlit nights in Salem, while grown-ups remained at home chatting or discussing some of their important domestic matters we, their children, went out to play in the open. Children of each age-group organized their own games which they played among themselves or in a team against children of other *borɔnoo* (quarters). Some of the competitive games were *ntɔmaa* when our cloths with looped ends were flung to hit at the opponents in vigorous encounters till a team disintegrated and gave up. Or, we might play hide-and-seek (*ahunta-huta*). At times we sat and told *anansesɛm* or listened to other stories told about witches and their nocturnal activities.

And we played witches, too, at times. Witch-playing was a daring game. A player collected a live charcoal and quenched one end of it with water leaving the other end live. The quenched end was put into the mouth and held with the front upper and lower teeth, thereby leaving the live and exposed end protruding through the lips, giving the impression of a flaming mouth. Players imagined themselves witches and with outstretched arms "flew" about naked, chasing the "victims" who were those wary boys and others who were not adventurous enough to put live charcoal in their mouths. As the imaginary witches "flew," they chanted what was said to be the witch-flying song:

Ɛna-a kyere me yɔ,
Punyem[1]
Agya-a kyerɛ me yɔ
Punyem!

(Mother teaches me the "do" of it),
Punyem!
(Father teaches me the "do" of it)
Punyem!

We "flew." We were witches, and chanted the witch-flying song in spite of all that was preached against witches. It was quite difficult to disbelieve all that was said about witches, especially when one saw and heard things with one's own eyes and ears. I recollect several occurrences and self-confessions I heard which left me in a quandary: "Who was speaking the truth, the missionary and his preachers who stood in the

---

[1] "*Punyem*" was the onomatopoeic sound that the flaming mouth of a flying witch was said to make.

pulpit to condemn outright the existence of witches, or the person, generally a woman or a young girl, who openly confessed she was a witch and able to bewitch her victim?" This was the question that I kept asking myself.

Eye-witness accounts were many but, because of the lack of space, only two of the puzzling cases of confessions I stole away myself to hear can be related:

Case 1

A continuous barking of dogs in the middle of one night awoke a father whose house was near the outskirts of the town (*mfikyire*). The barking became intermittent, but it never ceased. Wondering as to what might have been happening in the bush just outside the house to cause the unusual behavior of the dogs, the father rose from his bed, put on a piece of his wife's cover cloth and proceeded cautiously in the direction towards which the dogs had pointed their heads. He stopped after taking a few steps and stared intently. And there it was! The father saw his own daughter, who was supposed to be asleep in bed at home, standing naked in a crouching position as if in readiness to take-off.

In deep consternation the father said he asked his daughter, who also had noticed his presence and had gotten up: "Hi, Akua, what are you doing here such a time of the night?" The naked daughter stood dumb. He rushed to her, took hold of her hand and dragged her into the house. After persistent questioning to get a clarification for the Akua's strange behaviour, she confessed and said she was preparing to "fly" to attend a witch-meeting when the father saw her. "Where, and with whom, and why, and when and...?" the flabbergasted father probed and probed, determined to comprehend.

Akua coolly made her revelation and told her father that a shrubby plant which grew where he had seen her was the "take-off point." If she jumped on to the plant she was propelled to begin her "flight." She could not hop on to it promptly because each time she prepared to do so the dogs barked and she was "pulled" down. It was during one such attempt that she saw her father peering at her. Continuing her description, Akua mentioned that she was a member of a juvenile witch society whose "queen" (*bayi-hemaa*) lived in another quarter of the town. She described the "queen" as a girl of her age, breasts not developed (*ɔmmobɔɔ nufuo*), light in complexion with a slight facial mark (*paakrɔ*) on her left cheek (*n'afono benkum so*).

Early the following morning the father took Akua to the house where Yaa, the juvenile witch-queen was described to be living. Yaa, the queen, was away playing somewhere outside her house when the visitors entered. Her father was in and so was another girl of the same name, Yaa, younger and a little darker — Yaa Tuntum (Yaa Black) she was called for distinction. "Yaa, *bra ha*!" ("Come over here, Yaa"), the host father shouted. Yaa Tuntum who was then in the house ran quickly from a part of the yard and stood in front of her father, Agya Kwame. Akua saw her but could not identify Yaa Tuntum as the right person. "*Dabi, ɛnyɛ oyi a,*" ("No, that is not the right one"), she said, shaking her head. Yaa Kokoo was sent for from outside the house. Directly she entered and saw the visitors she winked at them viciously (*obuu wɔn anikye*) and left. To all in the house the action was suggestive. The visitors took leave of the astonished Agya Kwame.

Alone and in the presence of his wife, Agya Kwame called back their daughter, Yaa Kɔkɔɔ, and asked for her comments on what Akua's father had come to tell them. Very reluctantly, Yaa Kɔkɔɔ agreed to make a confession and to tell all about her witchery. She confirmed that she was a witch and the "queen" of her society. She had three other witches, all young girls of her age (*m'atipɛn-foɔ*), as her "bodyguard" (*wɔhwɛn me*). Her witch society meetings were held in the dead of the night. When leaving the house to "fly" to attend a meeting, she hopped over her brothers and sisters with whom she slept in one room and then changed into a mosquito. In that metamorphozed condition she "flew" to the meeting place which was far, far away. She kept in the fork of a stunted tree standing not far from the house her witch-pot containing witchery things (*bayi-senawa*). She made several startling revelations on the activities of her society.

When she was requested to produce her witch-pot, Yaa climbed the tree with the agility of a monkey and brought the thing down. It contained some strands of human hair, some copper rings and some shells in some pinkish slimy substance. Yaa Kɔkɔɔ, the juvenile witch-queen, was said to be known and called openly "Atu-faa" (Fast-Sky-Flier) by her playmates in the particular quarter of the town where she lived.

Case 2

Abena, a middle-aged woman, fell suddenly ill and seriously, too. She was in a deep coma. As was the practice in those days even as it is now, the alarmed relatives decided to take her to consult a fetish for divination as to what was the cause of the misfortune and what could be done to save her.

The fetish they first went to consult in Agogo referred them to another ɔbosom somewhere far away in the Bono (Brong) area. Without wasting any time Abena was hurried to the town and to the ɔbosom to whom they had been referred. At the shrine, Abena's relatives who went with her were told that she, Abena, was a witch and that if she did not make a full confession she would die and be given the treatment deserved by a dead witch. If she confessed, she would be treated and she would survive. Abena confessed readily.

In her confession, she revealed that she was a member of a witch society. When attending witch meetings in the dead of the night, members of the society transformed themselves into various animals such as vultures, snakes, owls, and many others. Parties were held very frequently at which they feasted on transformed bodies of physical human beings provided in turn by members of the society. A victim was to be a close relative of the supplier. She herself, Abena continued her revelation, had joined in feasting on the flesh of relatives of other members of the society. Her turn came to provide the festal meat of her relative. The sister, whose name had already been mentioned to them by the ɔbosom was the victim she had intended to kill for the next feast of her society. But when she went to the house of the sister she met a big and strong man at the entrance of the door to her room. He was holding a thick truncheon (aporibaa) with which he hit her hard on the head. She fell down in a swoon and had been unable to open her mouth to talk and her eyes to see since then. Confession accepted and the requisite fee paid in cash and in kind (wɔyɛɛ ɛho adeɛ), Abena was given some treatment and, in no time, recovered completely, physically, mentally and emotionally.

There was in Agogo, before I was sent to school, a little zongo — a quarter in which lived non-Akan people of the northern tribes, mainly Hausas, Dagombas, Moshis, Frafras, Dagartis and a few Kokombas. Among the Zongo dwellers was a Mallam (Kramo) who was said to have been to Mecca (Nyame-Frɛ-Bea) and was in possession of an Adi-Kura (El Koran). I knew Papa Kramo in person but did not have the opportunity of getting closer to him than an occasional passing by when I was on an errand in the *Zongo*. I found Papa Kramo was tall and slender. He wore spotlessly clean cotton flowing gowns (*batakari*) with a white muslin turban, a big silver ring on the second finger of the left hand, and was always holding in the right hand a string of beads wherever he went. He carried a strong scent of perfume about him and was soft-spoken. I often saw him squatting on a sheep skin in the yard of his house, facing the direction of the Afram Plains (East) counting his beads devoutly. Sometimes I could see him standing with his arms held up, then with his hands on his knees, bending the body. He stooped, sat and stood up again and again, mumbling something. On that occasion it was said of him that Papa Kramo was calling Allah, his God (*Papa Kramo rekana, ɔrefrɛ Nyame*).

Papa Kramo had many wives in his house including one Agogo woman married to him by an appreciative client. He was said to be a very powerful person, mystically, and was to be feared. The rumour was that the man at the Zongo could cure all ills, including impotence, barrenness and mental derangement and that he had the power to protect against attacks by witches and other evil spirits. It was also news that the Mallan wrote something mysterious (Arabic) on a wooden slate with some black liquid called *worowa*, which, when washed with water into a glass tumbler or calabash, served as a cure-all potion. Also it was said of the man in Zongo that he could prepare charms for young men which were very efficacious in enticing girls they desired to be loved by them. Tales, short and tall, were told about the Mallam, the mystic, and it was an open secret that many a client from Salem, mostly women of the community, paid Nicodamean visits to the Mallam, the Kramo of Agogo Zongo.

At one time news went round fast and suddenly that a "wonderful" man had come to Agogo from some far away place called "Nsemaa" (Nzima). The name of the extraordinary man was Kwasi Gyine. Kwasi was acclaimed a medium of indescribable power, capable of receiving and transmitting messages to and from spirits of departed relatives in *Asamando*, the Land of Ghosts. Many a credulous member of the non-Christian community of the town, especially old women, my own grandmother included, flocked to the house in which the strange stranger lived. They went there in their numbers to give urgent messages meant to be conveyed to mothers, sisters, brothers and fathers who had died recently or parted long ago. His service was said to be free, but a respectable amount was to be given to meet his "fare" to and from the Land of Ghosts. There were no qualms about the payment of the "fare" which was readily accepted as fair and reasonable: "*Ɔde twa ne ho asuo akɔ Asamando.*" ("It was to be used to pay to be ferried across the river lying between the Land of the Living and the Land of the Dead.") No one wished Kwasi stranded at the bank of that fearful river and so money given him to meet his travelling and transport expenses was generous.

Some years later, in our Ancient History lesson at the College, I learned of Charon, the squalid old man of Greek mythology, who was the ferryman who rowed the dead in his rickety boat to cross the hateful river Styx in the underworld. What agitated my mind was why the benevolent Kwasi Gyine should demand a lot more from his agents in Agogo than was Charon's standard charge of one Obol which was equivalent to a penny-ha'penny?

Kwasi Gyine "died," and "died" after he had been laid in a "coffin" made of raffia palm branches (*ntonton*). The "coffin" was left standing in a *pato* (open-front room) in full view of all who cared to go and see. It was covered with a piece of cloth. Kwasi was, at that stage, ready to receive from many anxious relatives of the departed, their messages together with the amount he needed for his "fare." Fetish drumming and dancing by his followers and adherents proceeded all day till a time in the late afternoon when the "coffin" was seen agitating, gently at first, and then violently and vigorously. Kwasi had "returned" from the Land of Ghosts (*Asamando*) to the Land of the Living (*Atease-foɔ*).

Visits to any place connected with fetish dances (*akɔm*) strictly forbidden, I could not stay long in Kwasi Gyine's house when I stole a visit to that crowded place. It was not therefore possible for me to gain much first-hand knowledge, much as I had wished it, about what messages he took to the dead or brought back to the living. I know, however, that an appreciative customer did name a son born at that time after the celebrated medium and that the young Agogo Kwasi Gyine child grew up to become a fetish priest himself.

All this, and more besides, was happening in Agogo. My dilemma at that time, and for many years after was: What was to be believed and what was not to be believed! Before I was sent to school, I lived in two worlds — literally and figuratively. I lived in the world of the young and in the world of grown-ups; I lived in Salem with my mother among Christians, and in town (*Ɔman-mu*), with my father among non-Christians. I lived too, with close relatives of divergent religious practices and beliefs. My grandmother, Nana Yaa Kwaane, for instance, was an ardent, unadulterated heathen to whom Fetish Bra-Kune was THE ALMIGHTY. She had travelled on foot, all the way, to Kranka in Bono (Brong) to "eat" Bra-Kune (*wakodi Bra-Kune*), and had by so doing placed herself in all respects of her person and personality — physical, spiritual and mental — under the protection of the fetish, Bra-Kune. She swore by Bra-Kune to prove her innocence, she swore by Bra-Kune to assert her determination and she swore by Bra-Kune to enforce her authority in the house. Everyone knew that when Nana swore: *"Meka Bra-Kune"* ("I swear by Bra-Kune"), she meant business and was to be taken seriously. But, for all that, she kept her obsession with her fetish, Bra-Kune and her unshakable belief in fetishism strictly to herself. She never did anything directly or indirectly to influence, much less force, any of her children and grandchildren to convert to her belief and faith.

Mother was a staunch member of the Agogo Basel Mission Church, a daughter of a senior presbyter and one of the founders of the church in Agogo. She later became an "Elder" of the local church and died peacefully, a senior leader of the women members of her church, in March 1965. One of the hymns sung at her church burial service was Twi Hymn 423, the first verse of which says:

Sɛ wosom w'agyenkw de kosi wum a,
wobedu soro Paradise hɔ;
sɛ woko na wudi mu nkomin a,
wobedi hɔ nkwadua aba.
Onyame mma no, wobedi n'ade;
Ɔno bɛkyekye wɔn werɛ daa.

(If you serve your Saviour unto death,
you will reach the heavenly Paradise;
If you fight and win a victory,
you will eat the fruit of the tree of life over there
Children of God, they will inherit Him:
He will comfort them forever.)

On sober reflection some time after the passing of a mother who had toiled ceaselessly and sacrificed so much for my well-being, I could not agree more with Svetlana Alleluyeva, daughter of Comrade Josef Stalin. "God grant an easy death only to the just."

Father, an apostate, lived in an apartment in his uncle's house in Wɔntoɔnase, the Asakyiri *Abusuafoɔ* quarter of the town, about three quarters of a mile away from Salem. He was quite liberal in his religious beliefs. He never went to church and never consulted any fetish (*abisa*). His religion, something he revered and sought to live after, was what he expounded briefly in a maxim: "*Mesom Papa. Mikyiri Bɔne*" ("I worship the Good, i.e., Fairness, Justice, Purity. I abhor the Bad, i.e., Evil, Injustice, Unyielding, Impure).

Whenever we were back home from our Apampramasu farm cottage, I spent most of the time during the day in my father's house, running errands for him, cleaning his eating-table (*didipon*) and staying about to render any service that he might request. Father had then married two other wives, both younger in age by far than my mother. The young wives were daughters of two of Father's uncles. I later learned that they were "marriages of convenience," arranged between uncles and nephew. One of the filial duties in his house therefore, was to clean and send back dishes (*adidi-wowa*) in which food was brought to the husband from the respective wives.

When in Father's house, I was free from Mother's vigilant surveillance and I often took the opportunity to sneak out to watch fetish dances. Father, of course, did not care a dime if I went to *akɔm-ase* (the fetish dance gathering place), provided that he knew beforehand where I would be. He always readily gave his blessing by saying, "*Wokɔ a, ɛnkyɛ.*" ("Don't be long.") There at the dance place, I was not in the least interested in what the grown-ups assembled there said or did, nor in what the ɔbosom was said to have said. What fascinated me and occupied my attention all the time was the dancer (*ɔsoam-nii*) and his movements and activities. I gazed at the brass basin wrapped in white cotton netting balanced nonchalantly on his head; the body all besmeared with white clay (*hyire*); the eyes in a trance; the strings of talismans crossing at the breast, one from the left shoulder passing under the right armpit, and the other from right shoulder to the left armpit; the *bodua* (cowtail swat) in the left hand; the ɔdɔsɔ (raffia skirt) on the waist moving up and down, swirling round and round rhythmically with the beating of drums operated by a group of enthusiastic adherents in a corner; the rattles from the *nkɔntoa* (long-headed gourd) held playfully by entranced women faithfuls singing moving *nkɔ-nnwom* (fetish dance songs); and, most impressively, the footwork of the dancer, especially, the stork-walk.

Interesting to me also was the dancer's attendant and his prompt attention to the dancer's frequent requests for *hyire* which he, the attendant, held in his hand following the dancer all about the place. The moment I eagerly waited for was when the dancer would signal for a *kosua-mon* (an unboiled egg) which he ate raw throwing the shell away adroitly, defiantly. And also for the rare occasion when he would request to be drenched with pots of cold water. Then the end came with the dramatic carrying away of the dancer on the shoulders of strong bearers, when all dispersed saying: "*Ɔbosom kɔda.*" ("The fetish has retired to sleep.") At a dance of a particular fetish one day, I recollect, I had a bewildering experience. The fetish was said to have a fetish-son called Abirim (Heavy-Beating Absorber). In the course of a normal dance, Abirim would suddenly "descend" on the dancer when there would be a stir of expectancy, with cries, "*Abirim aba o-o!*" ("Abirim, the Heavy-beating Absorber, has arrived!") On such an occasion the dancer would be seen stooped with all his body taut and arms stretched stiffly pointing to the ground and parallel to the thighs and legs. Abirim had, indeed, arrived and was, in that position, ready to receive heavy beatings. Men rushed on the dancer with firm clenched fists and gave him hard blows one after the other; women sought pieces of sticks and anything handy with which to beat Abirim. It was said that the heavier the beating or hitting, the more a hitter's worry was absorbed. To my surprise, Abirim took all the beatings, which were strictly administered at the back of the body and nowhere else, unflinchingly, without showing the least sign of feeling pain. Abirim was "off" when the dancer stood erect once again.

My rounds of the various fetish dances gained for me some knowledge of the principal *abosom* (fetishes) in Agogo. I had known that each one of them belonged to a particular *abusua* and that each had its day, days of worship, its abstentions, its own *ɔkɔmfoɔ* (priest/priestess) and its own *ɔsoam-nii* (carrier-dancer). As far as I can remember, the knowledge I gained in that way could be summarized as follows:

1. **Ɔbosom tano** (also called "*Taa-Kofi*")
   Abusua-owners:

Aduana (Amantinhene's section)

Days of Worship:
Dwoada Fɔdwoɔ (sacred Monday, occurring once in forty-two days)

Avoidances:
ɔmampam; amankani (cocoyam)

Remarks/Comments/Observation:
Taa-Kofi was the oldest of the Agogo *abosom* and still is operative (1982), the priestess being Nana Kwaakyewaa. Taa-Kofi was and still is one of the two State *abosom* whom the Agogohene and his Stool Elders went to consult (and continue to consult) in cases of imminent or prevalent calamity or of an unusual occurrence, to seek advice on measures to be taken in the interest of the community. The other State *ɔbosom* was and still is Afram.

2. *Ɔbosom afram*
Abusua-owners:
Aduana (Kootia Section)

Days of Worship:
Memeneda Dapaa and *Akwasidee*

Avoidances:
otwee;amankani (cocoyam); *ɔmampam*

Remarks/Comments/Observation:
Ɔbosom Afram is actively operating (1982). The present *ɔkomfoɔ* priestess is Aberewa Yaa Nsuo of the Agogo Etia Aduana. The *ɔsoam-nii* (carrier-dancer) is also an Aduana man, Agyekum.

The Coming of Afram:
The following account on the coming of Agogo Afram was what I heard: Opanin Duku of the Agogo Asona, son of Ohenewaa and grandson of Obiri Adaakwaa, was a professional big game hunter of Agogo. He was honoured by the Agogohene, Nana Tuuda, for his bravery and hunting exploits by conferring on him the title Atufoohene of Agogo. *Ɔbɔmmɔfoɔ* Duku lived in his hunting camp at Kurowireso, built at the edge of the Afram Plains, with his wife and daughter, Henewaa, whom he had named after his mother. In the evenings the family gathered and told *ananse-sɛm*. Daughter Ohenewaa, a teenager whose breasts were beginning to develop (*ɔrebobɔ nufuo*) proved to be an adept story-teller with a remarkable resonant voice.

One evening, the marvellous young story-teller could be found nowhere. All searching for her proved futile. The mother and father, alarmed, went to an ɔbosom to seek help (*wɔkɔɔ abisa*). The perplexed parents were told that the young Ohenewaa was not lost, neither was she dead, but was somewhere safe in the depths (*ebun*) of River Afram. The *ɔbosom* predicted that the young girl would emerge from the depths at a particular spot on a day he mentioned. The family was advised to gather at the spot at the material time to welcome her back.

Precisely on time on the day as foretold, the gathering on the bank of River Afram heard a rumbling sound from the depths, then the pealing of atumpam drums, accompanied by the beat of gong-gong and *nno-nno* drums. In a few moments, to the astonishment of the gathering, up popped young Ohenewaa, carrying on her head a brass basin wrapped in a white netting. She held a short *bodua* (cowtail swat) in her left hand and was wearing strings of talismans on her neck, knees and ankles. Young Ohenewaa was carried home, first to Taa-Kofi, the State *ɔbosom* and thence to the Agogohene's house to greet him and his Elders. *Ɔbosom* Afram had arrived.

3. *Ɔbosom anɔkye*

Abusua-owners:
Asona

Days of Worship:
Benada (Tuesday) and *Memeneda Dapaa*

Avoidances:
Nil, *Wadi Kunkuma*[2]

Remarks/Comments/Observations:
Ɔbosom Anokye is now (1982) dormant, having been so for sometime now. It has no *ɔkomfoɔ* (priest) and no *ɔsoam-nii* (dancer-carrier).

The Coming of Anɔkye
The spirit of the *ɔbosom*, Anɔkye, was said to have descended from the sky (*yɛsɔɔ no ewiem*), and came upon Naa Yaw Kɔdaa, an *ɔsonanii* (*ɛkaa* Nana Yaw Kɔdaa).

It was said that in those days, the Asantehene had decreed that no new *ɔbosom* was to be permitted to come into being in the Asante nation. In compliance with the decree, the Agogohene reported the "arrival" of the new *ɔbosom*, Anɔkye, in Agogo to the Asantehene. A court official was dispatched from Kumasi to execute the death penalty against Nana Yaw Kɔdaa for the

---

[2] "*Kunkuma*" was said to be an anti-avoidance course which a fetish itself took to qualify him/her to become immune to and therefore freed of all avoidances, hence the saying, "*wadi kunkuma*," applied to a person, meant he/she was immune to any mystical attack.

infringement of the decree. When he reached Amantena, then a main town on the Agogo-Kumasi road (*Asante-kwan*), the official was given the news of the death of the new priest, Yaw Kɔdaa, at Agogo. The mission, under the circumstance, had to be withdrawn.

Soon after, the spirit of Anokye "re-descended" upon Nana Kwaku Dwira, another *ɔsonanii* of Agogo. To escape the Asantehene's capital punishment, the new Anɔkye Kɔmfoɔ escaped, crossed the Pra, and settled in Akyem Kotoku where he operated for about ten years, returning to Agogo after the destoolment of the Asantehene, Nana Mensah Bonsu.

When *Ɔkomfoɔ* Kwaku Dwira returned to Agogo, the *Asonafoɔ* erected a mud and wattle hut, roofed with raffia palm leaves (*dahadan*) to house the *ɔbosom*. The last *ɔkomfoɔ* of the *ɔbosom* was Asadu Kɔmfoɔ, an *ɔsonanii*.

4. *Ɔbosom tano* (*antwiaa tano*)
Abusua-owners:
Agogo Ayokofoɔ

Days of Worship:
Dwoada Fodwoo Fofie — both sacred days occurring once in forty-two days.

Avoidances:
abirekyie (goat); *amankani* (cocoyam)

Remarks/Comments/Observations:
The *ɔbosom* is now (1982) inoperative.

5. *Ɔbosom ɔdomankama*
Abusua-owners:
Agogo *Asonafoɔ*

Days of Worship:
Thursday

Avoidance:
Nil, *Wadi Kunkuma*
(has undergone an anti-avoidance course)

Remarks/Comments/Observations:
The *ɔbosom* is now (1982) dormant and has been so since the death, some years past, of the last *ɔsoam-nii*, Ata Kɔmfoɔ. Its first *ɔkɔmfoɔ* was Kofi Aninakwaa. Whenever the *ɔbosom* was "carried," the dancer held dried plantain fibre (*baha*) and a broom (*ɔprayɛ*) on which was sprinkled white powdered clay (*hyire*) from time to time.

6. Akogya

Akogya was an *ɔbosom* of a singular standing, in the sense that it was not owned by a particular *abusua*. It was the exclusive patron *ɔbosom* of the Agogoman, the head of which was the Agogohene. It was said to be the spirit of Akogya, a small stream which ran across the road from Agogo to Hwidiem which was called *Asantekwan*. The physical Akogya stream was a small outlet of a nearby pool which dried completely during the harmattan season. But it was said that in days long gone, whenever any enemy set off to attack and invade the town, it reached Akogya in full flood, covering a wide stretch of the road with a deep unfordable flow of water of swift currents and whirlpools. In consequence, Agogo town could never be reached and attacked by any enemy, however brave and well-armed it might be. And so, like the moat around the castles and fortresses of the Lords, Dukes, Barons and other peers of the mediaeval Europe, Akogya prevented and warded off all invaders of Agogo town. The unqualified service of the brave guard of old earned for the *ɔbosom* the sobriquet, "*Akogya Baawɛ, Osiakwan.*" ("Akogya, the mighty guardsman, the blocker of roads.") Once a year on an *Akwasidee*, which was and still is a big occasion, the Agogohene, his Elders and his people, go in state to pay homage to the *ɔbosom* whose one-room hut is seen today situated midway on the Agogo-Hwidiem road where the age-long rituals continue to be observed. Akogya's avoidance is a sheep with a mutilated ear (*odwan a yɛatwa n'aso*). A sacrificial fowl to Akogya must be a male (*akɔkɔ-nin*). It was to be caught from anywhere in the town free, without payment, without begging for it, and without asking its owner for it.

7. Kurowire

One of the sources of the town's water supply was said to be a goddess, born on a Tuesday, hence the name "Kurowire Abenaa." She did not have a shrine which I knew, nor a priestess. Collecting water from the stream on any Tuesday in our childhood days was forbidden. All, including even us members of the Salem community, abided by the prohibition faithfully.

One other place, in addition to *akom-ase* (fetish dance place) that Mother had strictly forbidden us children of our house in Salem to visit in town, was *ayie-ase*, the place of a funeral. Taking advantage of my dual residency, I succeeded one afternoon, when I was supposed to be in Father's house, and Father knew I was in Salem, to sneak out to the funeral in a house where a prominent dead person was lying in state. And, Oh! what I saw frightened me terribly. The dead body had been put on a bed in a *pato* room. On the bed had been spread layers and layers of costly, indigenous blankets (*nsaa*), arranged in such a way that about six inches of the edge of each blanket showed below the one above it. The body itself was covered with several rich *kente* cloths (*nwen-tama*), similarly arranged. It was lying facing upward, and the face was studded in some intricate artistic design in gold dust against a background of some pale dark paint. The hands, put across the body, were adorned with heavy gold bangles (*bamfina*), and the fingers with several sparkling gold rings. An exquisite gold bracelet (*atwea-ban*) hung around the neck.

In front of the bed, and on a raised platform, were placed several dishes of cooked food of every description and type then consumable in the town of Agogo. These were whole-boiled fowls (*akɔkɔ-mua*) on which had been sprinkled palm oil, balls of *fufu* with big cuts of meat, boiled *ɛferɛ* (pumpkins), and what have you. Those, I heard, were send-off dishes for the departing relative to take with him to *Asamando*, which, they explained, was a place where dead men went to live (a place which, I learned later, the ancient Greeks called Hades). The time came for the body to be put into a coffin and the senior relatives of the deceased politely asked to be excused and be left alone to swear to him and bid him good-bye in secret. I left the house. All the way to my father's house in Wɔntɔnase Borɔnoo I kept musing:

And so when a person dies, he goes to live in another place called "*Asamando*," taking with him some of all the food that we eat here, to eat there; the best and nicest cloths that we wear Here, to wear There. He left bidding all goodbye, and was gone never to return, never to be seen by the living but he was about all the place and saw the doings of the living!

I must confess that I was bewildered for a long, long time by my boyhood experiences of religious incompatibilities and mysteries that could not be readily understood or rationally explained. All those imponderables weighed unbearably on me. They were compounded by the wise drummer in the language we heard transmitted on the *atumpan* drums on sacred days (*da-bone*), on *akwasideɛ* and *awukudeɛ*, saying:

Ɔdomankama, a,
Ɔbɔɔ Adeɛ;
Bɔrebɔre a,
Ɔbɔɔ Adeɛ;
Ɔbɔɔ Owuo,

Ma Owuo kum no.

(The Great Mighty who created the "Thing;"
The Creative Creator who created the "Thing;"
He created Death and Death killed Him)

Ɔdomankama created Death and Death killed Him, Ɔdomankama? I - N - D - E - E - D ! My inner puzzle deepened as I grew older and older. But our College Chaplain helped put my mind at ease and an inimitable social historian anchored it with the following thoughts:

We ourselves are failing to maintain our own once strong faith in civilization. It is important, I believe, at present time to remember what that faith was. It was founded on a belief that Christianity, however imperfectly expounded or observed, was the highest expression of God's purpose known to man, that all men should be free to follow it if they could; that the State should try to base its laws and actions on Christian principles; that men should be free to trade and make what peaceful bargains between themselves as they chose, free from the fear of violence; that justice as far as it could be ascertained, should be done between man and man and nation and nation and that lawless force should be resisted with patience, if patience could prevail and, if not, with the requisite force necessary to restrain it.[3]

---

[3] Sir Arthur Bryant, *The London Illustrated News* (December 19, 1957), 886.

—5—

A LAND OF MILK AND HONEY

For the Lord your God is bringing you into a good land of brooks, pools, gushing springs, valleys and hills; it is a land of wheat and barley, of grape, vine, fig trees, pomegranates, olives and honey; it is a land where food is plentiful, and nothing is lacking...

—Deuteronomy, 8, 10

If the Creator of the universe had graciously located an additional, reliable stream or two to well up from the valleys and hills of Agogo to complement the ever-faithful, ever-running Aboabo spring, one would have hazarded a guess that Agogo area was a Canaan, the Land of Promise about which Moses spoke in his address to the people of Israel when they were encamped in the valley of Araban in the wilderness of Moab, east of river Jordan. If the Mighty Creator (Ɔbɔɔ-Adeɛ) had just done that, what Moses, The Man of God, said, quoted above, could well have been applicable to the Agogo stool land.

The founding fathers of the town could not have chosen a more appropriate name for the town than A-go-go. Making the newly-found fertile land an analogy to a succulent fruit, ripe to the state that was just right for eating, *agon* (it is just ripe). Using the repetitive form of the verb *gon*, in the Akan grammatical manner, to stress the intensity of ripeness of the several fruits, the original name chosen for the place might have been A-gon-gon, meaning, it is all fully ripe here and in vast quantity. In the course of time, the final letter "n" of the word *gon* of each syllable might have disappeared, eventually leaving the compound word A-go-go, and, finally, Agogo, as the name of the new place where nothing was in want: A Land of Milk and Honey. Was it a coincidence that a word of French origin, A-go-go, also means, in English, "lavishly provided, galore" one might ask?

In the days of my childhood, we, the children of Agogo, found our town to be a land of milk and honey. Milk, as was imported in tins in later years into the town under brand names such as Ideal Milk, Carnation Milk, Butterfly Milk, Peak Milk, Cow & Gate Milk and others, was a rarity. Fresh milk in cartons or in bottles was an unknown commodity in Agogo in the days before I was sent to school. What we knew and understood milk, *nufu-suo*, to be was a real whitish-grey liquid that exuded from the breast of a human mother to feed a suckling child. From the mother's breast and its content we became aware of an important stage in the development of a child. When it had "passed" or "crossed" the stage of feeding on a mother's breast (*watwa nufuo*), we knew it was no longer an *asokɔnomaa*, infant, mewling and puking in the nurse's arms.

If through a misfortune such as premature death or some debilitating illness a child was deprived of its own mother's breast milk, there was one of two emergency measures which were taken in those days to keep fresh milk flowing for it. The immediate measure was to arrange with a mother in the neighbourhood still nursing an infant to feed the deprived baby also at her breast. The other measure which I recollect quite well because my grandmother, Nana Kwaane, was a specialist in its administration, was to groom a female relative of the deceased or incapacitated mother to undertake the care and feeding of the unfortunate infant. The relative who generally and preferably had not passed child-bearing stage (*ontwaa awoɔ*) was put on a breast-milk inducing course of treatment lasting from three to five or six days. At the end of the course the adoptive mother's breast produced healthy, fresh milk in sufficient quantity to feed the child. The principal ingredient of the concoction (*odudo*) for the woman being groomed was, I saw, the fruit of the *nufu-ten* (long breast) tree which was boiled in a small earthenware pot (*asenawa*) on a fire of three-piece wood of a particular tree. The medicine was taken orally several times a day.

Milk needed for infant-feeding was, therefore, not desperately in want in Agogo in those days. Besides, it was "portable" in a mother's breast, fresh and warm, and therefore available to satisfy a mewling infant at any place. Feeding was not scheduled and could be done even at such awkward times as when a mother had to balance some heavy load on her head on a narrow, bushy path crossed by logs of dead wood or swelled, swirling streams — a performance which many a bottle-feeding mother of these modern "civilized" days might find bewildering.

Honey, the ambrosia, the food for the gods of the ancient Greeks and Romans, was in abundant supply for the mortals of Agogo in those days, too. It could be had and sucked in combs, or eaten in its liquid form as it was poured from a gourd into a plate and licked with the right index finger. The more refined form of eating honey in Agogo, in our childhood days, was to lick it on a half-cut ripe lime fruit (*ankaa-dweaa*). Honey was harvested generally in the dry season of the year (*ɔpɛ-berɛ*), when it was said to be ripe and brimful (*adɔ*). Honey-harvesting was exclusively men's work done usually in the night when a flaming torch (*tɛnee*) made of dry palm branches was applied to the entrance of the hole to the hive in order to incapacitate the bees and to minimize what would otherwise be violent stings on the intruder. Bee-hives were located in hollows of trunks of many large trees growing in the forest fringing the Afram grassland plains. On food crop farms (*mfikyi-fuo*) near the town too were nests of some tiny honey-making flies called *mimina*. The little industrious insects were not as prolific producers of honey as the honey-bee, but their brand of honey known as *mimina-woɔ* had a distinct sweet taste of its own. *Mimina-woɔ* collecting was a profitable pastime that often kept parties of playmates rambling about in the wood for many hours. Wax, a useful by-product from honeycombs, was preserved and used by goldsmiths in Agogo in making, by *cire perdue* method, special gold ornaments for people of high rank, as well as trinkets for fashionable men and women of the town.

Meat and fish, as has been mentioned earlier, were in abundant supply in Agogo in my boyhood days. The supply, I recollect, was so plentiful that the lullaby sung by mothers to soothe and induce their fretful little babies to sleep was:

Akɔdaa ketewa mpotompo,
Gyae suu,
Gyae suu,
Na bɛgye adwene-tɔ

(Bonny little baby,
Don't cry,
Cease crying for a ball of mashed fish)

Agogo was, as it is now, blessed with salubrious air which, in conspiracy with the abundant supply of good nourishing food, produced a good breed of healthy, ebullient men and women. The exuberance, the energy and daring of such a people earned for the town the appellation *abɔ-din*:

Agogo, Okitikiri,
Mfante, Mfante -
Yaa-nom a,
Yɛne ɛkoɔ nante

(Agogo Okitikiri,[1]
Valiant Fellows,
Folk who walk in company of the wild buffalo)

The town's proud motto epitomized the typical characteristics of its people:

Yɛnsom obi,
Yɛnnan obi.
Nso yɛnne yɛn ho

(We serve no one
We depend on no one
And yet we are not independent)

Agogo itself sat in what appeared to be the crater of a volcano which became extinct some millions of years ago. Studded around the town in roughly two concentric circles were several steep-sided domes (*abodan*). The inner perimeter *abodan* fell on radii of between two to five miles. Among the principal Agogo *abodan* were:

Inner perimeter domes (standing within two miles from the town)	**Outer perimeter domes** (standing between two to five miles from the town)
Dɛntɛ-boɔ	*Nhama-nhama-boɔ*
Mponinsaa-boɔ	*Akwam-boɔ*
Ɔboɔ-Abenaa	*Ofori-boɔ*
Aborɔdesu-boɔ	*Bobia-boɔ*
Bɛposo-boɔ	*Kotobon-boɔ*
Kusibo-boɔ	*Ateban-boɔ*

---

[1] *Okitikiri* is the onomatopoeic word for the sound of a briskly, continuous stomping walk.

Atumpan-bɔɔ	Mpatampa-bɔɔ
Afrasua-boɔ	Nyanawase-boɔ
Mayera-bɔɔ	Magyeda-bɔɔ
Mantukwa-bɔɔ	Tetewabo-bɔɔ
Yaw Nkroma-bɔɔ	Anwanie-boɔ
Okomkuro-boɔ	Akyekyesu-boɔ
	Dankwabo-boɔ
	Tweasua-bɔɔ (with a waterfall)
	Krobaa-boɔ
	Akroma-bɔɔ

Considering all of these, one is inclined to conjecture that the many *abodan* scattered about within the radius of from two to five miles from the town might be some molten rock material ejected by the volcano and solidified in the course of years.

The vast **Agogo** stool land of hills and valleys in the rock-studded terrain with the adjacent Afram grassland plains was rich in natural resources. In the fertile forest areas grew a vast variety of tropical trees of very large girth. Timber industry was then a thing of the distant future. Forest trees therefore grew unmolested and, except the few which were unfortunate to be standing in an area cleared for farming, enjoyed their "natural right of peaceful coexistence." Those felled were not for any direct commercial purpose, but to remove a canopy which might hinder the proper growth of crops — both food and cash. Part of the path to our new Apampramasu farm went through a patch of virgin forest. As we crossed it, Father told me the names of most of the trees, shrubs and climbers growing in it. He also explained to me the sayings, expressions and proverbs connected with some of the trees and plants, all of which I found greatly interesting. From his useful and educative sylvan talks I still remember the following.

Osinnuro
The tree was also called *Onyame-dua*[2] (Sky god's tree). A softwood tree the cutting of which was planted in front of rooms of some

---

[2] Rev. J.G. Christaller has the following comprehensive notes on *Nyame-dua* in his *Dictionary of the Asante and Fante Language*. In the second edition (Basel, 1933) is recorded: "*Onyame-dua* (God's tree) the forked post to be found in most courtyards on which is placed a pot or bowl containing a stone-axe, water, certain herbs, and some offering to the spirits. People sprinkle themselves with water to be

Elders and Heads of Family (*ofie-panin*) for the purpose of offering sacrifice to God, the Supreme Creator (*Onyankopon Tweaduampon a Oboo-adee*). I saw one such tree standing near the entrance to the bedroom of Nana Kwadwa Bɔfoɔ, our *ofie-panin*.

Ɔwawa

Another softwood plant. The bark was used in making fences in cottages or as roof covers of huts in farm and hunting camps. The bark, *abena*, was the cheapest, though not durable, material for hut building. It was also used for collecting rubbish swept in the yard of a house. It was said therefore of a person who was in abject poverty, "*Ɔpra a onya abena mpo nsa.*" ("He has become so impecunious he cannot afford even a bark of common *ɔwawa* tree for the collection of his household refuse.") The trunks of bigger *ɔwawa* trees were cut and carved to make some useful household utensils, such as *apampaa*, for carrying goods; *apaawa*, for food-dish cover or *ɔkoroɔ*, vegetable grinding bowls.

Ɔpononoɔ

A very hard hardwood tree. Its logs cut into lengths of about ten to twelve feet were split into scantlings for house-building purposes.

Akusiaa

Another hardwood tree. From its trunk short pieces of about two feet were cut and carved to make mortars: *ɔwaduro*, for *fufu*-ball pounding; *ɔbɛwaduro*, for pounding oil palm nuts, fried groundnuts, maize and herbs to be used in medicinal soups.

Amire

A tree of medium hardness. Its trunk was cut into short pieces from which roofing shingles, such as those we had on our building in Salem, was made.

Ɔtweneboa

From cut pieces of the tree trunk State Talking Drums (*atumpan*) were carved, hence the prelude to the *atumpan* drumming which pealed on "sacred days": "*Tweneboa Kodua, ma wo omene so!*" ("Be astir and wake up, Kodua, the spirit of *ɔtweneboa* tree!")

Ɔframoo

(*Amire nua*: in the family of the *amire* tree). Like *ɔpononoo*, but of medium hardness, *ɔframoɔ* was used in house-building. Its timber

---

guarded against evil spirits . . . Onyd. "*A esi ahemfo pii aboboano no kyɛre sɛ wɔhyɛ Onyankopɔn pɛ ase,*" the *onyamedua* planted at the threshold of many king's houses is a sign that they stand under the protection of God."

was split into scantlings mainly for the construction of mud and wattle huts.

Ɔkyɛnkɛn

A softwood tree. Its fruits were favourite food for antelopes such as *ɔtwe, adowa, ewuo and ɔwansan.* Hunters therefore lay in wait near the tree early in the morning and in the late afternoon to kill animals which went there to feed. The bark of *ɔkyɛnkyɛn* tree was beaten to make a strong cloth called *kyɛnkyɛn.* I did not see myself the material being used as an item of apparel, but my grandmother said she did. I heard from her that she saw her mother's mother wearing *ɔkyɛnkyɛn* bark cloth which was then the fashion. In her grandmother's days, she related, there was not enough cotton cloth about. A whole family might possess one or two pieces for communal use. The one piece, according to Nana, was for use by all adults. A member going out of the house wore it. On his return home it was left and made available to another member who needed it to wear on a visit to a place outside the compound. The communal cloth for outside wear was hand-loomed cotton cloth bought and brought from Bontuku (Bondugu) by Agogo men who travelled to Bahuren to tap rubber. (*wɔkɔ ɔpowee-bɔ Bahuren*). Because the cloth came from Bontuku, it was called "*Bontuku kyekye.*" Nana had two pieces of *kyenkyen* bark cloth which I saw, but she never wore them. She used them as blankets.

Asia

The ripe fruits of the tree emitted some offensive smell. A story was told of an embarrassment that the scent of an Asia tree caused a woman and her son-in-law to be. The young man was said to be accompanying his mother-in-law to her farm to fell for her some trees in her newly-cleared farm. They reached a spot where the ripe fruits of Asia had fallen in profusion, creating a very unpleasant smell not unlike the belching of a human being. A situation was created which gave cause to one of the farm-goers to suspect the other of being the cause of the foul smell. Sensing the suspicion, the mother-in-law spoke reassuringly and said: "*Mase, ɛnyɛ wo a, Ɛnyɛ me a, Ɛyɛ Asia, a.*" ("My son-in-law, you are not the cause of it, I am not the cause of it. It is Asia that has caused it.") Hence, the expression came into proverbial usage, and was used to clear up a situation when blame for the cause of some unpleasant incident was not to be put on the first or second person, but on a third person or on some unavoidable circumstance.

Ɔsɛsɛ

A tree of the *ofruntum* family (*ofruntum nua*), was used in carving white stools for household use. It was one such stool, used by an Elder of an *abusua* in his lifetime that was consecrated, blackened and kept as his "Black Stool" after his death. From ɔsɛsɛ wood too was carved *baduaba*, the so-called fertility doll.

Odum

"The King Tree." It was believed to be one of the sacred forest trees which possessed "spirit" and was to be propitiated before felling it. The timber was pit-sawn when I was a child, to provide boards and scantling for building and furniture making.

Esa

The sapling of the tree was popularly used as a *fufu*-pounding pestle. The matured tree was generally killed by firing to provide first-rate combustible firewood material for cooking and snail broiling.

Odwuma

A softwood tree. It was felled for the log to be split into some light boards for fencing, generally. The fruits it bore had a velvety covering which could easily be mistaken for a real velvet cloth. This had prompted a saying: "*Odwuma horɔdoɔ, Woyɛ wo ho sɛ agoʃ*" ("Young budding *odwuma*, you delude yourself into believing that you are a piece of genuine velvet cloth.") The saying was quoted when referring to a low class person who assumed some air of superiority to boast his standing in a society. Rafts used for fishing on Lake Bosomtwe were, I was told, logs of the *odwuma* tree.

Tweapea

The "chewing-stick" tree. In the days before the introduction of the toothbrush and toothpaste, *tweapea-duaa* was an indispensable article in every home in our town. It was chewed (*we*) to clean the teeth first thing in the morning by grown-ups; after a meal and, before any self-respecting person went to bed after his last meal, the chewing of *tweapea-duaa* was a must.

Ɔtannuro

The name of the tree, *ɔtannuro*, it was explained to me, was a contraction of "*ɔtan nni aduro*," meaning "there is no remedy for as a cure for hatred." The ripe seeds of the tree were favourite food for large birds of the forest, such as *ɔnwam* (horn-bill) and *akyenkyena*. The proverbial name of the tree was used in an involved statement: "*Akyenkyea se, onya obi akɔka akyerɛ Ɔnwam Kesebrekuo sɛ, onnyae Ɔtannuro di, na ɔno a odii kan dii no, asram atɔ nitrim.*" ("Akyenkyena, the Bird, says she wished she could have someone to carry a message to warn Ɔnwam Kesebrekuo to desist from eating the seeds of *ɔtannuro*, for she, Akyenkyena, the first to eat the seeds, had contracted a fatal cranium disease, *kokoram.*") It was a sarcastic expression meant to insinuate an upstart who indulged in unhealthy competition to undo an experienced rival.

Akuekue-nsuo

A soft wood, quick-growing tree. It bore large scarlet petals which caught and stored clean, clear water. We collected the flower and squeezed the water into our eyes to imitate tears from our weeping mothers.

Prɛkɛsɛ

The tree bore large fruits, bits of which were used as spice in soups. The pungent scent of its fruit earned for it the appellation: "*Prɛkɛsɛ, Ogyaanaku, Ofiti Kurotia a ne ho bon afie mu.*" ("*Prɛkɛsɛ*, the insuppressible, whose presence permeates houses as he touches at its outskirts.") The expression was used in reference to a notorious character whose crafty deals instantly revealed his presence on arrival at a place or in a community.

Bedi-wonua

The latex from the tree gave such a pleasant and alluring scent that its application as a perfume by a woman was said to be so effective that it could seduce her own brother.

Ntommɛ

A quick-growing, hardy tree which was planted to mark boundaries of farms or for fencing. It was cut pieces of the tree that I saw used in making *nkyerɛɛ* (men's place of convenience) when we returned to Agogo from Kwaaman.

Ɔbonsannua

"The Devil Tree." It was so named, I was told, because of the colour of its bark was red, which was said to represent the eye of the Devil. I was also told that the bark of the tree was an essential ingredient in some medicine prepared to drive away evil spirits and witches.

Akɔnkɔdeɛ

It was a popular tree in our boyhood days. We went in groups to collect for our games its pink-coloured, stiff large-petalled flowers held in a deep basin. We picked up all the flowers which had fallen from the tree. At times we had to wait patiently for some hours for one flower to fall when we rushed and scrambled for it. *Akɔnkɔdeɛ* trees growing near the town were named after handsome persons or respectable people to symbolize the beauty of their flowers. Two such trees, I recollect very well, were *buosie* in a *borɔnoo* in town, and Akɔnkodeɛ Akwasi Pong (named after my uncle) in Salem. Dwarfs (*mmoatia*) were said to have their home on top of the tree. For that reason, when a boy in a collecting group screamed:

"*Mmoatia, Sankuo - O - O, Hwane na ɔbɛkɔ fie - e - e?*" ("Dwarfs, the music players, Who will go home?") we all ran helter-skelter back home in fear.

Atewa

A tree dear to us children. From its long pods which split by themselves when mature, flat seeds were scattered about in all directions under the tree. They were collected avidly and jealously kept for use as a plaything in our competitive *atewa* spinning games. The husks, too, were gathered and kept in heaps for our bonfires around which we sat and sang carols on Christmas Eve and after New Year's Midnight Church service. Several climbers combined with large trees in the forest and competed to reach high in the sky to catch the sun's light and some of its heat.

As in the case of trees, Father took the trouble to tell me the names of the larger and most useful ones, including:

Nnɔtɔ

A woody climber. It was cut and split into strands which were kept for use mostly in mud and wattle hut construction. It was supple and could be stored for a reasonably long time.

Ntwea

A climber much like *nnɔtɔ* but a little coarser. It was cut, treated and used in the same way as *nnɔtɔ*.

Odufee

A woody climber which was cut and beaten for its strands to be used in making fences and cocoa drying mats.

Nwerɛ

A woody climber with prickles; gives some tender, pliable fibre useful for making cocoa drying mats (*asrene*). Its thick, sharp thorns made its handling risky and difficult.

Sapɔ

The climber was of direct commercial value during our boyhood days. It was cut, beaten and treated for use as sponges for bathing and washing of utensils. Sponges prepared for sale were specially treated and made into round fluffs, each about twelve inches in diameter, six of which were, at that time, sold for three pence (*sempoa*).

Hama-kyɛm

"The Leopard Climber." It was said to be sacred because it had *sasa* (spirit). Fetish priests and medicine-men who needed cuttings from the climber for use as medicine had to observe some rituals, I was told, before the sun rose and after an egg had been thrown to hit it.

Agyaamaa
A useful, well-known climber. Its white latex was tapped, coagulated and used for trapping birds such as parrots on top of high trees, and other smaller birds, by streams, in the dry season, in an operation called *amantoɔ.*

Mmata-twenee
A climber with clasping roots. Its tough, almost waterproof fibre was used mostly for weaving *adwokuo* (fish traps).

Among the variety of canes of which Father taught me names and uses were:

Ɔyeɛ
It was used in making more durable baskets than those made of palm and raffia branches. It was also used for making stronger cocoa bean drying mats.

Demire
The cane was slightly smaller in size than *ɔyeɛ,* but served the same purpose which was the making of cocoa drying mats and baskets.

Kete
The stalk of the cane was prepared for making a type of a flute used in a *kete* drum dance band.

Mfia
The smallest of plants in the cane family, it grew mainly on dry lands unlike the others which grew in marshy places. Because of its suppleness, *mfia* was used in bindings requiring finer finish and perfection.

Any account of forest products from the Agogo Stool land would be incomplete without a word or two on the oil palm tree. Everywhere in the forest area of the land, the tree could be seen growing. The belt that fringed the Afram Plains grassland was the home of the tall stately palm tree, *ɔbɛten,* that bore several clusters of nuts perennially. In cleared areas of farms, the oil palm tree grew uncultivated. One particular locality of such a profuse growth of the tree earned the name *Abɛten-Tiase* (the place of oil palm trees). It was the place that was leased to the pioneer Basel Missionaries for the development of their Salem – the quarter for the first Christian community of Agogo. I knew of four varieties of the oil palm trees, namely:

Abɛ-pa

The ordinary thick-shelled oil palm tree. It grew in abundance all over the land.

Abobɔ-bɛ

It was the type that had smaller nuts with thin soft shells which could be easily broken with the teeth, hence the name, easily cracked palm nuts. When cooked in salted water, the nuts of *abobɔ* were delicious, chewed whole.

Abɛ-hene

"King Oil Palm Tree" was very common. What was nice about the tree, and what might have earned it the royal name, was its stately appearance with leaflets that branched, not at right angles as the ordinary oil palm tree, but at neat, acute angles to the frond. There was not much to differentiate the nuts of *abɛhene* from those of *abɛ-pa*.

Abɛ-dɔm

The tree resembled *abɛ-pa* but had larger kernels. Its unripe and young fruits were green but they turned reddish orange with green yellow tips when ripe. It was said that *abɛ-dom* was a taboo for a slave. It was held that a slave who ate the nuts of *abɛ-dɔm* or drank its wine lost his senses and became crazy. Whether this was credible or not, I could not say, but it was an oft-quoted saying: "*Ɔdɔnkɔ ba kyiri ɔbɛdɔm.*" ("An off-spring of a slave has the *abɛ-dɔm* as a taboo.")

The numerous products and by-products of the oil palm tree are too well known to require repetition. However, for the purpose of reinforcing the point that Agogo was blessed with innumerable natural resources in my boyhood days, it is felt that a remark or two on how this useful tree contributed to the richness of life in the town might not be a bore.

When we were boys, and before I was sent to school, people of our town made their own sweeping-brooms (*prayɛ*) from the spines of the leaves on the branches of the tree. Parts of the leaves left after the spines had been removed were bound together and tightened at one end to make a plaything used by teenage boys in a game called *ɔsɔma*. Whole branches of the tree were used as roof-covers on sheds and farm-cottage huts, hunting camps and several forms of shelters. The fronds were used in weaving baskets of all sizes and shapes, including *kentenku*, the largest, for the storage of every conceivable article including personal properties, such as cloths and other apparel. From the frond was also woven *asrɛnɛ*, the cocoa bean drying mats. The nuts (*mmɛfua*) were an important item of food. They were boiled and pounded to prepare nourishing palm-soup (*abɛ-kwan*), or pounded for the extraction of rich vegetable oil (*abɛ-nno*). Stews were cooked with palm-oil, and palm-oil was used in making local "black soap" (*samina-tuntum*). The fibre from the pounded nuts (*mmɛ-fee*), which was the residue when the liquid had been squeezed out, was burned for the smoke to blacken earthenware dishes (*nwowa*) and washing-pots (*dware-sen*) and to give them a lustre. The smoke from the burning *mmɛ-fee* was also utilised to improve the taste of water in earthenware drinking-pots (*pun ahina mu*).

Palm-kernel oil (*adwe-nno*) extracted from the kernels inside the nuts was, in those days, mainly used medicinally. The hard covering of the kernels were collected by Agogo blacksmiths and burnt in their sheds (*tonsuom*) to heat pieces of iron which, when they became red-hot, were hammered on anvils to produce hoes (*nsɔ*) for women, earth chisels (*nsɔsɔ*) for builders, cocoa-plucking chisels (*kokoo asosowa*) for farmers, and felling-axes (*nkuma*) for all. The tree was tapped for its wine (*nsa-fufuo*), which, when fresh and undiluted, made a refreshing drink. When left for a long time, the wine fermented and became so intoxicating that many a man fell victim to its snare and became inebriated. Palm-wine left overnight (*ɔdae*) was drunk and enjoyed by hardened habitual palm-wine drinkers (*asa-dweam*).

On dead wood of tapped palm trees grew a kind of popular mushroom called *domo*. From eggs laid by a fly called *asɔmmorɔdwe* in the hole of an abandoned tapped palm tree grew some large edible larvae, *akɔkone*. The fat-filled grubs were dug out from the decaying log of the tree and, when roasted, became a delicacy which went very well with roast plantain (*borɔde-dwo*), a snack which was very much enjoyed by us children in those days.

Wine from the oil palm tree was the main drink for the ordinary Agogo man on all occasions of sadness, merry-making or social gatherings and functions. The gods and *ɔbosom* of Agogo, it appeared to me, did not enjoy drinking *nsa-fufuo* (palm-wine), the drink of the common man, very well but preferred imported gin (*mmorɔ-sa*), which I saw was always offered them during libation pouring functions by linguists of the Agogohene and owners of all fetishes. Palm-wine was cheap and readily available. A standard size palm-wine drinking pot called *adama-hina* (a two-penny worth pot) was used for the collection of the wine. A drinking pot brimful of the stuff cost tuppence, hence the name. It is worth remarking that the same quantity of the drink sells for over C10 (£5—) in our modern days (1982). Expenses for drinks at funerals were greatly minimised by "self-supply" palm-wine. The practice was that, when a member of a family was critically ill and there was no hope of his/her coming through, the head of the family (*ofiepanin*) arranged for some trees growing on the family land to be felled and tapped in readiness. If death did occur, drinks were ready, free and in sufficient supply for serving friends and sympathisers who went to mourn with the bereaved family. From this practice came the expression, *"yɛreto ne mmɛ"* ("palm trees for his funeral are being felled") which, when made in reference to a person who was very seriously ill, came to mean, "he is on the brink of death."

Fish was also in abundance in the Agogo of my childhood days. Fishing was concentrated and seasonal, the business taking place in the major dry season of the year (*ɔpɛ-berɛ*). Fish were caught in large quantities from the Afram River and his "wife" (tributary), Ɔnwam Yaa, which flowed east south-eastward through the Afram Plains, some twelve to fifteen miles from the town, to join the Volta River.

We often heard at the beginning of the dry season a gong-gong beating to announce that some person had been granted fishing rights over a named section on the Ɔnwam or a depth in the Afram, and that any person who wished to participate in the operation was welcome. Men and some daring women of Agogo as well as some non-Agogo people from nearby towns rushed to the particular place to fish in groups. I was too young to understand most of what it was all about, but a relative, Kwabena D., who always accompanied his father, an experienced entrepreneur — *ɔsa-hene*, they called such people — every year to the operation, has given me the following account of fishing in the two rivers before the Volta Lake inundated the Afram Plains.

Before we went to a fishing camp, my father approached the Agogohene and his Elders to negotiate for the right over a particular fishing section on River Ɔnwam or a depth (*ebun*) on River Afram. My father was asked to pay a fee together with three bottles of gin and one fowl. One of the bottles was used for a libation in the Ahem-fie to the Chief's Stools. The second bottle was taken to Afram-fie (the house of the Fetish Afram) for a libation to the *ɔbosom*. The third bottle and the fowl were carried with us to the fishing camp and given to the *ɔdekuro* who, in the morning following the day of our arrival at the camp, used them for some ritual on the bank of the river. In the course of the performance of the ritual the *ɔdekuro* spoke to the spirit of the river and said:

Asuo Afram/Ɔnwam,
Woakoa Kwame D. aba ha sε, ɔrebεpe bribi kakra akodi. Okura ne
nsam nsa akɔtewa ne akɔkɔ a, ɔderema wo. Mesrε wo, mma bribiara
nyε no. Mma bɔne biara nka nnipa a ɔde wɔn aba ha rebedi dwuma yi
no. Obiara a, obesi wo nsuo yi mu, mesrε wo, mma ɔmfa nsapan nkɔ
ofie. Kwame D. se, sε woboa no ma ne dwuma a ɔrebedi yi yε yiye, na
bribiara anyε no ne obiara a waba ha rebedi dwuma yi a, okura ne
nsam edwan pa, a otua dua, bεba abεda wo ase. Agogohene nkwa so,
ne mpaninfoɔ nyinaa nkwa so!

(River Afram/Ɔnwam,
Your servant Kwame D. has arrived here to find something little to eat. He has brought to you a bottle of gin and a fowl. I pray, let not anything ill befall him nor any of all those who have come here with him. I pray, let whoever enters the water of your river obtain something. Do not let anyone come out of it empty-handed. Kwame D. promises you a whole live sheep if you guide and direct all operations about to start to a successful end. Long life to the Agogohene. Long life to all his Stool Elders)

Meantime my father had advertised the operation widely. The reason was that the more people who took part in the fishing, the bigger the catch, and the bigger his share of the takings would be. He took a third of all the catch in his section or depth of the river during the season. The first four days of our arrival at the fishing site were spent on active preparations. Huts were erected; fish-smoking platforms were put up by groups, and everyone collected firewood which was piled up ready for smoking the catch. Two methods of fishing were employed in those days, namely: *Anuu* and *Ahwee*.

Annu fishing

This was the method employed to catch fish by drugging. One of the following two kinds of drugging-material was uses: (a) *εhweε*, (leaves of *εhweε* shrub), or (b) *adede*, (latex from *akane* tree).

(a) Preparation of εhweε for fishing

The shrub was gathered in bundles and dried in the sun. The dried leaves and stem were crushed with earth and pounded into a moist, coherent mass which was rolled into balls. The handy balls were carried to the river and dissolved into the water at a point where fish were suspected to be living in large numbers. The irritating property of the *ɛhweɛ* stupefied the fish in the depths and caused them to rise to the surface, throwing themselves about frantically. Fishermen and women who had stationed themselves at vantage points in anticipation of the forced emergence of their quarry cast their nets and caught the paralysed creatures.

(b) Adede was the latex of a tree called *akane.* The tree was tapped and the grey liquid stored in containers that were carried to the river's edge. When poured into the water of a depth, its poisonous effect on the fish dwelling in it was the same as *ɛhweɛ.*

Ahweɛ fishing

This was the method employed to catch fish from rivers without drugging. To reach the creatures a dam for the purpose was constructed at a convenient spot upstream to arrest the flow of its water. The dam was built by first fixing in the river strong wooden pillars, the height of each was not less than twice the depth of the river at the point of construction. To the pillars were attached cross-pieces, which were fastened with the fibre of the *nnɔtɔ* climber. On the upstream side of the fence, palm branches were fixed against the erected framework. Soil was dug from the bank and dumped thick and tight behind the leaves and branches. The fishermen and women made quite sure that the swish had been rammed so firmly that no water could penetrate to flow downstream. The dam thus erected, the fishermen and fisherwomen, working in groups, dipped and threw away (*hwe*) the water standing in pools with pans and scoops. In a short while the aquatic inhabitants were uncovered, grabbed into nets and carried into pits dug ready on the banks. To and from the river they went, catching and unloading fish into prepared pits, till all edible creatures in a pool had been cleared. Fish caught in the Ɔnwam and Afram Rivers by either *anuu* or *ahweɛ* method in those days included:

Apaterɛ: same species as those in Lake Bosomtwe
Apate-bire: ditto
Okyikyie: which grew a set of three horns on their head
Adɛɛma: which resembled Okyikyie and grew three horns
Ɔbɔre
Osusuakye: one of the three biggest fish in the two rivers
Aprukusu: its touch gave an electrifying shock

Ɔdom
Ɔsrayɛ
Ɔdweam
Osapa
Apraneɛ
Nkonturo: same species as were caught in large quantities in
   the Ankobra River in the Nsema area
Opitire: a prize fish; one of the largest fish in the two rivers
Otikwafɔ: another one of the largest fish
Ɔkyɛɛ-mmire: resembled Apatere but it was so large that it had to
   be cut into about 12 or 13 pieces for effective smoking

Osudanna, also called "*osu-kyekyedeɛ*" (river tortoise) and
apɛtɛ, another river tortoise, but bigger, were often caught in
the two rivers. Kwabena D. continued his story:

My father, the *ɔsahene* (operation-promoter) who had taken the
fishing right of a particular section or depth, took as his share a third
of all takings. To be able to collect his share effectively, he engaged
helpers called *gyaase-foɔ*, agents who were his authorised collectors
and "watch-dogs," vigilantes, as it were. Fishermen and women
employed as *gyaase-foɔ* retained the third share which should have
gone to the promoter. An *ɔsahene* had the full authority to seize and
confiscate part or all the catch of a fisherman who proved to be
dishonest and unscrupulous. In a temporary fishing camp where
there was no resident *ɔdekuro*, the *ɔsahene*, for all intents and
purposes, acted in place of the Agogohene with all the delegated
authority and privileges. In such a place it was a part of his duty to
collect all *ahen-nam*, the share which would go to the Agogohene,
and arrange for it to be dispatched to Agogo. *Ahen-nam* comprised
the largest fish of the catch, such as *apitire, atikwafoɔ*, or a quantity
of such fish caught which the *ɔsahene* might consider deserving of a
gift to the Chief. In a village with a resident *ɔdekuro*, it was his duty
to collect and dispatch *ahen-nam* to Agogo. If not properly organized
and if insufficiently advertised, an *ɔsahene* might run into debt, but
shrewd and experienced promoters always found the venture
profitable and worthwhile. Some young men and women who could
not do the actual fishing benefited by going to the camp to buy head
loads of fish which they brought to sell at Agogo. Meat and fish-
sellers were, in those days, all men. A woman was expected to sell
food crops such as plantains, garden-egg, pepper and okra. Hence, it
was said in those days: "*Ɔbaa tɔn nnuadewa, ɔntɔn atuduro.*"
("Woman's wares are garden-eggs, not gunpowder.")
   The intensive fishing period in Afram and Ɔnwam lasted about a
month when fishers worked full time all day except on Thursday, in
the case of fishing in the Ɔnwam River, and Saturdays, on the Afram

River. When fishing for the season ended and before we left the camp, the ɔsahene, my father, redeemed his pledge by presenting a live sheep to the ɔdekuro for a sacrifice to the Spirit of the River.

Group fishing apart, individuals caught fish in rivers by *kwagyan-too*, another drugging method. *Kwagyan* was a woody climber whose sap was poisonous. The stem was cut into pieces and beaten into pulp. The preparation was taken to a river and stirred into water near a hole, at the entrance of which a fish-trap, *adwokuo,* had been set. In a rush to escape from their unbearable abode, the disturbed fish swam into the trap and were caught by trappers who stood by waiting for the escaping creatures.

The Volta Lake, Kwabena D. observed, has now changed drastically the pattern and mode of fishing in the Afram and Ɔnwam rivers. Almost all the designated fishing depths have been levelled by the lake and in their place stretches of large expanses of water now flow. "Professional" fishermen from the Volta and the Northern Regions have taken permanent residence on the Afram River. Seekyeso, for instance, where the depth was the deepest, is now a sizable fishing village of Ayigbe (Ewes) people, and Punaase as well as Dawiaso depths are worked by some fishermen from the north (*ntafoo*). The "alien" professional fishermen work under the traditional agreement whereby a third of their catch went to the Agogohene. In place of *anuu* and *ahweε* methods which the indigenous Agogo people employed in group fishing within a limited period of about one month in the dry season, the professional non-Agogo fishermen have taken permanent residence on the banks of the river and employ the following three main methods, namely:

Twii, by which a wide nylon net is stretched across the river, from bank to bank, to catch all fish which happen to pass up or down the river at a point where the trap is fixed;

Cast-nets with lead-ends thrown to catch fish at a particular spot on the river;

Adwokuo traps made of canes or palm branches are placed in openings and gaps left in a fence erected in the river to catch all fish that attempt to cross to either side of the blockade.

Kwabena D. ended his account on a rather depressing note. One very disturbing fact, he deplored, was that some unscrupulous people now catch fish in the two big rivers of

Agogo by using deadly and poisonous chemicals such as cyanide which does not only kill all fish and any living creatures in a very wide area of each river, but render every fish so killed highly dangerous for human consumption. Maybe, he ended dejectedly, this too is one of the prices of "civilization" (*anibue ne ɔpɔ*) that the modern Agogo man has to pay.

Women of Agogo, too, went a-fishing in my childhood days. They employed the *ahweɛ* (direct catching of fishes) method on a small sale. Small, in the sense that the fishing was done, not in deep waters of big rivers, but in smaller streams that ran not far from the town or farm villages, in particular, Kurowire-Atifii, Aborɔdesu, Supuni, Apampramasu, Ntɔn and Pɛmfɛn. Their fishing was also done in the *harmattan* season, when most or all the streams dried out. They did not fish to sell but for the consumption of the family.

My mother took me to *ahweɛ* in the Apampramasu stream one afternoon. I can recollect that we went with a group made up of most of the women from the nearby cottage. They carried enamel and wooden basins (*korɔɔ*), hoes, scoops, machetes and large sieves made of the spines of raffia palm leaves (*sɔne-yɛ*). An important item they took with them was a short piece of wood with live fire at one end (*gyentia*). At a rendezvous on the bank of the stream the women stopped and got themselves prepared for business. Fire was set while they changed dresses. They removed and put aside the neater and better cloths they wore to the place. Some of them put on *pieto* (short underwear). Others, tighter cloths which were held above the knee. Our mothers were ready to start fishing.

A dam was erected. We, their children who accompanied them, assisted by carrying dug-up earth to ram in the dam. In groups of threes and fours the women attacked stagnant pools, dipping out the water. The exposed fish including *nkawa, mmɔbɔnsɛ,* medium-size *mpatewa,* a few small-size *apitire* and some prawns, were caught. The children carried their mothers' catch of fish to the fire and emptied them into receptacles brought for the purpose. Movable rocks standing in the stream were heaved aside single-handed, or with the help of a co-fisher, if it was a big and heavy rock. Crabs hiding under them were grabbed with both hands and killed by deeply pressing in the underside of the eight-legged broad-bodied shellfish with the thumb of the right hand. It was, to me, a startling exploit seeing mother catching live crabs and killing them in such a way that not a single one of them could bite her with its fearfully big pincers.

When one pool was completely denuded of its useful contents a group moved downstream to tackle another one. The operation continued in that way until daylight began to fade when all the women retired to the fire to share their booty. My mother worked in a group of two other women. Their joint catch was therefore shared into three equal parts. The oldest woman of the groups who did the sharing asked her junior partners to collect their shares first, remarking, "Ɔkyɛ, adeɛ nyɛ atu-kanee." ("A sharer must not be the first to pick.") Once the booty had been shared, holes were pierced through the dam for the volume of water that had, by then, collected high behind it to rush gushing downstream. Our mothers once again changed their attire and put on respectable cloths for their return home. Thus prepared, they set off for their respective cottages. Mother's share of the day's catch could feed us for about a week, and sumptuously too.

Mushrooms (*mmire*), too, were plentiful in Agogo. They grew wild all over the place — in the deep forest and on cleared farms. The edible ones, I knew, were classified into two groups: *esi-bire* and *mmirebia*. *Esi-bire* comprised two large types of mushroom which grew on anthills. They were *ɔnoo* and *nkyemmire*.

Ɔnoo

This mushroom was tastier and fluffier and grew only one crop once in a year in the minor rainy season from about the beginning of August to about the end of November. The sprouting of the plant was so regular that, it was said, it could be timed to within a week The mushroom was, in our boyhood days, the exclusive property of the person who owned the farm on which the anthill (*esie*) was situated, if weeds growing on it had been cleared by the owner in anticipation of its sprouting. In such a case, it was the owner only who had the right to uproot the crop. Any other person who passed by and saw the growth might either inform the owner or could uproot the mushroom and carry the whole lot to the rightful owner who gave the picker a share for the service rendered. Whoever uprooted sprouting *ɔnoo* mushrooms from a cleared anthill and failed to deliver it all to the owner, committed a theft and could be punished if found out. If the poacher could not be traced, the owner could inflict a curse on the thief. It was then believed that if some of the soil removed from the roots of a stolen *ɔnoo* mushroom was moistened with water and placed back into a hole of an uprooted plant, the pilferer was sure to contract a damaging disease called *ahonhono*. *Ɔnoo* mushroom was never, never, never to be salted when on a fire cooking. It was said that if salted in that way, the particular anthill on which it grew ceased producing mushroom (*esie no wu*). It was a known characteristic of the *ɔnoo* mushroom. It was said of it: "*Ɔnoo nyin horan, horan, horan; na ewu ntɛm, ntɛm, ntɛm.*" ("*Ɔnoo* mushroom develops very, very rapidly, and dies very, very, very quickly.") The owner of its anthill, therefore, had to keep a vigilant watch and pay frequent visits to the farm during the week that it was expected to sprout.

Nkyemmire (saltable mushroom)
As the name implied the mushroom could be safely salted while cooking without "killing" the anthill on which it grew. It sprouted once a year at the beginning of the major rainy season, which was in about February, March and April. Several crops, as many as six, could be collected from one hill in a season. No one person could claim the exclusive ownership of *nkyemmire* mushroom. Whoever reached it and spotted it first was the rightful owner, whether it was seen growing on somebody's farm or in an uncleared forest area.

Mushroom gathering was the work of women and children in the days when I was a child. The plant, when uprooted, was smoked to dry and kept for use. Properly treated, mushrooms could be preserved for as long as two years and would retain their wholesomeness, particularly, when used in palm-soup (*abɛ-kwan*). Some of the mushroom collected were sold, fresh or smoked, for small amounts. Now *nkyemmire* gathering is a big business in Agogo in which not only women and children, but also many young men fully engage themselves, gaining, in some cases, substantial amounts of some C200 or more for a day's collecting mainly from the Afram plains fringing the forest. Buyers of *nkyemmire* travel from several places in the country and take away loads of the mushroom.

The *mmirebia* species comprised all smaller-size mushrooms which grew not on ant hills in particular, but on logs of dead wood (*dufɔkyeɛ*), of palmtrees (*abɛ-fun*) or on the ground in unspecified places in the forest or in farm areas. *Mmirebia* of all kinds grew mainly in the rainy season, and like *ɔnoo* mushroom, *mmirebia* I knew in my childhood days included:

Domo
It grew on dead and decaying logs of the following trees: oil palm, *ɔkyɛnkyɛ*, *ɔnyina* — all soft wood trees. *Domo* could be cultivated

on palm-nut clusters (*mmɛtema*) and on heaped *kookoo-puo*, the core in the cocoa pod on which the beans clustered.

Esaseɛ

It grew on logs of soft wood trees, except the oil palm tree. As the name implied, the mushroom grew on dead roots of the *esa* tree.

Gyamadusuo

It also grew on the logs of soft wood trees. A *gyamadusuo* mushroom soup looked blackish and was very tasty.

Mmɛwereɛ

The mushroom was white in appearance and brittle in touch, and grew on oil palm trees.

Mpempena

It grew on the ground and at unspecified places. It grew in a mass which covered several square yards of ground. *Mpempena*, seasoned with pepper, salt and onions and baked in *anwonomoo* (one-leaf plant), served with roasted plantain or cocoyam, was another delicacy for us children in those days. Grown-ups, too, liked it.

Kyikyirikyi

Place of growth: As *mpempena* mushroom. It sprouted generally in October when the minor rain, *kyikyirikyi suo* fell briskly in the night, hence the name of the mushroom. Snails were available at that time of the year, and so with *kyikyirikyi* mushroom, it was possible for mothers to provide delicious palm soup (*abɛkwan*) of the two cherished ingredients.

Nsosaa

It could, like *nkyemmire*, be salted when cooking without any harm to its place of growth.

Ɔdabɔ

This *mmirebia* had a little red patch on top of it. As the colour resembled that of the *ɔdabɔ* antelope, the mushroom was given the name, "*Ɔdabɔ*." When a person sighted the mass of growth and shouted aloud, "*Ɔdabɔ, trɛ trɛm ɛ-ɛ-ɛ*"("grow and spread, *dabɔ mmirebia*"), the mushroom, it was said, grew fast and spread.

Ntrotrowa or adiabronsa

Ntrotrowa implied sliminess, and *adiabronsa*, a state of drunkenness, after eating a thing. The two names of the one mushroom, therefore, defined the qualities of the plant. When cooked, it became slimy like an okra (*nkruma*) and tasted so nice that the temptation was to eat one's fill. There was nothing wrong about that, provided that the consumer of any quantity of the palatable *ntrotrowa* soup did not take any intoxicating drink, palm-wine included, either soon after the meal or later for as long as about ten to fourteen days. Unlike the lotus-eater of Greek mythology in *The Odyssey*, who subsisted on the lotus shrub and lived in the dreamy indolence it induced, it was said that the Agogo *adiabronsa*-eater who took any strong drink, lived in agony of acute headache, violent heart-thumping and general restlessness which, more often than not, ended in his death. *Adiabronsa* or *ntrotrowa* were, therefore, women's or children's mushrooms. A man who dared eat its soup and then drank any alcoholic liquid after the meal did so at his own very fatal risk.

One valuable Agogo forest product was the edible land-living snail (*nwa*). Then, as now, snails emerged from inactivity (*fi*) twice a year in the wet seasons. The first emergence was expected about three to four months after Christmas — in March and April, generally. They disappeared (*wɔhyɛne*) in the minor dry season (*ofupe-bere*) — in about July and August — and came out of concealment again in about the ninth month, September/October. Snails lived in the forest areas of the land and fed mainly by night or at dusk. They sometimes came out by day when it rained or when the sky was overcast (*osuo muna tumm*). Snail hunting (*awa*) was prohibited (*bra nwa*), and until a proclamation removing the ban had been made by the beating of the gong-gong (*yeatue nwa*), it was an offence to bring home from the bush even a single snail. The officials of the Chief's court (*nhenkwaa*) saw to it that the prohibition was strictly observed by all. They had the power to go on roads to stop and search head loads and other packets being brought home from anywhere in the bush. When it was considered that the snails were reasonably mature the Chief, in consultation with his Elders, caused an announcement to be made by gong-gong. Such announcements were generally made on a Friday evening. The day following the announcement removing the ban was generally a busy one as all able-bodied young men, women and children of Agogo and the neighbouring towns rushed to hunt for snails (*kɔ awa*).

On several occasions, I accompanied my mother and some of her relatives snail hunting in the forest adjacent to our Apampramasu cocoa farm. We took with us machetes, small and big enamel basins, empty sacks and bags of narrow-meshed nets. We searched for snails at different places on different days, but wherever we went we prepared a stopping place where we set fire and left all the big containers. The place became, as it were, our "central depot" from where we dispersed in several directions in our search. Snails sought cover under fallen leaves in the daytime. A bulge formed by the snail and its leaf-cover (*nwa-boa*) betrayed the hiding place of the animal. They were hunted by using a short stick of about three to four feet long (*prɛ-duaa*) to remove dead leaves on the bulges suspected of sheltering them. The operation was referred to as *aprɛ*, baring by removing coverings. One by one bared snails were picked and kept in a receptacle which, when filled, was taken back to the "central depot," and emptied into a bag, a sack, or an enamel basin. Care was taken to ensure that all snails brought to the "depot" for storage were kept tightly in containers. The operation continued till one's container was full or it was time to go back home. Many a time, a bulge did not harbour a snail but another creature such as a millipede (*kankabi*). If a bulge dweller was a millipede, a hunter tapped it gently with his/her hunting stick (*prɛ-duaa*) thrice, muttering each time:

> *Kankabi e-e-e-,*
> *Gye wo poma,*
> *Gye wo poma,*
> *na fa me kosi awa-dwaa.*

(Hi-i-i Millipede,
Take hold of your stick,
Take hold of your stick,
and lead me to a colony of snails)

The belief was that, by making the plea to the millipede, the hunter would be led to a large colony of snails. It did often happen that a protrusion contained a nocturnal snake called "*ɔnanka*." In such a case the hunter might withdraw the hunting stick quickly and leave the wallowing serpent alone, or, if he were brave, cut a big stick to crush it to death in its sleep. I never encountered a sleeping *ɔnanka* snake in a bulge, but I came face to face with something more frightening. Engrossed in my pickings in a large colony of snails, I raised up my head. And what did I see? There it was! Right in front of me and curled round an *mpawuo* sapling, was a red-eyed green mamba (*ɔkyereben*) with tongue twirling from the mouth. The instinct of fear took the reins and commanded. I obeyed and took to flight. I ran away fast from the venomous thing. All mother's admonishments about manly behaviour she so frequently dished out to us sank into oblivion. "*Ɔbarima nsu; Ɔbarima nnwane.*" ("A brave man never cried; a brave man never ran away from danger.") They could go to hell. I ran away fast and frantically, trembling to the bones. Out of danger and safe from the mamba, I consoled myself and to hide my shame by muttering incoherently: "I am not a grown-up yet; I am not a man, anyhow!"

Snails were sold unshelled (*awa-kro*) by the unit of tens, or were processed and preserved for sale or for home consumption. Preservation was done in five stages, namely:

1. *Nwa-bɔ* (unshelling)
This was done by putting a whole snail, one at a time, on a flat stone and hitting it with a smaller stone to release the flesh and remove the entrails which were thrown away. Alternatively, a stick sharpened at the end was pierced through the body at the head-end of the shell to dig out the flesh with the entrails left in the shell.

2. *Nwa-sina or nwa-ntoabɔ*
The de-shelled flesh of snails without their entrails were strung on skewers (*nwa-duaa*) made from raffia palm fronds. It was a straightforward operation performed by women and children.

3. *Nwa-kyɛn*
The process required expert handling and was generally done by men. Shelled snails pinned on a stick in stage two, were pressed down tightly on a three-line formation to look like an equilateral triangle at each point on the stick.

4. *Nwa-hoo* (snail broiling)
The sticks of fresh snails were put on a fire to broil, on a grid constructed with stems of pawpaw tree that rested on cross-pieces of banana or plantain stems. The stems of pawpaw, plantain or bananas were used as they were succulent and could stand better and as they were needed for a long time while the sharp heat of the fire broiled the snails which were full of slime. For the same reason fire from special trees such as *esa, kyee, ɔnakwa* and *odum* was preferred as it could not be easily quenched by the slime from the broiling snails.

5. *Nwa-barɛ*
It was the last step in the process in which the neat sticks of broiled snails now called nwa-dwanee, were prepared by experts and bound into units of twenty sticks called *nwa-kyɛm*.

Broiled snails (*nwa-dwanee*) were sold in bundles of twenty sticks, which, in my boyhood days, cost 1s. 6d. Now one *nwa-kyam* of twenty sticks can fetch anything between C200 and C300, depending on the length of the stick and the quality of processing. A stick of broiled snails, *nwa-bena*, was measured in *nsaama*, the distance between the tips of the smaller finger and of the thumb of a man's hand. A three-*nsaama* stick taking about one hundred and twentu single snails, was of a Grade One standard and was priced higher than a shorter stick of about two — or two and a half — *nsaama* which took between fifty and sixty single snails. Snails broiled for one's home consumption were treated with some special care and attention to last for as long as two years.

Any able-bodied person, a native or non-native of Agogo, could hunt snails from anywhere on the Agogo Stool land when the ban had been raised. The Agogohene was, however, to be given his traditional share by all who engaged themselves in the snail-collecting industry. About two weeks after the ban had been raised, *nhenkwaa* (court servants) went round all houses in the town and to all villages and cottages in the area to collect *awa-feɛ*, the Chief's share. They usually went round on Tuesdays and Fridays, snail collecting taboo days, when people where at home working on their takings. In villages, they called on the *odekuro* or the headman of a cottage whose duty it was to assist the court officials in the collection of all that was due to the Chief. The size of the Chief's share was left to be decided at the discretion of the officials who, on the whole, were always quite fair and considerate to honest snail hunters. After a sufficient time had been allowed for the hunting, the season was closed by reimposition of the ban, again by a gong-gong announcement, when snails were left to lay eggs to replenish themselves.

Buyers of snails, in shells (*awa-kro*) or broiled (*nwa-dwanee*), flocked to Agogo during the snail season and brisk trade was always transacted. The District Council has now replaced *nhenkwaa* in the collection of the Chief's traditional share of snails (*awa-feɛ*). When the ban on hunting prohibition is lifted by the Chief and his Elders, the District Council officials issue snail hunting licenses at the entrance of the Chief's house to prospective hunters for a fee, a part of which is paid to the Chief in lieu of snails that would have gone to him traditionally.

Another minor but by no means insignificant source of meat supply in Agogo in my childhood days was the edible bat, *apan*. The flying mammal had two habitats in the forest fringing the Afram plains. One such place was in the area of Anwama and Dukusɛn, and the other, in the neighbourhood of Kurowireso. They migrated to these two places in the major dry season (*opɛ-berɛ*) (November, December, January) and in the minor dry season (*ofupɛ-berɛ*) in about July and August. In each such season the animals alternated their stay in their two habitats, living a few days in the Anwama/Dukusɛn area and from there to the Kurowireso area, returning in rotation to the first habitat for a few days and then to the second.

Bats were nocturnal, roosting in clusters all day in bunches of about two hundred heads in each. At night they fed on fruits and fresh leaves in the particular area. In wet season they went away to some far away place and returned regularly to their Agogo habitats upon the approach of the dry seasons. The *odekuro* of Dukusɛn or Kurowireso would inform the Agogohene of the return of the animals to their feeding grounds and recommend that a gong-gong be beaten to declare open the bat hunting season. Until that was done, it was an offence for any hunter to shoot at any bat colony in the Agogo area. The ban raised, bats were hunted in the afternoons between three and five o'clock only. Two or three hunters usually teamed up and fired simultaneously into a cluster. That was a clever move to kill as many of the creatures with one joint shot in order to lessen the chances of a large number of those that were not hit flying away. Bat hunting lasted about two weeks in one season until the ban was reimposed. The Agogohene's traditional share was a stick of six bats for one shot into a roosting cluster. Any Agogo hunter could take part in the hunting in a declared season.

It is worth noting that the seasons for snail collecting in Agogo generally coincided with mushroom-sprouting period. As land tortoises also fed on mushrooms, the shell-encased reptiles were out of hiding during the same season. Ingredients for soup making, therefore, were, in my childhood days, no serious domestic problem. In the wet seasons there was ample supply of snails, mushrooms and some tortoises; fish and bats were easily available in the dry season, and meat from the forest and the Afram plains area were in abundance all the year round.

Some forty years later I had the opportunity to gain some firsthand knowledge of the extent of the Agogo Stool land and an inkling of its vast natural resources. In the mid-fifties, the Agogohene and his Elders appointed a committee to ascertain on the spot: a) the extent of farms within the Agogo Stool land area owned by non-Agogo citizens, a majority of whom were from the Eastern Region of Ghana, and b) the terms of Agreement, if any, under which each such farm was acquired. As a member of a delegation that toured the north-east, east, and south-eastern sections of the land, I became deeply impressed with the benevolence of Providence for the bounteous blessings bestowed so generously onto Agogo and its people. Standing at the confluence of the Afram and Onyem Rivers close by Kansanso, the boundary village of Agogo, and surveying intently the vast, luxuriant forest lying before me; the fish-swarming River Afram behind; the crab-filled River Onyem on the left; small birds twittering and singing joyfully on trees; great birds flying gracefully, unmolested above, and, seeing with my own eyes chunks of wild game meat piled high on smoking platforms in almost all houses in the village, a passage that I learned by rote in my Class 1 Catechism lesson suddenly surfaced from the sub-conscious mind. It became meaningful and applicable as I recited it to myself: "*Sɛ wudidi me a hyira Yehowa wo Nyankopɔn wɔ asaase pa a ɔde ama wo nti.*" ("When you have eaten your fill, bless the Lord your God for the good land He has given you.")

6

HEALTH PROTECTION AND HEALTH HAZARDS

Community health was the concern of all in Agogo in my boyhood days. The *abosom* (fetishes), the Agogohene and his Stool Elders, men and women as well as children, all contributed to keep and maintain the town in what was, at the time, considered the highest sanitary condition. It was the practice in those days, even as it is today, for the Agogohene and his Elders to consult (*kɔ abisa*) one or other of the two state *ɔbosom*, namely Tano (*Taa-Kofi*) and Afram, on matters concerning the general welfare and progress of the town. The *ɔbosom* consulted, I was told, might predict the imminence of a calamity and prescribe measures to be taken to avert the occurrence of any danger. In all cases of predicted outbreaks of a plague or an infectious disease such as smallpox (*mpete*), the *ɔbosom* always directed that the town should be kept scrupulously clean. That meant that all nooks and corners were to be swept clean; broken bottles and pots (*nkyɛmfehena*), pans and disused mats (*nkɛte-go*), discarded baskets (*nkɛntɛnno*), filthy rags (*ntamago*) and rubbish of any description (*nkuntunkamago*) were all to be cleared away and carried from the town for disposal at a particular spot.

All took part in the town-cleaning operations, as enjoined by the *ɔbosom*. Men brushed off weeds around the town, women swept houses and their surroundings, and children swept the streets and gutters. In long lines women and children trailed along the footpath leading to Kwawu (*Kwawu-kwan*) to *Prayareɛ-so* (disease-swept-away hillock), a spot about a quarter of a mile beyond the Kurowire stream. On top of the hillock and across the footpath, the rubbish from Agogo town was piled "to bar the plague's entry into the town" (*si yareɛ kwan*).

Regular brushing of weeds around the town (nsɔsɔɔ-bɔ) was a communal duty undertaken by men on the order of the *asofo-akyɛ* (leader of youngmen, i.e. non-elders) of the town who summoned them to work by the sounding of a double-headed gong-gong (*nnawu-ta*). Women, in addition to sweeping compounds and their vicinities, were responsible for keeping water-supply places on Aboabo and Kurowire clean (*nsuom-teɛ*). Boys kept men's latrines and their vicinities clean, and women's places of convenience, as well as rubbish disposal places (*suminaso*), were in the care of girls.

Failure to attend communal labour was punishable. Punishment for us boys, imposed and executed by our boy-leaders, varied in type and in severity according to the nature of the "offence" and the frequency of its commission. The most dreaded punishment which every boy of our group feared and tried to avoid was deliberate exclusion from games (*yɛpae wo*). Punishment for failure to take part in the sweeping of the path to the place of convenience and its surroundings was a fixed one: the culprit was barred from using the latrine in his neighbourhood for one week.

The type of latrine I grew to know, and the first I learnt to use by myself, was the most primitive one called *nkyereɛ*. The place of convenience was an inclined platform constructed with logs of some hardy trees. The logs rested on wooden beams supported by stout forked sticks fixed firmly in the ground. Looked at from the end, it was in the form of a right-angled triangle ABC, with side AB, the perpendicular, being the forked-stick pillar of about six to eight feet high; side BC, the base, being the ground level, and side AC, the hypotenuse, the inclined wood platform. At the highest point of the platform a user would squat to do the dropping. He reached there by walking on closely placed stout logs bound tightly together with strong *nɔtɔ* fibre.

Baha, a finely dry-fibre fluff of plantain stem, the refined name being *mposa*, was used by some men in place of the fashionable "toilet stick", but *mposa*, strictly, was a toilet thing for women and girls of those days. Men used a toilet stick, which was either an empty corn-cob (*burodua*) or a short piece of a special climber cut into suitable lengths of about one foot and left in the sun for some time to dry and be rendered firm for effective scraping. It was from the use of such a stick for the toilet that the euphemistic expression *merekɔto abaa* (I am off a-stick throwing) came to mean, "I am off to the toilet." The second stage in the evolution of places of convenience in

Agogo, as I saw it, was the unroofed, unfenced pit-latrine (*tonko*).

There was no hospital anywhere near Agogo. Words such as *dɔkotoa* (doctor), *asepiti* (hospital) and *paneɛ* (injection) were completely outside our everyday vocabulary. Diseases were treated by herbalists and medicine-men (*nnunsin-foɔ*), most of whom were fetish-priests or priestesses. In addition to herbalists, who were regarded as "professional" healers of diseases, some individuals held in private ownership medicines for curing some particular diseases or illness. The range of such people and their knowledge in particular medicines was as wide as there were different diseases. A person might, for instance, be reputed for having in his possession the knowledge of what to add to produce a particular brand of medicine that could cure a particular disease. My mother's sister, for instance, was known to be a "specialist" of repute on arresting vomiting, however violent the condition might be. The knowledge was passed on to her daughter who, in turn, passed it on to her twin daughters, who now administer it effectively. Yet another person might hold a "brand" medicine for a snake-bite. It might be in the form of black powder (*mmɔtɔ*) or in the form of a traditional pill (*dufa*).

In addition, there were popular medicines for the most common ailments. Such medicines were applied as first aid only in all households, and were referred to as "medicines kept for self-treatment" (*nea yɛde hwɛ yɛn ho*). The following, for instance, were common knowledge:

Afama: for the cure of stomach upsets (*ayɛm-keka*)
Some leaves of the herb ground together with one or two nhyeraa: pepper and a few pips of guinea-grains (*wisa*) made a mixture which, dissolved in cold water and strained, was commonly used as an enema, potent for the cure of stomach upsets.

Bontorie: for the cure of constipation (*ayɛm-tim*)
A piece of bark of the tree ground and boiled with pepper and salt was drunk for the cure of the illness.

Toa-ntin: for cuts and bruises
Tender leaves of the herbaceous climber were ground in the palms of both hands and the juice squeezed into the affected part.

Krutu: for the cure of fever (*yare-fufuo*)

The leaves were used in preparing medicinal palm-soup (*abε-duro*) for the cure of fever.

Obodwe: for the free movement of the bowels of an infant child
A piece of bark of the tree was put in the drinking cup of an infant child and fed to it with its drinking spoon (*saawa*) to give free bowels.

Nunum: for use as a general tonic and for good appetite. Some leaves of the shrub were boiled in a small earthen-ware pot (*asenawa*) with pepper. A pinch of salt added to the decoction (*ɔdudo*) was taken first thing in the morning and at convenient times of the day.

Ɛgorɔ: for the treatment of boils (*mpɔmpɔ*)
A leaf of the herb, softened by the heat of fire, was used to cover a boil on which palm oil had been applied.

Akakaduro: a cure-all ready-to-apply medicine (ginger)
Akakaduro was kept in every home for the cure of cough (*ɔwa*), chest pains (*mu-yareɛ*), common colds, headache (*ati-payeɛ*), or sore throat (*ntasua-krowa*). A piece of the bulb was chewed raw, with or without sugar to cure stomach upset (*ayɛm-keka*). What stamped *akakaduro* firmly in my little mind was not its medicinal use, but the use to which the ubiquitous bulb was put as a punitive instrument. Many stern mothers were unsparing in its application by pushing a little ball of ground ginger through the anal orifice in the rectum (*tua*) of a naughty child or urchins who disobeyed their parents or neglected the discharge of their filial domestic duties.

Nufusuo: for curing conjunctivitis (*anii*).
Human mother's breast milk was squeezed into the affected eye or eyes several times a day as might be required.

In general, a medicine-man was consulted only after a first aid treatment had proved ineffective. When consulted, a medicine-man (*odunsi-nii*) accepted a patient for treatment on payment of a first fee called *ntoaseε* which was, in those days, a small amount of *doma-fa* (3s.6d) or *doma* (7s.). Full payment called *adoma-deε* or *aboadeε* was paid on full recovery from the disease or affliction. In some serious or fatal and "bad" diseases (*yare-bone*), the cure was confirmed by the healer in a ritual ceremony called *asubɔ* (sanctification) which, when performed, a sick person under treatment was declared completely fit (*yi no aduro mu*) and absolved from all avoidances. There were some diseases which attacked children only. The common ones were:

Asram

A child might have the disease at birth or be attacked later. The head bones of the victim were said to be so soft that pulsation was distinctly visible on the crown of a little child (*ne ti home*). Its breath was in the form of snoring. It looked feeble and was lacking in the normal body movements. The disease was said to be deadly in those days, claiming the lives of many newly-born babies. The belief was that some mothers had the disease inherent in the breast, causing the death of any child they might bear. A mother whose babies one after the other suffered from the disease sought treatment from an *asram* healer for herself as soon as she became pregnant. Immediately on delivery she put the child under the care of the *asram* "specialist."

Asabra

Asabra was a disease of the digestive system of a newly-born child. Its stool was darkish-green in colour and the victim cried unceasingly. It was a case for a "specialist" to whom the sick child was taken for treatment.

Ɔsorɔ (Convulsion)

The disease attacked children up to the age of about four or five years. It was said to be of two types: the violent type which was diagnosed by the child's violent cry and muscular spasms and the slow, silent (*aka-nyaa*) type. In either case the victim was rushed to a "specialist" herbalist who was known to make a small cut on one cheek into which was pressed some *mɔtɔ* (black powder) or *dufa* (a traditional healer's pill), rubbed on a flat stone in the juice of fresh lime or in a few drops of gin. A little of the mixture was poured into the mouth of the sick children and air blown into its mouth to facilitate swallowing. The disease was a dreaded killer of children in Agogo in those days. In consequence, a mother whose child suddenly caught it panicked and behaved hysterically as she followed a man who, for safety's sake, was to carry the child in his arms to the house of the healer. Many a time, we stood by and looked pitifully at such mothers in distress.

Roughly between the ages of three to eight or ten, the Agogo child encountered two common diseases, both of the skin. They were yaws (*dɔeɛ*), the most serious and painful one, and itches (*ɛboro*).

Dɔeɛ (Yaws)

The disease, regarded as normal, was accepted as marking a stage in the development of a child. I was fortunate to escape a yaws attack, but from what I saw of my playmates who had the ill-luck to be its victims, and what I heard from the account of their experiences, I was left in no doubt that *dɔeɛ* must have been one of the most painful diseases which attacked children of those days. When yaws attacked, every part of the body of its victim from head to toe — the head, the lips, the arms, the legs, the palms, the penis, the testicle, the sole of the feet — everywhere was covered with running sores. Painful as yaws itself was, it was on the day of its treatment that the victim went to real hell on this earth. It was said to be a day of intense suffering and extreme agony in the life of an Agogo child in the days I was young. A yaws-treating day (*dɔeɛ-mu-hyɛ-da*) started early in the morning. If the victim happened to be unfortunate enough to have sores on the soles of the feet (*namuromdɔeɛ*), he was seated for all areas around each sore to be cleared of skin cover. The operation was performed with a sharp razor and so there was every chance of the sharp thing cutting into a sore as the poor child struggled desperately. That was said to be painful enough, but only the beginning. The victim was bathed in warm water with harsh fibre sponges and biting black soap (*samina tuntum*) until the sores were all scrubbed and oozed blood. That also was painful enough but the worst was yet to come. And it came with the meticulous application of a mixture of some blue-greyish chemical called *brisitoo* (brimstone — the biblical fuel of hell-fire) and palm-kernel oil (*adwe-nno*) on all of the visible sores. The operation was referred to as *dɔeɛm-hyɛ* (yaw-sores dressing). From the way I saw victims behave at the final stage of yaw-sores dressing, there did not appear to be a word sufficiently strong enough to express the feeling of pain that a pathetic sufferer went through. Excruciating was a very mild word. And the indescribable pain lasted the whole day. Notwithstanding the fanning of the body that went on all the time, the cooked egg held tightly in the hand of the screaming child, the nicest of words that were spoken to soothe him, the pains could not be abated — nothing could, until they had run their full course late in the evening. The intense feeling of pain made the young sufferer temporarily insane, and, in consequence, he did things which a child in his sober senses would not contemplate, much less dare do to his own parents. The poor child openly cursed, swore and abused his parents. He damned all and everyone who took any part in the treatment, charging them to be fools and idiots (*nkwaseafoɔ*), murderers (*awudifoɔ*), thieves (*akrɔmfoɔ*), mad men (*abɔdamfoɔ*) and uttering much more unprintable words. It was said that there were a few cases in which victims who could not bear the intense pains succumbed and died.

Ɛborɔ (Itches)

Ɛborɔ was another childhood skin disease which attacked children between the ages of about five to ten and above. Itch-pains, however, were milder and the dressing more tolerable compared with yaws. The disease attacked the skin on all parts of the body, particularly the softer parts. As in the case of yaws, itches where treated by a thorough scrubbing of the affected parts of the body with native sponge (*sapɔ*) and black soap (*samina-tuntum*), which was made locally. In place of *brisitoo* (brimstone), a mixture of some yellow chemical crystals called *sɔfe* (sulphur) and shea butter (*nkuu*) or palm-kernel oil (*adwe-nno*) was applied. It was soothing and not at all maddeningly painful. Some juice from green pawpaw fruits was at times used before scrubbing. The application of the juice on the sores induced an intense desire to scratch, thereby obviating pains which otherwise would have been felt by the raw application of fibrous sponge and black soap. It was said that the sap of a tree called "*bɔmpagya*" was the traditional medicine for the treatment of itches before the introduction of *sɔfe* (sulphur). The belief was that if a child ill with itches (*ɛborɔ asi no ataadeɛ*) went and stood under a *bɔmpagya* tree, bared its buttocks, and danced round and round the tree and sang the following pleading song earnestly, the spirit of the tree caused the itches to vanish and the sufferer recovered:

Bɔmpagya e, hwɛ me toase O.
Bɔmpagya e, hwɛ me toase O.
Bɔmpagya e, hwɛ nea mahunu O,
Bɔmpagya e, hwɛ nea mahunu O.

(Hi, *Bɔmpagya,* look at my buttocks.
Hi, *Bɔmpagya,* look at my buttocks.
Hi, *Bɔmpagya,* note my trouble.
Hi, *Bɔmpagya,* note my trouble.)

Itches were said to be caused by the bite of larvae called *nsaase-boaa.* Children in those days did not generally sleep on beds, but on mats spread on floors made of beaten soil which was occasionally daubed (*kwa*) with red-ochre earth called *ntwoma.* The mats were woven locally and were named according to the material with which they were made. There were *ntɔn-kɛtɛ* (from the leaves of the *pandamus* tree), *sibire-kɛtɛ* (from the stalk of the *sibire* plant) and there was *gowa* (from the straw of the *anwonomoo* plant). If a child was a bed-wetter (*dwensɔ-krobo*), the floor on which he/she slept offered a favourable breeding place for the fly. *Asomtakom,* the mother-fly, laid its eggs in cracks in the mud floor where they hatched into *nsaase-boaa.* The larvae hid themselves in holes in the floor in the daytime and wriggled through the mat in the night to feed on the blood of the sleeping child. From the bites itches were said to develop and spread to cover the skin on several parts of the body. It was for that reason that the *asomtakom* fly was chased and killed whenever it was found. From the perpetual chasing of the fly arose the expression: "*Awo bɔnee nti na yekum asomtakom.*" ("Asomtakom fly was killed because she begat a dangerous child.") This is said in reference to a parent who had to suffer in any way for the misdeed of her child.

Nkantamase (Jiggers or Chigoe)

This affliction in our childhood days in Agogo was prevalent in the dry season of the year. It was known to us that a sand flea burrowed into the soles of the feet. Tiny at first, it swelled into a small but visible white-grey ball that contained its eggs. The developed eggs inside caused severe irritation at the spot they had lodged themselves. A dark brown speck seen on the skin, said to be the mouth of the flea, betrayed its presence. The parasite was dug out of the skin with a needle and a sharp penknife. A few drops of fresh lime (*ankaa-dweaa*) squeezed into the hole left in the sole upon its dislodgment cured the wound. Some of our playmates were prone to jigger attacks. One such earned the nickname "Jigger". He continued to be called so even when he grew to be a man. It did not bother him a bit. He took it all as fun and each time he was addressed "Jigger," he responded jokingly "*nkantamase.*" It was erroneously held by us children that *nkantamase* was brought into the town by cows which the fleas followed from the North. Consequently whenever we saw a young Northerner of our age following a herd of cows to a feeding ground, we ran after him and taunted him by singing in unison: "*Opepenii akɔdaa, Nkantamase, mmowa mmoawa.*" ("Northerner Child, Little, little Jigger parasite.")

Aprɔprɔ or nantetare (Foot rot)

In the wet damp season some of us children of Agogo were afflicted with foot rot (*aproɔprɔ*). The wearing of sandals, shoes or any covering for the foot in any shape or form by children was not in vogue in our childhood days. Not only children, but most adults also, male and female, moved about on bare feet night and day, in wet or in dry. I recollect that it was only senior Elders, Stool Elders and the Ɔhene of the town who had to wear *mpaboa* (native sandals) all the time. The sandals they wore were made from dried skins of ɔtwee (an antelope) by skilled local sandal makers. Occasionally, some wooden footwear carved from the *ofruntum* tree were worn by men in their farm cottages. They were called *nkuro-nnua*. I never saw any man wearing the type of wooden (*nkuo-nnua*) sandals in a public gathering anywhere in the town. In the wet season, therefore, when much walking had been done in damp places, water collected under the toes. If not thoroughly cleaned and kept dry, rot set in and developed into sores which ate into the toe joints. The sores were not themselves fatal, but were a nuisance and unpleasant and could cause some deformity, as happened to the second toe of my left foot.

Diseases that attacked grown-ups were talked about much, but as they were all adult matters, they fell outside my interest as a child. Any account that I attempt to give now of such diseases as prevailed in those days in Agogo is a recollection of what I heard said or of the little I saw of the victims. They included:

Babaso (Syphilis) and **Kekayɛ** (Gonorrhoea)
Some young men and women were said to be victims of one or the other of the two communicable venereal diseases, the former said to be more virulent and difficult to cure. Often I overheard mothers warning their daughters to take good care of themselves, emphasizing that the disease could cause barrenness (*etwa awoɔ*). In town there lived a charming, fashionable, unmarried young woman notorious for being badly contaminated with syphilis. She was nicknamed "*Afua Owuo*," (Afua, the Killer). What puzzled most sober elderly persons was that, even though aware of the danger, some young men were foolhardy enough to risk copulating with her and got themselves contaminated. As the practice was in those days, syphilis and gonorrhoea were treated by "specialist herbalists." It was said that the victims were put on a strict diet and were, in almost all cases, forbidden from eating fresh meat or any meat containing fat. It was said also that chronic syphilis could be fatal, causing death or bringing upon the victim other afflictions such as blindness, impotence and imbecility.

There were a few cases of dreaded diseases in Agogo, including *kwata*, (leprosy), *nkwantu*, *kokoram* and *otware* (epilepsy).

Kwata (Leprosy)
The disease was so dreaded that its name, *kwata*, was not to be mentioned to the hearing of anybody. It was euphemistically called *mekura-duam* (touch wood). Two victims of the disease were said to be in Agogo. I did not see any one of them. They were kept in two separate removed villages, undergoing intensive treatment. The disease was talked of as being a "bad" disease (*yare bɔnee*) and so its victim was not given the normal funeral, but was buried in an anthill to prevent his/her reincarnation into the *abusua* (lineage).

Nkwantu
The second "bad" disease (*yare-bɔnee*) was *nkwantu*. I had the opportunity to see one of the two victims in Agogo when young. The building next to our house in Salem was that of my mother's

father's brother, and so Mother called the owner "Agya" ("Father"). Agya had five children: three sons and two girls. The eldest of them, a boy called Kofi H., was one of the first boys sent to the Agogo Basel Mission School. He was therefore one of the few lettered persons in Agogo at the time we returned from Kwaaman. Kofi H. had secured a job in a place in Adanse near the mining town of Ɔboase. One afternoon, news flashed through the community that Kofi H. had been brought home sick. Mother was one of the first to go to Agya's house to see her sick "brother." She returned a little later and I heard her telling Nana Kwaane rather dejectedly, "*Me nua Kofi de nkwantu na aba.*" ("My brother Kofi is back home with *nkwantu* disease.") She added by way of explanation that it was the same disease a person in a quarter of the town had contracted. On an errand to Agya's house two days later, I caught a brief sight of poor Kofi H., my mother's "brother" (so he was my "uncle"). He was sitting in a corner, moody, morose and dejected. His body was all distended, and he was staring absent-mindedly, vaguely, at nothing. It was rumoured that he ate quite a lot, insatiably, and that most of the time, he was in a state of dormancy. Kofi H. was taken to a remote village on the Agogo-Kumawu road for treatment and died there after a short time. He was not given the normal funeral because it was said that *nkwantu* was, like leprosy, a "bad" disease (*yare-bɔnee*).

The disease was so dreaded in Agogo in those days that it was one of the curses someone who swore on a fetish invoked on a person they wished ill. I had a shocking experience of such cursing one afternoon. We, the children of Salem, used to go to the Kurowire stream at the other end of the Town to swim on hot days. There we met other children from town who had also gone to swim or collect water for some domestic purpose. Unlike us Christian children, the young townsfolk were not restrained from swearing by anything. They could swear and curse uninhibitedly "by the Father's foot" (*meka agya nan*), by a fetish, by the spirit of a river or by God the Supreme Being (*Onyankopɔn Tweadumpɔn*) Himself.

On the bank of the stream that afternoon was a teenage, saucy, garrulous pert of a girl, Abena B. Abena had no respect for anybody, young or old. She was standing there haughtily, haranguing, ranting and cursing because, she complained, her drinking calabash had vanished and she suspected that someone had stolen it. In the end she picked up a pebble from the ground, held it in her raised right hand and cursed, saying: "*Nana Afram, Nana Anɔkye, Deε wafa me koraa ye, sε wamfa amaa a, mo ma nkwantu nyε no.*" ("Grandfather Fetish Afram, Grandfather Fetish Anɔkye, Let him/her who has stolen my calabash fall ill of *nkwantu* if it is not returned to me.")

Abena B. hit the pebble onto the ground as the curse ended to confirm it. It worked. Standing aghast staring at the contemptuous little quarrelsome thing, I saw a timid, innocent-looking girl who stood at the other bank and who had all the time been behaving as if she was unconcerned, becoming suddenly agitated. Trembling, she bent down and removed the object of complaint from her earthenware pot (*ahina*). She hurried to the girl who had uttered the curse and handed the calabash to her. Abena B. accepted it, picked up another pebble which she threw back to the ground to repeal the curse by saying: "*Nana Afram, Kɔ-kɔ-twea, Nana Anɔkye, Kɔ-kɔ-twea.*" ("Grandfather Afram Fetish, the curse is revoked Grandfather Anɔkye Fetish, the curse is revoked.") Both girls appeared happy, the pilferer of the calabash looking greatly relieved.

Kokoram

The third deadly disease in Agogo that attacked adults was *kokoram*. I saw some of its victims. One was a woman past middle-age. She had scars on her arms and legs. The disease, which attacked the nose, had eaten it and had destroyed the bony and cartilaginous structure which are the nostrils, exposing, thereby, the purple-coloured nasal cavity. *Kokoram* was said to be a very difficult disease to cure. Consequently, there were many harsh abstentions connected with its treatment. They were all to be observed strictly by the patient, some by the person attending to him/her and others by any person who went near the treatment area. For that reason, a *kokoram* patient was always put in confinement in an isolated place in a remote area. In such isolation, the patient was said to be "under special medical treatment" (*ɔda adurom*). It was said, however, that *kokoram* was not infectious, but rather hereditary (*abusua-yadeɛ*). The rigid observance of abstentions was enforced, not for prevention of infection, but to avoid doing anything that would nullify the potency of special medicine prescribed for its cure. A deceased victim of the disease, unlike those of the other "bad" diseases such as leprosy and *nkwantu*, was accorded the normal funeral as it was not regarded as communicable or "bad." *Kokoram* was said to have preference for handsome, comely persons and, in consequence, had gained the nickname *odi-ayie* (he who consumed only the best).

A cured *kokoram* patient went back home from isolation to live a normal life in the community without any stigma. He was, however, a totally deformed person when the nose was attacked and the external part eaten away. We, the young children, were always scared by the look of such a noseless person and each time on approach, we moved far away to give him/her, as it were, a wide berth. The defect of a principal organ of the most exposed part of the body, causing serious deformity in the appearance of a person, led to an aphorism: "*Wo hwene bu a, woanim dua asɛe.*" ("A broken nose is a deformity of the whole face.") It is an expression meant to emphasize the point that the disgrace of a principal member of a community affects all its members.

Otwarɛ (Epilepsy)

The fourth morbid disease (*yare bɔnee*) I encountered in Agogo was epilepsy (*otwarɛ*). The victim was the only one I saw in the town. He was a little past adolescence and was called Kwasi S. He lived in Salem in a house a few blocks away from ours, with his mother, brothers and sister, but his father, like mine, lived in Town. He was older and therefore not a member of my play group. Kwasi S.'s playmates often ran to tell us stories about him and his frequent bouts. From their accounts I gathered that Kwasi went to join his group at marble playing, hale and sound. But in the course of the game, he suddenly acted abnormally when he was seized by the disease. His eyes were said to turn pale as he swooned and fell to the ground with foam gushing out of his mouth. His limbs stiffened and he struggled violently as he hit the ground hard and repeatedly with his fist and feet, bit his tongue and lips, lay prostrated and looked quite aggressive. One of his mates would then run to let his mother know of the condition of her son. Kwasi S. did not live long. He died and was not given the normal funeral as he was said to have been killed by a "bad" disease (*yare bɔnee*).

Ɔdam (Insanity)

Near my father's house in Town was a house in which lived a mentally deranged man (*ɔbɔdamfoɔ*). He was the only one that was said to be a victim of the disease in the town when I was young. I saw him one afternoon when I had taken Father's meal to him. As he was away on a short visit to a neighbour, I took the opportunity to go and look at the maniac. Through a gap in an *odwuma* fence screening the yard I saw the unfortunate man sitting alone in a *pato* (open-front room). His left hand was in a chain which was fastened to a log lying by him. He was stark naked. He talked to himself, jabbered, laughed at times. His behaviour appeared to me quite abnormal and childlike, but he was a fully grown person. I learned later that the man had been put in chains by his relatives (*yɛato no duam*) to prevent him from going about the town naked. I was not in Agogo when the madman died and no one told me what happened to his dead body or the funeral that he was given.

Men and women, old and young, died in Agogo in my childhood days. Deaths however, were quite infrequent and almost all those who departed and went to *Asamando* (The Dwelling Place of Ghosts) died a natural death, that is: they were killed by one disease or the other accepted to be normal or ordinary. Cases of accidental death were few and far between. Such few unexpected deaths which occurred by chance in those days, as far as I can recollect, were caused by:

Ɔwɔ aka no or **ɔwɔ aforo no** (Snakebites)

Among the dangerous killers were *ɔkyereben* (green mamba), *ɔpramire* (black mamba), *akwatia* and, on rare occasions, *ɔnanka*. Most snakebite cases were treated quite successfully by traditional medicine-men and some herbalists who also administered anti-snake bite treatment for a small fee.

Dua abu abɔ no or dua akasa no (trapping by falling trees)

Asuo afa no

Drowning in the Afram River while on a fishing operation.

There was a horrid case of a man who committed suicide by hanging himself (*ɔhyɛɛ akɔmfo*) on a beam in his bedroom. He was buried hurriedly with no funeral. It was said that his ghost became *ɔsaman twɛntwɛn* (an evil haunting spirit) because he was refused admission to the Land of the Ghosts (*Asamando*) for his misdeeds in the Land of the Living (*Ateasefoɔ*).

7

MEN FROM NEAR AND FROM FAR BEYOND THE SEA

The Agogo I knew was a well-organised, homogenous community, the bulk of whose inhabitants was almost entirely indigenous. The few non-Agogo natives comprised some Akans from Kwawu, Akyem and other Asante towns, some non-Akans from the North, and a handful of Lagosians (*Alatafoɔ*) from Nigeria. The Northerners, mostly Moshis, Dagartis, Busangas and Frafras, lived in a small *zongo*. There were a very few persons of Northern extraction who, however, did not reside in the Agogo Zongo. They lived in a small community in a quarter in Salem, *Sukuum*, where a mango tree grew. They were, in consequence, referred to as *Amanno-asefoɔ*. They were just five families, in the proper English sense of the word, that is a "family" of a father, his wife and children. Each family lived in a compound house of their own. They were: *Opanin* Kofi D. (Thomas), the oldest and head of the community who was over sixty years of age and an Elder of the Church, *Opanin* Y, who was about sixty; Charles K., a little over fifty, Andrea N., about fifty; and Kwasi K. (N), the youngest, who was about forty.

The five men were, at the time of our return from Kwaaman, completely integrated into the Agogo community and, but for their intonation and some tribal marks on their faces, would have easily passed for pure Agogo natives. Three of the men, Opanin Y., Andrea N. and Kwasi K. (N), had married native Agogo women with whom they had had children. The head of the community, *Opanin* Thomas Kofi D.'s wife, Aberewa N., a Northerner, was seen most of the time sitting under the mango tree which had given the quarter its name, painstakingly cracking palm-nuts for kernels from which she extracted kernel oil (*adwe-nno*). *Opanin* Charles K.'s wife was also a

Northerner, but christened "Maria" with an Asante name, "Dapaa," added as her surname.

Kwasi K. (N), the youngest man, was a hardworking person, tall and slim, light in complexion, stern and serious in his deportment. I never saw that man ever laugh or smile. He was a carpenter, grim but competent in shingle-roofing. He was the first carpenter that I knew and saw at work. Whenever he was at work, sitting high on a roof frame on top of a building, most of us children of Salem ran to give him a helping hand by collecting and throwing up to him odd pieces of wire nails that dropped by chance from a pocket on the khaki apron that he wore at work.

I learned later that the five Northerners (turned Agogo Basel Mission Church members) were formerly slaves. Three of them, Kofi D., Andrea N., and Kwasi K. (N), were known to have been the property of a neighbouring *Ɔmanhene* (Paramount Chief) and the other two, *Opanin* Y. and Charles K., had joined them at Agogo from some other places whose names I was not told. They all became free when the Treaty of Fomena, in February 1874, concluded the Sagrenti War. It was said that on regaining their individual freedom, the five ex-slaves left their former masters, travelled to Agogo, the nearest place where a church had been established, and there, rehabilitated themselves as Christians and free persons.

No non-African, as far as I can recollect, lived anywhere near Agogo. The first European (*oburonii*) I saw was a man said to have come from somewhere far, far away beyond the sea (*aburokyire*). Where that place was I could not imagine, but could understand vaguely that it was the place where my grand's cocoa went when it was purchased from our Apampramasu cottage and carried to Asokore. It was from that place, too — *aburokyire* — that the cloth and *pieto*, biscuits (*krakase*), and the rockets that father bought for us for Christmas, came. That first *oburonii* I saw came to Agogo from Abetifi, Kwawu, on foot, and stayed in a room in the compound of the teacher/catechist. He left in the manner he came, no fanfare, no pomposity, but gently, after he had preached a sermon to his congregation in their small local chapel.

Another "White-man" called *Komisa* (Commissioner) visited Agogo from time to time. Unlike the other "White-man" from Abetifi who arrived quietly and left quietly, the visit of the *Komisa* was a town-wide stirring affair. Weeks before his arrival, a gong-gong was beaten at intervals of a few days to announce the visit. He arrived by way of Kumawu or via Asokore. The gong-gong ordered all able-bodied men to work on certain days on the footpath along which he would travel to Agogo. Weeds were to be cleared, log-bridges put across rivers and streams, fallen trees across the path removed, all gullies filled and all narrow passes widened to facilitate the passage of a hammock. In addition, the men were ordered to brush off weeds all around the outskirts of the town. They called that *nsɔsɔɔ-bɔ*.

Women were ordered to sweep around their houses and all open spaces. Their other duty in preparation for the *Komisa's* visit was providing the supply of water and all firewood that would be required for the services of the august visitor. Under the direction of an elderly woman who was the "caretaker" of the "White-man's" house (*oburonii-fie*), the women of Agogo stockpiled in the rest house good firewood and pots full of water from the two streams in Agogo. The floors of rooms in the rest house were daubed lustrously with red-ochre earth called "*ntwoma.*" Everything in the vicinity was kept scrupulously clean. Agogo was ready to welcome the *Komisa*.

He arrived on the scheduled day. He never failed. The morning of his arrival was a hectic time, indeed. All domestic animals were chased, caught and kept in confinement. The operation was not to prevent a nuisance but to save the heads of the birds and beasts, for, on arrival in the town, carriers (*apaafoɔ*) of the *Komisa*, without obligation for payment or request, caught and killed for the preparation of their meal domestic animals they found straying anywhere outside a house. From all over the place one heard the "*m-m-ɛ-ɛ-ɛ, m-m-ɛ-ɛ-ɛ*" of sheep and goats, and the *tw-a-a-a, tw-a-a-a*," of cocks and hens. For their own safety, the animals remained in close confinement for the duration of the stay of the *Komisa* and his carriers.

The first of the *Komisa's* entourage to arrive were the carriers of his personal effects and official documents. With them were the cook and the head steward, then junior clerks, followed by the registrar (*krakye panin*), the *Komisa* himself guarded by a busybody orderly (*wɔdre*), the trusted "Small Boy," and, finally, the remaining carriers of important chop boxes and packages. The *Komisa* was carried in a hammock borne in relays by selected strong men called "*ahamankaa-soafoɔ*" and was taken to the rest house. The clerks were accommodated in a house rated as the best in the town in those days, close by the rest house.

The *wɔdre* announced the arrival of the *Komisa* to the Chief and his Elders who, all this time, had waited assembled in the *ahemfie*. They went immediately to bid the visitor welcome, moving in a procession led by young girls carrying head loads of gifts comprising fowl, eggs, yams, oranges, garden-eggs, pepper, pawpaw, onions and other items for the preparation of his meals. The *Komisa* reciprocated with gifts of gin, tobacco and other articles. The Chief briefed the *Komisa* briefly on a few important matters of the state, after which the traditional ruler and his Elders took leave of the *Komisa* and parted in a most friendly and cordial atmosphere, to meet again, formally, the following day.

It was the first *durbar* that I witnessed. As I stood by my father craning my neck nervously, I saw him — "the White-man." He sat under a state umbrella, provided for protection against the sun, and yet he was wearing a white helmet in spite of the wide-brim cloth canopy. In a few moments he rose up and addressed the gathering. It was, again, the first time that I heard an *oburonii* speaking English. He spoke in what they said was "*Brɔfo*"(English). I did not, of course, understand what he said, but that did not matter much to me. I was not in the least interested in what came out of the man's mouth. My interest was in his physical appearance: the long nose; the bright, clear eyes; the straight hair that was auburn; the neat, smart dress, the man's mien, his tone, his generous height, and the strangeness of what I heard coming through his lips. The registrar who stood by the *Komisa* interpreted what he said, clause by clause, in Asante, for all to hear.

It was the Chief's turn to address the visitor. He spoke in Asante through a linguist who spoke eloquently as he held his *akyeame-poma* (the linguist's staff). The registrar, still standing, interpreted what was said to the *Komisa* in *Brɔfo* (English). That was my third "first"that morning: the first time that I heard an *obibinii* (an African) rattling off English to an Englishman who, from the repeated nodding of his head left no doubt that the registrar was in fact translating the Chief's address intelligently to him. And oh! how I wished, from that moment, I could speak proper *Brɔfo* (English) like that confident registrar I saw standing by the white *Komisa*.

The time came for the hearing of complaints. Every person in the gathering who had any complaint to make was invited to come forward to speak. A few complaints were brought up that morning and were all disposed of expeditiously. Judgments were given promptly, fines imposed and paid on the spot, and everybody seemed satisfied. I heard it said that the *Komisa* was, on the whole, just, fair and impartial, and that in one or two cases of misgivings, the slip was regarded as a genuine error. The blame was understandably put on the White-man's ignorance of some particular aspect of the customary law as practised in Agogo. From a sympathetic complainant I heard the remark: *"Ɛnyɛ ɔno a, ɔnnim Asante amaneɛ. Sɛ omin a, anka wanka no saa."* ("He is not to be blamed. He is ignorant of our Asante customary law. Were he conversant with them he surely wouldn't have adjudged in the way he did.")

The following day the *Komisa* was gone. During the *Komisa's* departure, some of us boys from both Salem and town hid ourselves behind a nearby house. As soon as he had vacated the rest house and was out of sight, we rushed to the house to collect, as playthings and mementos, "leftovers" including, in particular, empty small soda canisters from which aerated water had been produced through a siphon for mixing whisky and gin consumed by the *Komisa*. We also collected emptied cans and a few jam jars. There were also quite a lot of cigarette-ends which, for obvious reasons, we, the boys from Salem, left alone for those from town to scramble and fight for.

One day the gong-gong announced the visit of someone said to be "A Very Big Man" — *Asante Buronii Panin* — the Chief Commissioner of Ashanti. Preparations for the visit were similar to those made for the *Komisa*, but on a more elaborate scale. For instance, on the morning of the Big Man's arrival, gunners were sent to wait for him at a spot on the Kumawu footpath about a quarter of a mile away from the town to fire musketry into the air in his honour. *"Yɛkɔhyɛɛ no atuo"* was what they called that. Directly he arrived at the spot, volleys flew high, loud and repeatedly: *"B - U - M - M, B - U - M - M, B - U - M - M!"* All were astir. Everywhere the cry was, *"Waba, Waba, Waba!* ("He is in. He is in. He is in!")

In the forenoon of the following day there was a big *durbar* at *Adwabɔ-yɛ*, an open space in front of the *ahemfie*. It was a thick crowd. All in Agogo attended, except the sick and the dying. The Agogo Brass Band was stationed at the entrance of the *durbar* ground. As soon as His Honour, the Chief Commissioner of Ashanti, arrived at the place, the National

Anthem, "God Save The King," was struck. All stood at attention for the duration. I watched His Honour keenly. He was said to be the *Aban* (the Government), the representative of His Majesty the King in Ashanti. That added more interest to my desire to see him in person. He appeared to me a great man in whom nobility was personified. He was in full uniform, consisting of a brilliant white dress, some medals on the breast, a white helmet topped with some dazzling plumes on his head, a scabbard dangled by the thigh of a long leg, complete with a neat white glove in the right hand. Routine greetings, return-greetings, addresses, and replies followed. The middle-aged man of honour and dignity left the *durbar* ground. Merry-making continued as many non-Christians of Agogo danced happily to an *atumpan* drum orchestra, which continued playing well into the evening. It was one of the few occasions on which I saw members of the Basel Mission Church mixing freely with non-Christians in an assembly outside Salem.

8

FATHER IN AN
OATH-SWEARING CASE

Two years after our arrival from Kwaaman, Father had settled himself as a full-time cocoa farmer. The two year-old clearings had been planted with cocoa and the young seedlings were shooting with healthy, purple-brown leaves. The plantain suckers which Mother planted as cover for the seedlings had sprouted, giving much needed shade in the dry season. We continued to stay in our *apampramasu* farm cottage for most of the year, one or the other, or both parents, coming to town once a while to settle some important domestic or social matters, returning the same day as soon as it was possible to do so. Mother did not miss her Sunday forenoon church services. She left the cottage regularly each Sunday morning and returned in the evening. When Father had nothing in particular for me to do for him, she took me along with her. Nana Kwaane was quite pleased with the good progress her son-in-law was making on his new cocoa farm.

A few weeks before Christmas each year, Father returned home from our cottage and engaged himself, once again full-time, in tailoring. The well-oiled, stored machine was back in service. It was the major cocoa season and there was money to spend. Providing fathers travelled to the nearest shopping centres at Asokore, Effiduasi and Kumasi to buy things for Christmas and the New Year. The principal items that men bought for their wives, their children and or themselves, as well as their dependents, included cotton prints, khaki and white drills, headkerchiefs, cutlasses (machetes), soap, tobacco, gem biscuits, pomade, bath-towels and other essential household articles. Cotton prints were bought by the unit of a piece, twelve yards in length, a half-piece of six yards, or a quarter-piece of three yards. Dutch and Manchester wax prints called *"daa-no"* were the most fashionable and preferable. Prints bought were taken to a local tailor to cut and sew into dresses for Christmas. For the woman it was a half-piece (*ɔpo-fa*) length which was cut into what was called *"ɔsoro ne fam ne kaba"*, (up-piece, down-piece and cover-shoulder piece). Men required a one-piece cloth of nine to ten yards, and children, a one-piece cloth of three to four yards.

Tailors in those days were generally men. My father, popularly known and called "Tailor Nkɛtea," was a reputable tailor who was held in high esteem by many in the town for his self-respect, competence and fair dealings. He was often spoken of as *ɔbarima a, ɔte ne ho aseɛ* (a man who lived and let live). Many customers brought to him, day and night, their pieces of prints which he cut and sewed into dresses for them. Prints sent to him were of two different widths: short-width prints called *"mpo-trawa,"* twenty-four inches wide, and long-width prints called *"apo-kɛse,"* thirty-six inches wide.

I often sat by my father and watched him work all day and most part of the night when some demanding customers insisted that their dresses be completed for them. One such busy afternoon he took a break in order to go to Salem to discuss some urgent matter with my mother. I accompanied him. We left the Agogo High Street (*Abɔnten Kɛseɛ*) and turned on to the main street that led to Salem. On reaching an intersection of the street and a lane, I saw an enraged man of Father's age approaching from our right walking furiously in our direction. Quite unexpectedly, he shouted at my father querulously: *"He, Kwabena Nkɛtea, Kwasea. Wo na woafa me yere ntama no?"* ("Hi, Foolish Kwabena Nkɛtea. Is it you who have wrongfully seized my wife's print cloth?") Father stopped, surprised. He turned in the man's direction and asked him coolly: "What exactly do you mean? Me, having wrongfully seized your wife's print cloth?" Yaw P., growing more angry, retorted, "I mean exactly what I have said. You have stolen my wife's cloth. I, Yaw P. say it", knocking the fist of his right hand on the chest to give emphasis to the personal pronoun "I."

Father, still surprised at such an unprovoked affront, asked calmly: "Yaw P., don't you think it would have been sensible if you had gone to my house to talk about your wife's cloth? Do you not realise it is disgraceful for two grown-up men to be seen and heard quarrelling in an open street in this way like teenage girls?"

Yaw P., now in a fighting mood, approached Father and, thrusting a challenging right index finger at my father's nose, replied angrily:"Going to your house? You thief! Do you have a house? Aren't you staying in your uncle's house? I have said you are a thief. I say you are a THIEF. I will forever say you are a THIEF. You have stolen my wife's cloth. It is I, Yaw P., say so!"

The scene created by Yaw P.'s rantings had, by then, drawn a crowd of idle spectators. Patience ran out, and Father swore, "*Meka Nana Praso sɛ, Minwiaa wo yere ntama biara.*"("I swear by Nana's Praso that I have not stolen your wife's cloth.")

Yaw P. responded instantly:"*Kwabena Nkɛtea Krɔmfoɔ, Mesrɛ Nana Praso me ka sɛ, woawia me yere ntama!*" ("Kwabena Nkɛtea, the Thief, I pray to swear by Nana's *Praso* that you have stolen my wife's half-piece of cloth.")

Some onlookers were heard saying aloud: "*Ɔde abɔ so! Ɔde abɔ so!*"("He has responded to the oath. He has responded.")

An *ahenkwaa* (court official), who happened to be among the crowd, tapped at the shoulder of each of the litigants and said, as he did so, "*Me gyedua ne wo!*" ("You are my prisoner.")

Father, a prisoner of the State arrested before my own eyes! He asked me to continue to Salem to inform Mother what had happened, as he returned to his house, followed by the *ahenkwaa*, to pay the traditional confirming fee of one *doma* (7s.) on an oath-sworn (*nte-hoo*). The other litigant also, I was told, paid the *nte-hoo* fee of a *doma* to the same *ahenkwaa*, who took them prisoner. A date was fixed for the hearing of the case. Meantime, each of the two contestants had paid the customary *dwem-taa-deɛ* of *asuaa-nu* (£4—), which was an amount to be deposited at the Chief's court before an oath case was heard. A litigant who lost his case forfeited his deposit.

At home that evening, I asked my mother to explain to me what "*Praso*" meant. My grandmother, who had been greatly upset by the news of her son-in-law's confrontation, sat by the fireside, deep in thought and smoking a pipe. She offered to answer my question addressed to her daughter. The gist of her explanation, as far as I can recollect, was this:

Many years past (*akyɛ*), the Asantehene had many wars with the people living at the other side of Pra, particularly the Asins and the Akyems. In one of the wars the Asantehene sent the Agogohene, Kyei

Panin, the Amantrahene Asumadu and the Adansehene Kyei-Yeboa, to punish the Akyems and their allies. The attack was delayed at Prasu and so the provisions for the Asante army ran short. Many of the fighting men were therefore sent out back to their own towns and to the neighbouring places to collect food. The three Chiefs did not leave their camp. This was because when an ɔberempɔn (a person of noble rank and royal birth) swore to the Asantehene that he was going to war, he fought to win or die. He never "turned his back" to the enemy under any circumstance. The three Chiefs therefore had to stay on and wait for the return of their men.

The enemy took the opportunity of the absence of a large number of the Asante fighting men, and attacked. They put their troops into three formations. The first detachment crossed the Pra at night at the lower end of the Asante army Chiefs' camp; the second took position on the Asin side on the bank of the river, and the third forded it at the upper end (asu-tifii). A palm-wine tapper who had gone to the riverside to wash and clean his pot saw the water of the river had become suddenly unusually muddy. His deduction was that the disturbance might have been caused by a mass crossing, no doubt, by the enemy. He ran quickly to the camp to alert the Chiefs of the suspected movement of the enemy, but alas! it was too late. The Chiefs had been fallen upon from all three sides and there was no way of escape. "Yɛkyeree wɔn sɛ mmaa" ("They were caught like women."), said Nana, poking the fire deliberately. All the three Chiefs were killed, continued Nana, and so was the brother of Kyei Panin of Agogo, Kyei-Ansa, who accompanied him to the war. She concluded, "Asantehene hyiraa Ntam Praso so maa wɔn" ("The Asantehene consecrated the oath Praso for them, i.e. for the three stools whose occupants suffered tragic deaths in the war on the bank of River Pra.")

The day fixed for the hearing of the case arrived. I accompanied my father, mother and other relatives to the *ahemfie*, the Court of the Chief. It was the first time that I entered a Chief's house. Stool Elders had already arrived at the house and were sitting, waiting, on their sheepskin-covered chairs in a spacious *pato* room. They sat in a semi-circular formation flanking the Chief, whose arrival was soon announced. As he came out of an adjacent room and entered the courtyard, all, including the Elders, rose up. He sat gracefully on his *asipim* chair which was standing vacant. All Elders sat after him. There was complete silence. An ɛsɛn (court crier) who sat at the foot of the Chief called aloud: "Yɛntie! Tie-e O - O - O, A! Yɛntie! Yɛntie!" ("Listen! Let all be quiet and listen! *Voyez, Voyez!*) The Agogohene's Court was in session. Father's oath case was the first to be called. The two litigants rose up as their names were called out and moved to stand in the yard facing the Chief and his Elders. The only one among the Elders I knew and could identify was Father's uncle, the Akwamuhene. He sat quietly and looked thoughtful and somewhat embarrassed. The Chief, I found, was a middle-aged person, slender in build and of medium height. His uncovered head was shaved bare and looked shiny with a light, smooth smearing of what might have been shea butter (*nkuu*). Everything about him looked neat and simple, and there was an air of sincerity around him. Before Father was called to state his case, he and Yaw P. were asked separately if they had any witness or witnesses in the case about to be heard in the yard. My Father mentioned Abena K., the wife of the Respondent, Yaw P. Yaw P. also said his wife was his only witness. The *ɔkyeame* ordered Abena K. be taken and kept out of hearing by an *ahenkwa* until she was sent for. The hearing started. My father gave his name and occupation, and stated as follows:

"My Lord, *Nana* Agogohene and *Nananom* Stool Elders. I am a tailor/farmer. As a tailor I receive cloths in lengths which I cut and sew into dresses for men, women and children. I do not sell material myself. Anyone who needs a dress brings to me his or her dress-material and directs me the style he/she prefers. In the few weeks before Christmas many people rush to my house with their pieces of dress-material to be cut and sewn for them. It was a rush period when everybody requested that his/her dress be completed for use on Christmas or the New Year's Day. To be fair to everybody, I work on the materials in the order they are brought to me. A person who comes first is served first. I spend the daytime taking measurements and cutting the material to style as directed by a particular customer. The day's cutting is put together for sewing almost all night. In my view that is the only way by which I can be fair to all my customers, most of whom rush to me at the last moment and make importunate requests to be served out of turn.

"About a week ago Abena K. brought to me one half-piece of wax-print cloth to be cut into *ɔsoro ne fam ne kaba* (three-piece dress). She insisted that the dress be completed for her the same evening to be taken with her on a journey the following morning. I told her that was not possible and explained to her the system according to which I work. She still pressed and requested that she should be given a special consideration. I refused and asked her to try another tailor or leave the material with me for collection of the dress on the fourth day. Abena disagreed and left sulkily with her half-piece of cloth.

"Four days later the wife called again with the same half-piece of cloth for cutting and sewing and requested that the work be completed for her that same evening. Once again I explained patiently to her my system of working and told her firmly that I was not prepared to make any exception in her or anybody else's case. Abena K. agreed somewhat reluctantly and left the cloth with me to work on it on my terms. I took her measurements and cut the material to the style she directed.

"Abena was in my house early the following morning and said she had called to collect her dress. She was told she could not have it that day, but in three days as agreed. Still not satisfied and pressing, I offered her two alternatives: either that she wait and come back for her completed dress in three days, or that she take away the already cut piece for another tailor to complete the sewing for her. Abena K. left my house in a very impudent manner. I took no notice of her disrespect to me.

"I was on my way to Salem in the evening of that same day when her husband, Yaw P. met me on the street and confronted me quite unexpectedly. He openly abused me and charged that I was a thief who had stolen his wife's half-piece of cloth. Yaw P. was not prepared to listen to any explanation from me. He went further to challenge me to an open fight on the street. He rained abuses on me and repeated over and over that I was a thief who had stolen his wife's dress-material. He said all that to the hearing of a large crowd of idle spectators which the scene he made had drawn to the place. Nana, Yaw P. disgraced me unjustifiably in public. He had soiled my good name. I had therefore to swear your great oath, *Praso*, to compel him to come before you to prove to you, the Elders and all in Agogo that I, Kwabena Nkɛtea, am not a thief. Nana, I am not a thief. I have never stolen a thing, and will never steal a thing in my life."

There was a look of concealed satisfaction all around on many faces as my father completed his statement. Yaw P. was asked if he had any questions to put to the complainant. Yes, he had, and he asked, "Kwabena Nkɛtea, do you have my wife's half-piece of wax-print cloth in your possession as you stand here in this Court?"

"Yes, indeed, I have it."

"Does it belong to you?"

"No, it does not belong to me, it's your wife's, Abena K.'s."

"Would you agree therefore that by keeping someone
else's property and refusing to give it back to the owner
you have stolen it?"

There was an uproar from the audience. Someone was heard shouting Yaw P. down, saying, "*Firi hɔ kɔ, sɛ wunni asɛm pa biara bisa a*" ("Clear out of here if you have no better question to put to him"). Father was not pressed to answer the question. Yaw P. said he had no more questions to ask. One of the two ɔkyeame (linguists) present stood up and asked,

"Nkɛtea, you have just told us that you have cut the print ready for sewing. Can you produce the cut cloth for us to see?"

"Yes, Nana, I have it here!" At a signal Father's youngest wife, tender and fair Afua T., carried cuts in three separate bundles to Father. He picked up the first bundle wrapped in a blue head kerchief, showed it to the Elders and explained: "This is the bundle containing cuts for Tuesday night's sewing." Then he picked up the second bundle wrapped in a piece of calico cloth and said, "In this bundle are cuts for my Wednesday night's sewing." The third bundle, wrapped in a green piece of cloth, was picked up and shown to the Elders with the explanation that it contained cut pieces for his Thursday night's sewing. He loosened the knots and exposed the contents, among which he picked out one pack. "This is the cut of the print Abena K. brought to me," he said as he raised it up for all to see. The ɔkyeame-questioner sat down. Father put the print in question back into the third bundle and retied it. He was asked to leave all the bundles where they were in the yard. The witness, Abena K., was brought in. Having sworn by the Fetish Afram that she would speak the truth, the ɔkyeame asked her if she knew the complainant. "Yes, Nana, I know him. He is Tailor Nkɛtea", she replied. Then followed a barrage of questions, the pertinent ones being:

"You know him as what?"

"As a tailor, Nana."

"Do you have anything belonging to you that is with the tailor at this moment?"

"Yes, I have."

"What is it?"

"It is a half-piece of *daa-no* (wax-print) cloth."

"How did your half-piece of *daa-no* cloth get to the tailor?"

"I took it to him myself to have a dress of *"Ɔsoro ne fam ne kaba"* cut and sewn for me."

"When did you take it to him?"

"About six days ago."

"Why is the material still with the tailor?"

"I went to collect the dress but he wouldn't give it to me."

"Did you find from the tailor his reason for not giving back to you your material?"

"Yes, I did, Nana. He said he had not completed sewing the dress."

"Could you identify your dress material if you saw it?"

"Certainly, I know my cloth. I bought it myself with the money that my husband gave to me to purchase it. I selected the material myself."

The *ɔkyeame* requested that the first bundle of cut materials be loosened. Abena B., Father's second wife, tall and stately, who was sitting by the bundles, gracefully untied the knots of the blue headkerchief package. *Ɔkyeame*, turning to Abena K., asked; "Abena K., is your material among the lot?" Abena K. ransacked the contents, shook her head confidently and told the *ɔkyeame*, "No, Nana, I cannot find mine among this pack." The second bundle was unloosened for Abena K.'s inspection, but she again shook her head and said she could not find her dress material in that lot. The third bundle was unloosened. Abena K. quickly pounced on a pack, that same one that Father had described as belonging to her. She held the pack high and told the Chief and his Elders that it was the right material she sent to the tailor. She was dismissed and told to go and wait outside till she was sent for. Yaw P. was called to state his case. It was a short one:

He gave his wife money to buy for herself a half-piece of *daa-no* cloth for Christmas. He chose a very good cloth and took it to tailor Nkɛtea to sew for her an *ɔsoro ne fam ne kaba* dress, but he would not accept it that day. Three days later she went with the material the second time to the tailor who accepted it. The following day she went to collect her dress but he refused to give it to her. Yaw P. maintained strongly that a person who accepted someone else's property, kept it and refused to give it back when the owner requested it, was nothing but a thief, a crafty thief and that, he concluded, was exactly what Kwabena Nkɛtea was.

Asked whether he had any question to ask Yaw P., Father said he had none. And none of the Elders had any question to ask either. The Elders retired for a brief consultation. They were back in their seats in a few moments. The ɔkyeame rose and addressed the Chief and said:

"*Daasebrɛ,* your Elders are back from consultation (*agyina*). We are all of the opinion, unanimously, that Yaw P. has been unable to prove the accusation he made against Kwabena Nkɛtea."The Chief spoke and gave the verdict, his utterances interposed with the Court Crier"s call: "*Tie - O - O - O - O - ...A! Yentie!*"

Said the Chief: "*Ɔkyeame,* I agree with the Elders. Yaw P. has not been able to prove his charge. He has disgraced Kwabena Nkɛtea unjustifiably. He has soiled the tailor's name in a public place without provocation. He has violated the Great Oath. Pronounce Yaw P. guilty!"

The ɔkyeame, who had all the time been standing while the Chief spoke, pronounced judgment. Solemnly he declared: "*Yaw P., sɛ woamfa aso pa bi antie, na womaa abaa so de bɔɔ Kwabena Nkɛtea a, wukum no a, anka wudi no aboa.*" (Yaw P., had you not listened with good ears and had taken a stick to hit Kwabena Nkɛtea and had killed him, you would have dealt with him as if he were a beast.")

The pronouncement was greeted with a thunderous acclamation: "*Heeh - e- e- e...e!*" The Court Crier dabbed Father's right shoulder with a pat of powdered white clay (*hyire*), the same stuff I saw used at fetish dances.

Yaw P. rose and went dejectedly to one of the Elders to ask him to plead for him (*odwane tooa no*). Just at that moment, I saw Father's three wives leaving the yard together. Not long after, I saw a man climbing the platform (*ɛsɛ*) on which sat the Chief and the Elders, and whispering something into the ears of the Akwamuhene, my Father's uncle. The Elder rose up at once and left the house in a hurry. I followed him unnoticed. A few yards away, at a corner of the *ahemfie*, stood Father's wives, all looking very aggressive. Nana Akwamuhene, the father of my father's second wife, reached them. I saw him speaking to them earnestly and in a pleading manner. The co-wives were nodding their heads, apparently in agreement with all that the Elder was saying to them. Satisfied with the women's response to whatever it was that he told them, the Elder returned to join his colleagues in their deliberations on the appropriate *mpata* (compensation) to be awarded to Father.

I learned later why the three co-wives left the *ahemfie* together at the time they did. They had conspired to teach Abena K. and her husband, Yaw P., a lesson they would never forget in their lives. They were going to engage the couple in some sharp and bloody fisticuffs. The "Amazons of Agogo" were on a war path! Their plan of operation had been very carefully laid: they would first attack the husband and incapacitate him by pulling some delicate parts of his body. That done, they would fall on the wife. Her hair would be torn off the scalp and she would be disgraced in an indescribable way. As a permanent reminder of her husband's impudent action to defame their husband, Abena K.'s face would be disfigured. And they were prepared for the operation, for they had all put on tight fitting *pieto* underwear, breasts were firmly banded, and their hair done in such a way that it could not be pulled. One of them had sharpened her fingernails in a way that could cut deep into the flesh of Abena K.'s face. On the Akwamuhene's advice, the co-wives abandoned their planned open fight and went to join their husband's jubilant supporters just as he came out of the *ahemfie* and was carried on shoulders to his house in the Wontonase quarter of the town. The crowd of supporters which followed thickened and the women danced and sang:

Oseee - e - e , Yee - e!
Ɔtweaduampon e - e - e - e!
Yɛda wo ase O - O - O,
Yɛda wo ase Amene, O!
Atadwe e, Ɛnnɛ yɛate dɛ nnɛ!
Atadwe e, Ɛnnɛ yɛate dɛ nnɛ!

(Oseee - e - e, Yee - e!
The Supreme Creator,
We give thanks to You,
We thank You graciously.
Sweet as tiger-nuts is the news we have heard today!)

Mother danced too. It was the first time I saw her dance so happily. Jubilation continued all day in Father's house as pots and pots of palm-wine were consumed. It was a day I never forgot. I had been to the *ahemfie* for the first time. I had seen the Agogohene and his Elders sitting in state deciding an oath case, and, most memorable of all, I had myself heard Father cleared of a very disgraceful charge levelled against him by Yaw P., a very mean man.

9

"AFRINHYIA PA O - O - O!"
(MERRY CHRISTMAS AND
A HAPPY NEW YEAR)

To me, as a child, Christmas (*Buronya*), the festival of the birth of Christ, was an occasion of one solid week of merry-making which occurred once a year. It started in the afternoon of the day on which the Christmas tree was put up, nostalgically called "*Buronya-dua si da*", the Christmas round-off day, and ended a week later on a day that was to us children, "*Da a yɛyi Buronya ano.*" The New Year's Day was not seen as a separate occasion marking what I later grew to know to be the start of a New Year, but the tail-end of Christmas festivities.

Buronya was a period of great expectation and a happy fulfilment. What contributed to give the occasion its lasting memory was the elaborate preparations that were made for its advent. Men, women and children all prepared seriously for Christmas in our childhood days. For men, as has been mentioned earlier, it was the time that they were expected to present the wife or wives with at least two sets of "*ɔsoro ne fam ne kaba*" (up-piece, down-piece and cover-shoulder piece) cloths, complete with headkerchiefs to match. A marriage could founder if a husband neglected unreasonably to discharge that marital obligation. His repeated failure to provide the wife with *Buronya Ntama* could give her a good ground to initiate dissolution of the marriage. The charge, "*Buronya si a, ɔmma me ntama*" ("He fails to give me a cloth/dress for Christmas"), was accepted as substantial. A husband against whom it was made had to be prepared to defend himself convincingly to avert a divorce, especially if throughout the year the wife had helped him conscientiously in all his farmwork.

We, the children, likewise expected from our fathers at least one or two different piece-cloths (*ntama*) of three to four-yard cut-lengths and a *pieto* (underwear). With luck we might have a pair of trousers or shorts (we called them knickers) together with a long-sleeved white cotton shirt. Some boys of "progressive" fathers could expect to receive a pair of trousers or white drill trousers and a coat complete with a white shirt for Christmas. A provident father therefore started preparing for Christmas weeks before the actual day of festivities. He got the required piece-lengths purchased and cut ready for presentation any time before the day.

A few weeks before Christmas Day some discerning couples travelled together to Asokore, Effiduase or Kumasi to buy good quality wax-print cloth (*daanoo*). Hawkers of cloth in Agogo did brisk business in the preceding few weeks and some itinerant peddlers, mostly Northerners, went from house to house to bargain their wares. In some leather bags slung over their shoulders they kept assorted pieces stuck under their arm-pits. As they entered a house they drew attention by crying aloud:

Pe! Pe!
Pe, Memaa, εha da,
Εnnε na maba ha.
Mikyiri nkontompo,
Mikyiri ahuna huna.

(Pe! Pe!
Never before have I been here,
Here am I today.
Lies, I hate, threats I abhor.)

The cry, "*Pe! Pe!*" earned for the Northern peddler the name "*Pe-pe-nii*" (a "*Pe-pe*" person), and for more than one of them "*M-pe-pe-foɔ*" (*Pe-pe-persons*). In due course, the word "*Ɔ-pe-pe-nii*" and its plural form, "*M-pe-pe-foɔ*", were associated with that class of peddler, and the term "*Ɔpepenii*" became generically applicable to a Northerner, irrespective of whether or not he was a cloth salesman who went from house to house. Because cut-cloth pieces sold by the "*Ɔpepenii*" peddler were always seen held under his armpit (*mmɔtoam*), they were referred to as "*Pepe-mmɔtoam ntama*". As good quality Dutch and Manchester wax-prints became readily available and in large quantities, women spurned "*Pepe-mmɔtoam*" pieces which were all of inferior quality. The contempt for the cloth as a Christmas gift consequently led nagging wives to sing a song composed to tease tardy husbands indirectly:

Asomasi, Wokɔ mpoano a,
Tɔ daanoo brɛ me,
Na Pepe-mmotoam afono me.

(So-and-So, when you travel to the coast,
Buy for my present a wax print cloth,
For I am now fed up with the inferior type of the Northerner peddler's under-armpit cloths.)

It was the wife's responsibility in those days to provide all food items except meat. The husband supplied game meat (*mpunam*) or fish (*adwene*) which he bought from a male meat seller's stand at the market (*konko-pon ho*). Many a time, he succeeded in trapping or killing some small game or big birds which went to the wife or, if a polygamist, was shared as equally as possible among his wives. The sale of meat, like most other items, was then the proper function of men. A woman's wares were the produce from her foodcrop farms, hence the maxim, "*Ɔbaa tɔn nnuadewa, ɔntɔn aduduro.*" ("A woman sells garden-eggs; she does not sell gun-powder"), the underlying meaning being that there was a limit to which a woman could go. A wife therefore started her preparations for the provision of quality food in sufficient quantity for Christmas weeks before the start of the festivities. Every industrious woman in Agogo at that time worked two or more farms. She worked on her own foodcrop farm (*mfikyi-fuo*), which was situated within a mile or so from the town, and at the same time, assisted her husband in working his cash-crop farm (*kwae-fuo*) some distance away from the town. Most elderly women, in addition to one or two *mfikyi-fuo* farms, had their own cash-crop farms in the forest areas.

My mother had an *mfikyi-fuo* at Nkwantam on the Agogo-Hwidiem road on a site about three hundred yards from the present Agogo Magistrate's court building. A part of the land is the Agogo Presbyterian Training College playground. It was a well-cultivated and neatly kept food-crop farm, with plantains and coco-yams grown in the previous year's clearings (*dada-so*) and mounds of yams, suckers of plantains and cocoyams, seedlings of pepper, garden-eggs, okra, *akatewa*, beans (both *apatram* and *adua-apea*) some beds of groundnuts, tigernuts and Bambara beans (*akyii*) planted in the current year's clearing (*afu-foforo*). She also grew a few sticks of a new variety of cassava called "*bɛdɛ-Kofi.*" It was a type of cassava with bigger tubers of ivory-coloured skin. Cassava, it is to be observed, was not an important or popular item of food in those days. It was grown mainly to feed pigs. The few cuttings of *bɛdɛ-Kofi* cassava which Mother planted in her farm was therefore not for feeding human beings but for the novelty of it. A small quantity of its harvested tubers was, however, occasionally cooked with plantains and cocoyams and pounded into mixed fufu balls. Yams were the principal crops grown in Mother's Nkwantam farm in mounds of several varieties including:

Pona (Mother's favourite)

Dabrekɔ -(Grandmother's favourite)

Kuntuo, which was good for *fufu* balls

Nananto, also good for *fufu* balls

Baye-deɛ, another good *fufu*-ball yam

Ɛyerɛ (Grandfather Kwaku Pepra's favourite)

Kuru-kuru-pa

Akwaa-kwaa-mpakyiwa (Father's favourite)

Asɔbayerɛ (my favourite)

Mensa

Akwa or **afun** (Great grandmother Afua Adɛm's favourite)

Pasadwɔ (Another of Nana Kwaane's favourite)

Afaseɛ (Water Yams) of many varieties such as, *Afase-pa, Kɔ-aseɛ-kɔhwɛ, Apoka, Akwaa-Tibire*

Nkamfoɔ, one of the avoidances imposed on me by Herbalist Kwaku Boaten of Boanin and was still being observed. It was grown specially for Grandmother who enjoyed eating it with *opotonsu*, a stew of uncooked pepper seasoned with salt and onions)

Mother harvested her yams a few weeks before Christmas and had them preserved on a *putuo*, a wooden rack erected on the farm in the cool shade of a tree. Before they were stored, she inspected each tuber critically for a cut or bruise that might have been made unnoticed in the course of digging. If any was seen it was treated with some green juice from tender leaves of *apatram* beans squeezed into it. A treated tuber was left in the sun to dry firmly to prevent it from rotting. Certified healthy tubers were fastened with the fibre of an *odufeɛ* climber to the erected framework of the rack which measured about ten feet long and six to seven feet high. Father built my mother's *putuo* for her when the yams were all harvested. He fastened the tubers on the framework, not haphazardly, but in a distinct pattern. At the bottom of the framework, he put some logs of wood to prevent the yams coming into direct contact with the ground. Layer by layer and in sizes, the yams were mounted onto the rack, the whole structure when completed tapering perpendicularly with the smallest tubers topmost. Tubers reserved for immediate consumption were not stacked on the rack but were kept separately in a heap at the foot of the *putuo*. Among the reserved lot were those to be selected specially for Christmas (*nea yɛde bedi buronya*), including those to be presented to friends and relatives on the morning of the great day.

If by some unfortunate chance a bush fire, which always plagued Agogo in the dry season, reached a *putuo*, it might burn the whole rack with all its attachments. The affected farmer's plight was very pathetic: a whole year's labour was lost and the previous harvest destroyed just in a moment. The loss, however, provided free and abundant roasted yams for anyone who chanced to be at the scene of misfortune. To him the burnt *putuo* was hardly an ill-wind. The mass roasted yams in the farm could not be left to go to waste and so must be eaten. From such a situation arose a saying: "*Obi nka sɛ, Putuo nhye ma yɛnwe dwo, na sɛ ɛhye de a, yennya mma ɛnsɛɛ.*" ("No one wished a yam rack on a farmstead destroyed by bush fire in order to have abundance of roasted yam to eat, but if it did, the yams were not left to rot.") The proverb was quoted to emphasize the point that some misfortune could bring in its wake some pleasure which, of necessity, must be enjoyed.

One other way in which my mother prepared for Christmas was black soap making. Elderly relatives in those days appreciated a Christmas gift of sponge and locally made soap. The sponge, as has been mentioned earlier on, was a climber that grew wild in the Agogo forests. It was sought and cut into pieces and carried home to be beaten on a log with a mallet. The fibre it released was taken to a stream to wash, dry and make into fluffy balls each between nine and twelve inches in diameter. The treated sponges were either preserved for family use or were sold at the then prevailing price of six for three-pence. Choice ones were reserved for presentation as presents on Christmas Day. Sponge gifts always went with some balls of home-made black soap (*samina tuntum*). My mother was famed for the quality black soap she produced. The lathery soap she made was in great demand. I learned later that her home soap making business helped her in no small measure to earn enough money to meet the cost of her children's education.

I observed that my mother never threw away peels of plantain (*borɔde-hono*), but saved them for soap making. Each day's peels were spread in the sun to dry. When sufficient dry peels had been gathered she burned the lot. The ash was collected carefully into a basket lined with some old discarded mat (*kɛtɛ-fun*). The basket with its contents was placed on supports on top of an enamel basin. Water was poured on the ash in the basket from time to time to drain the potash content into the enamel basin. The dregs left in the basket were thrown away, but the liquid that drained into the receptacle was poured into a cauldron to boil. Palm-oil, previously extracted and stored for the purpose, was added to the boiling content of the big pot and stirred round and round. Black soap to be presented as Christmas gifts was specially treated by the addition of a few leaves of white Jatropha (*Nkrannyedua*) plant to increase its lather. The thickened mass was removed from the pot and spread out on a neat floor to cool. Finally the solidified drained-potash liquid was pounded in a wooden mortar (*owaduro*) to a desired consistency and moulded into balls called *samina-toa*. The balls were wrapped in twos in dry plantain leaf. Mother's black soap was then ready for use by the family or for sale to the public. Christmas gifts packets were put aside for the occasion.

Our preparation for Christmas, as children, took the form of firewood stockpiling. Weeks before the great day we went in groups to the bush in search of dry outer coverings of *atewa* seeds. *Atewa-abena*, as the husks were called, were hard and highly combustible and offered an ideal fuel for bonfires on Christmas Eve and New Year's Night.

The day before the Christmas Day itself was particularly busy for us. It was the normal practice that we accompanied our mothers to farm in the morning of that day to fetch the last batch of foodstuffs or firewood that would be needed for the celebration. We did not stay long in the farm and were usually back home before midday. All the afternoon was left free for us to go in search of a Christmas Tree (*Buronya Dua*). Much time was spent on the search. The problem was not finding a young palm tree, but selecting one that met our high standard of suitability. In our search for the ideal tree, we moved from thicket to farmstead and from farmstead to thicket, digging one tree here, discarding it there on seeing another one considered better than the one previously dug up. Finally a medium size young tree with luxuriant leaves on symmetrically shaped branches was spotted. It was dug up with eager contentment and carried back home.

The exciting moment arrived when the tree was stood in our *pato* (open-side room), and the box containing it covered with a nice piece of headkerchief which Mother had kindly lent to us for the purpose. It was a sweet and happy moment when I stood aside to admire my Christmas Tree on Christmas Eve. Elated, I skipped lightheartedly to the rhythm of a pun composed extempore: *"Buronya o-o! Buronya. Buronya asi nnɛ o-o, Buronya. Ɛnne yeasi Buronya Dua o-o, Buronya!"* ("Hurrah, Christmas! O, Christmas. Christmas is dawn today, Christmas. Christmas Tree is up today. Hurrah, Christmas!") My Christmas Tree was completed with a decoration of garden-eggs, pepper, gem biscuits and a few sticks of candles fastened to the lower ends of some of the branches.

Soon rockets were heard firing from near and afar. Up above in the Salem sky rose sky rockets that were seen soaring higher and higher, exploding into some multi-coloured flames which vanished in a few seconds. The long awaited moment had arrived. Already one heard cries of *"A F R I N H Y I A P A - O - O - O!"* wishing all neighbours a Merry Christmas. The still evening air was stirred by the church bell ringing, *"Kron-kron! Kron-kron! Kron-kron!"* to summon all to the church room to hear the good tidings of the birth of the Saviour of the World. It was the same old church bell that I heard ringing, but on that particular evening the sound it made was exciting, cheerful, exhilarating — surprisingly extraordinary.

The Agogo Basel Mission little church building was filled to capacity by the time the third bell ceased ringing that "Holy Night." The Catechist, in the mood of the night, recited the Introit:

Munnsuro, na hwɛ, me de anigye kɛsɛ asɛmpa a ɛbɛyɛ ɔman nyinaa dea merebrɛ mo; sɛ ɛnne woawo Agyenkwa a ɔne Kristo, Awurade no ama mo wɔ Dawid kurom.

(Don't be afraid. I bring to you the most joyful news ever announced, and is for everyone. The Saviour — yes the Messiah, the Lord — has been born tonight in Bethlehem.)

Zestfully the congregation of regular and occasional churchgoers sang the opening Hymn:

Yesu awoda yɛ me fɛ koraa
Yesu Kristo me m'agyenkwa
Sɛ woanwo Yesu a, anka, yɛbɛyera
Yesu Kristo meda w'ase
            — Twi Hymn 57

(The birth of Jesus is gratifying to me,
Jesus Christ is my Saviour.
Had Jesus not been born, we would have perished.
Jesus Christ, I am grateful to you.)

In front of the platform in the room where Church Elders and distinguished visitors sat at church, stood a full-size palm tree which was well-decorated for Christmas. On its leaves hung selected garden-eggs, pepper, gem biscuits strung on threads, as well as sticks of candles which were fastened to branches at regular intervals. Perched on top of the highest branch was a star-shaped tinsel. Outside the church building some young adolescents kept firing rockets causing church ushers to dash out furiously, but in vain, to silence them.

The church service was programmed for adults whose hymn singing continued all the time with breaks for the reading of passages on the birth of the Little Lord Jesus from the Bible. Most of what was said or read did not interest us children in the least. We were looking forward eagerly to the end of the service and, on hearing the final "A - M - E - N!," rushed to an open space behind the church where our pile of *atewa-abena* (husks of *atewa* seeds) was set ready for our Christmas bonfire. Live coal was fetched from our house, the nearest, which was only about twenty yards away at the other side of the church building. Flames shot high and sparks from the burning husks enlivened their brilliance. The biting cold of the night harmattan air mellowed the sharpness of the *atewa-abena* bonfire heat and enhanced its enjoyment as we sat round singing Christmas songs all through the "silent night."

At cock's crow, our leaders organized us for the annual early morning house to house carol singing to wish inmates in Salem houses *AFRINHYIA PA!* (Merry Christmas). When we entered a house, one of our leaders knocked gently at a door and woke the head of the family as we, the remaining members of the group, sang merrily: "Good morning, Sir! Good morning, Sir! *Damfo a woasa, sɔre bra.* Halleluia, Halleluia, Praise ye the Lord." As the head of the house came out and stood at the entrance of his/her bedroom door or sat at a convenient place in the yard, we sang Christmas hymns, the most popular ones being; *"Yesu Awoda ye me fe koraa,"* and two or three of the following:

Anadwo a yɛkae nnɛ yi,
Aman nyinaa nkaakae bi!
Ɛyɛ Osor'abɔfo fɛ
sɛ woawo Yesu Kristo nnɛ
　　　　　— Twi Hymn 56

(The night we remember this day
Let all nations join in its celebration.
It has delighted the angels in heaven
That Jesus Christ is born today.)

Abofra Ketewa a,
nnɛ yedi n'awoda,
ne m'agyenkwa.
Ɔba ahohiam,
Ɔda mmoa 'dakam.
Yɛn nti na
wɔawo no saa.
　　　　　— Twi Hymn 58

(A little child
Whose birthday we celebrate to day
Is my Saviour.
He came in poverty;
He lays in a manger,
For our sake

He was been born in such a condition.)

O Yesu, ye da wo ase
sɛ wufi sro baa wiase;
Maria na ɔwoo wo ampa,
eyi ma nnipa anika
ne ahotɔ
                    — Twi Hymn 59

(O Jesus Christ, we are grateful to you
For having come from heaven into the world.
Mary it was who truly begat you.
This has gained for men gladness
And happiness.)

Onyame bɔfo fi soro
bɛsee nnuan-hwɛfo no sɛ:
'Munnsuro hwee, maani nnye,
mo bo ntɔ mo yam kɛse!'
                    — Twi Hymn 60

(The angel of God from heaven
came and said to the shepherds:
'Don't be afraid; be glad,
keep your hearts very calm!')

Mifi soro no ho maba.
Asɛmpa na mede maba,
a munnsuro, moani nnye!
mo bo ntɔ mo yam yiye
                    — Twi Hymn 61

(I have come from heaven afar
Bringing to you good news.
Don't be afraid; be glad,
Keep your hearts very calm.)

Our host, the head of the house, expressed his/her appreciation with a cash donation of 3d., 6d., 1s. or 2s. At the end of our rounds, our leaders commended all members of the group on their excellent performance, which had resulted in a handsome total collection of 11s.3d. The appreciable amount was spent on buying pieces of fireworks that were shared with all of us who took part in the early morning carol singing. To the older ones went rockets and to us, the younger ones, "Christmas Stars" (*Buronya Nsoroma*) and boxes of coloured matches we called "*ayerɛmoo.*"

Back home we rushed to the riverside thrice to fetch water. Then followed one of our most pleasant filial Christmas duties: that of carrying Mother's gifts to her friends and relatives, the principal ones of whom, I recollected, were:

Nana Pepra (her father) in Salem:
3 tubers of *ɛyere* yams + 3 sponges and a packet of black soap.

Nana Yaw Nkroma (her grand-uncle) in Salem:
tubers of *Kuntuo* yams + 3 sponges + 1 packet of black soap.

Nana Panin Afua Adem and her sister **Akua Adwapa** (her grandmothers in town):
4 tubers of *Akwa* yams + 4 sponges + 2 packets of soap together with 3 pieces of firewood of dead *Esa* tree.

Papa Kwaben Ofiri (her brother-in-law) in Town:
2 tubers of *pona* yams + 3 sponges and 1 packet of black soap.

Nana Kwadwo Bɔfoɔ (her uncle) in Town:
2 tubers of *dabreko* yams + 3 sponges and a packet of soap.

Nana Yaa Kuma (her mother's sister) in Town:
2 tubers of *nanantɔ* yams + 3 sponges and a packet of soap.

Nana Kwaben Atobra (her uncle) in Town:
2 tubers of *nanantɔ* yams + 3 sponges and a packet of soap.

Nana Adwoa Bruku (her mother's sister) in Town:
2 tubers of *nanantɔ* yams + 3 sponges and a packet of soap.

Nana Daatano (my father's uncle) in Town:
2 Tubers of *nanantɔ* yams + 3 sponges and a packet of soap.

The Catechist (Agogo Basel Mission Church) in Salem:
1 fowl + six eggs + 3 tubers of kuntuo yams.

The Catechist reciprocated by sending to Mother a beautiful headkerchief, plus a quantity each of cooking salt and gem biscuits. Other male recipients of her Christmas presents also reciprocated with cash gifts of 4s. and one or two of the following articles: cooking salt, shea butter (*nkuu*) or gem biscuits. Cured tobacco (*tawa*), sold by the head called "*tawa-bɔn*," was a valuable and appreciable Christmas gift especially to elderly women (*mmerewa*), but as Mother was young and was known to be a non-smoker, her gifts did not include any tobacco.

Mother's two grandmothers went themselves to Salem to thank her for her presents and to wish us, their great-grandchildren, a Merry Christmas (*Afrinhyia Pa*). They hobbled together, trusted walking sticks in right hands, with short black clay-pipes held firmly at corners of their mouths by the few remaining teeth. The coming together on a Christmas Day of members of four generations was, in itself, a happy moment. It must have been particularly so for the oldest ones, whose prolonged handshakes betrayed a feeling of happy fulfillment as they wished us individually and collectively, and repeating over and over, the season's greeting: "*Afrinhyia pa*, (Happy New Year) and *Afe nkɔ nsan mmɛto yɛn mfeɛ so* (Many happy returns)."

Presentation of gifts over, we bathed, dressed and got ourselves ready for the Christmas Day church service. As always, but particularly on such an important occasion, Mother saw to it that we had bathed ourselves thoroughly, shea-buttered every part of the body evenly, and that our talcum powder application was just right. Having been "passed" as properly dressed we set off to church, which was only a few steps away from our house. Everything we wore that day was new: our cloths were new, our *pieto* underwear was new, and our singlets were new. One thing, however, was puzzling to me on that day of days. It was the incongruous behavior of almost all adults in Agogo, but particularly the women of Salem. On a day that was, we had been told several times before it arrived, the remembrance day of the birth of Christ the Saviour, when all were bidden to "be glad," those same grown-ups were mourning! They mourned, grieved and wept irrepressibly, we heard, for the loss of some dear relatives who passed away a long or short time before that day! Because of the incomprehensible action of many of the adult members of the Agogo community, the atmosphere of Christmas Day itself was rather unhappy and funereal.

In town, the situation was no better, if not worse. It was a day of hard drinking and wanton drunkenness. The attendance at the church service that morning was, in consequence, seriously affected, with most of the few members present dozing most of the time.

The day after Christmas Day itself was the real merry-making day in Agogo — a day of unbounded jollity. Animals

bred for Christmas were slaughtered: fowls in their tens by the
very ordinary folk, and sheep and goats in their numbers by
the relatively well-to-do, who distributed some parts of the
mutton to friends and relatives. In every home in the town
that day, it was fresh meat consumption. She was regarded an
odd fad of a woman who did not prepare Christmas Soup
(*Buronya Nkwan*), but cooked the common, everyday soup of
lean meat and smoked herrings (*ɛman*). The exception was, of
course, in the case of sick persons on diet including venereal
disease patients. It is worth observing that chicken soup
(*akɔkɔ-nkwan*) was highly valued because it was an uncommon
meal in those days. It was prepared and eaten on special
occasions, particularly in times of gladness when one could
truly say: *"Asɛm yi dɛ nti, mekum akɔkɔ madi."* ("For such a
happy news, event or occasion, I will kill a fowl for a meal.")
Another occasion for *akɔkɔ-nkwan* was to honour a
distinguished guest (*ɔhɔho pa*). It did often happen also that in
a case of some misdemeanour proved against a spouse, a
friend or some close relative who went into the case asked the
guilty wife or husband to pacify the aggrieved partner with a
fowl and some number of eggs, usually six. The fowl so
provided was killed and used to prepare *akɔkɔ-nkwan*, which
was eaten to reconcile the discordant couple.

Eggs, like fowls, were not normally an item of everyday diet
in those days. They were collected or bought at six for three-
pence for presentation to visiting missionaries and high
ranking government officials. There were two occasions apart
from Christmas festivities on which, I recollect, eggs, as an
item of food for the ordinary person, was a necessity. Both
occurred in town and were of some ritual significance. One
was connected with the observance of a nubility rite (*Bra-
gorɔ*), when an adolescent girl undergoing the performance
was fed with a generous supply of eggs of which her mates-in-
attendance had a fair share. The other ritual ceremony that
offered the opportunity for much consumption of eggs outside
Christmas was *Ano-hyira-Da*, when a man decided to offer
sacrifice to his soul so as to sanctify his whole personality.
Ano-hyira ceremony became necessary on several grounds. It
was performed for instance, to give expression to the inner
feeling of happiness that rose out of some unexpected
deliverance from what could have been a calamity. Also to
propitiate an aggrieved soul as might have been advised by a

Fetish on consultation, or to express appreciation for complete success in an undertaking.

My father performed an *Ano-hyira* ceremony once when he won his oath-swearing case. It took place on a Tuesday, his natal weekday. Early that morning I saw that his second wife, who was not a Christian, brought to him a dish of mashed yam without oil (*εtɔ-fufuo*) with several boiled eggs studded on it. Normally he took his meals in a *pato* (open-front room) in his part of his uncle's house. But the ritual meal that morning was placed on his short eating table (*didi-pon*) at a corner of his bedroom. He wore a pure white cloth (*ntama fufuo*) and sat on a white stool by the table. He had woken me up early that morning to fetch fresh water from the stream at the topmost end of the general collecting place. A calabash full of the fresh water I brought was placed on the table by the dish of mashed yam. Standing behind a half-opened door to the bedroom, I saw Father dip some fresh *adwera* herbs collected early that morning three times into the water which was sprinkled on to all parts of the body: the head, the trunk and the limbs (*Ɔdwera ne ho*). That done, he uncovered the dish, picked up a small morsel of the mashed yam and touched it to the tip of his tongue. Three eggs were "fed" to his soul in like manner. Each action was repeated thrice, and each time he did so, Father muttered, "*Kosε, Okra Nkεtea, Kosε, Kosε, Mihyira m'ano.*" ("Bless you, Soul Nketea, Bless You, I sanctify myself.") At the end of the short ceremony in the bedroom, I was asked to remove the table with the dish to the usual eating place in the *pato* where, together with another dish of specially prepared early morning *fufu* (*anopafufuo*) with a lot of boiled eggs, the "Soul Cleansing" meal was distributed to some close friends and relatives.

The slaughter of a sheep or a goat by an ordinary person for home consumption was quite unusual on an ordinary day except on an occasion such as Christmas. It was, in fact, a notion widely upheld that "*Wukum odwan di a, wo ho dwan wo.*" ("He who killed a sheep/goat for his own consumption brings a nuisance unto himself.") In the case of sheep-slaughtering in particular, the involved procedure of obtaining the Chief's prior consent through an *okyeame* (linguist) militated against any desire, however strong it might be, for killing one for household consumption. Christmastime, therefore, offered an opportunity, once in a year, for anyone who had a domestic animal, including sheep, goats or pigs, to kill and enjoy it as part of the festivities, without any restraint or inhibition. Hence the added extraordinary cheeriness of the occasion.

The day after Christmas day itself was said a day of remembrance for someone called "Stefano," who was said to have been stoned to death somewhere a long time ago. All the Catechist's talk about that Saint Stephen and his fate did not make much sense to me at that time, particularly so on a day of dishes of good food and heavy eating. It was a puzzle that was readily dismissed as another one of grown-ups' inconsistencies. The church service was a short one, happily. The afternoon of that poor "Stefano's" day was, for us children, a big time. We were free to go a-roaming (*yekotwa ntɛn*), apparently to greet parents' friends and relatives, but ostensibly to display the beauty of our new Christmas cloths and dress. In some houses genial hosts gave each young caller a handful of gem biscuits which we called *krakase* (crackers). By the close of the day some thrifty girls had accumulated a sufficient quantity of *krakkase* to string them into a long necklace.

Gem biscuits of our childhood days were real biscuits from the world-famed biscuit makers Huntley and Palmers and Peak Frean & Co. of Reading, England. Their simple product which reached our remote corner of the world was simply delicious — tasty, crispy, crunchy, palatable. I ate their make of gem biscuits by the handfuls within the week of merry-making, at odd times and at all times, without any stomach upset. No amount of the biscuit I chewed caused indigestion (*ayɛm-tim*) or stomach-running (*ayɛm-tuo*). Compared with the nice Huntley & Palmers or Peak Frean & Co. gem biscuits of my childhood days, most of the crumbly, tasteless things that pass now-a-days for gem biscuits are spurious imitations. Most of the so-called gem biscuits that we have had to buy for our children for Christmas these days are an insult to that genuine gem biscuit which we received as welcome gifts for Christmas when we where young.

Other Yuletide activities in Agogo which contributed to a happy memory of *Afrinhyia Pa* in my childhood days were organised dances in the non-Christian section of the town. In vogue were two dances: the Agogo Brass Band and *Ositi*.

The Agogo Brass Band of Long Ago

Members of the band were the cream of young men of the town — handsome, vigorous and brimful of life. They, too, started to prepare strenuously for Christmas, weeks before the time. They attended regularly afternoon practices which they called *"Padeeti"* (Parade) at a prepared spot under a big *odum* tree about a quarter of a mile away on the Kwawu footpath. To polish their performance for Christmas engagements, the members employed a dashing coach from Asiakwa in Akyem Abuakwa. He was said to be proficient in the handling of all the band instruments, with the cornet as his special part. A likable young man, he soon made friends, including any unmarried women, some of whom were detailed to cater for him in turns. It did not take the players a long time to master a few pieces for play to entertain merry-makers in the evenings of the Christmas week.

An incident occurred at the time that offered the young Asiakwa coach an opportunity to demonstrate his creative ability. It happened that a hideout of a gang that stole goats and sheep was uncovered at Atara, a village a few miles from Agogo off the Agogo-Kumawu road near the confluence of two streams. The members of the gang were all caught red-handed as they were enjoying a hearty meal prepared with the mutton of a fat sheep they stole the previous night. Their leader, a lanky middle-aged man with a slender nose and a pair of small piercing eyes set deep in their sockets, was Ad. Men.

The brilliant coach promptly composed a short piece themed on the theft. It became an instant hit, just in time for the Christmas week dances. Immediately the tune was called, the whole crowd of dancers was thrown into a wild ecstasy and spectators ravished with delight. The players, too, enjoyed it. They could be seen twisting, bending and shaking their bodies to the rhythm of the tune as the dancers and all hilariously sang:

E - E - E, Dwan-sadeɛ O-OO,
Ad. Men. e-e-e,
Dwan-saadeɛ O -O
Ɛhe na ɛwɔ O- O- O?
Dwansaadeɛ O-O-O!

E - E - E, Dwan-saadeɛ O - O
Ad. Men. e - e - e,
Dwan-saadeɛ O -O

Atara afuom O -O
Dwan-saadeɛ O-O-O!

(Yes, the fatty mutton,
Ad. Men, Yes
The fatty mutton.
Where is it?
The fatty mutton!

Yes, the fatty mutton,
Ad. Men, Yes
The fatty mutton,
In Atara farmstead
The fatty mutton is!)

As the band played and the crowd that followed it surged from one quarter of the town to the other, we, the children-spectators, followed wildly, bravely, unmindful of gutters or of any obstacle that happened to be in our way. Those of us who stumbled and fell ignored cuts and bruises and continued on doggedly.

From a vantage point at an open space where the band stopped to entertain the residents of the neighbourhood, I had the opportunity to watch the players and their instruments closely. My eyes roved searchingly,

From the Euphonium to the Tuba and the Cornet
To the Trumpet and the Trombone;
To the Bass-Drum and the Side-Drum;
To the Cymbal and the Triangle;
And from the Triangle back to the Euphonium.

The Agogo Brass Band gratuitously enlivened our Christmas with captivating music that reverberated in the distant encircling rock-caves, and drew a jubilant crowd of spectators including even elderly women whose cries echoed the season's greetings: "A-F-R-I-N-H-Y-I-A P-A-O-o-o-o!"

The Agogo Ositi Dance Group of the Mid-1910s

A second dance in our childhood days was *Ositi* whose members were exclusively unmarried youth. Each major quarter (*borɔnoo*) of the town, Salem excluded, had its well-organized *Ositi* dance group. Inter-quarter competitions were frequently arranged. Some persons of distinction from other places in Asante often came to spend Christmas in our town. I recollect one such person quite vividly. He was Paa Koo. F., a man of wealth and a native of a town in Asante-Akyem, our District. I learned later that he was the founder of a quarter in Kumasi which, to date, bears his name. Paa Koo. F. was the proprietor of a trading firm which had many branches in many big towns in Asante. He was said to be so rich he had been able to employ some expatriates (*aborɔfo*) on the staff of his establishment. He was in Agogo that Christmas, I heard, as the guest of the Agogohene. An *Ositi* dance competition was organized in his honour. The function was held at the upper end of the Agogo High Street (*Abɔnten-Kɛseɛm*) on the fourth afternoon after the Christmas Day. The crowd, including even some Christians from Salem, was already thick by the time the august visitor and his royal host arrived at the place of the dance. They took their seats on a decorated dais at the Hwidiem end of the Main Street with the various dancing groups and spectators facing them in a wide semi-circular formation. All eyes were on Paa Koo. F., the Agogohene's honoured guest. I saw him. He was medium in height, corpulent in build, and the air of well-being around him gave credence to his much talked-about opulence.

The *Ositi* groups danced in turns, one *borɔnoo* group after the other. The most exciting moment came when the leader of a group styled "*Ositi-Kɔmfoɔ*" (the ace of *Ositi* dance) and his "queen," *Ositi-hemaa*, took the floor. The crowd would suddenly surge forward, everyone making a frantic effort to catch a glimpse of the adroitness and skillful bodily movements of the two acclaimed most handsome youngsters of the particular *borɔnoo*. The tempo of the dance rose to its highest pitch when their group, joined in by many of the enthusiastic spectators, sang the rousing song:

Ositia Komfoɔ asi dwem O-O
Yɛnnye no yɔɔ,
Yɛnnye no yɔɔ,
Ɔbɛba O-O?

(The Ace of Ositi is on floor,
Let's all hail him,
Hail him respectfully,
He'll have the day?)

Another moment of intense joy at the dance came when a dancing maiden was honoured in public by her friends, relative or lovers. It took the form of an admirer placing a gift on her back between the shoulders (*n'awan-mu*) as she stooped dancing. The bestowal of honour in public at a dance in such a manner was an expression of regard that was highly esteemed. Articles presented included petty cash, pads of shea butter, handkerchiefs, and other hand things bought at the site from shrewd vendors who took advantage of the spending proclivity of people at the material time, to display wares suitable for the occasion. Young men in love, in particular, bought lavender water and soaked the body of the dancing lover from head to toe with the whole content of a bottle. Florida Water, a brand of lavender water, was the most fashionable and highly valued item of such gifts. Satisfied, the male lover doing the honouring strutted away from the arena in a manner supposedly befitting a true lover.

Some spectators at the dance displayed their affluence by throwing into the air coins specially changed for the occasion. Boys, girls and some young women scrambled furiously for 1d., 3d., 6d., 1s. and 2s. pieces that fell to the ground from the displayer's throw. In spite of some tight squeezes or minor cuts and bruises sustained in the struggle, the display achieved its purpose and helped create an enjoyable side attraction.

It was time to close and the guest of honour, Paa Koo. F., rose and said a few words of thanks to all the members of the various dancing groups for their smart turnout, their skillful dancing and their melodious songs. He ended with a promise to visit the town again the following Christmas, and wished all who had gathered together there, "*Afrinhyia Pa,*" to which all responded in unison: "*Afe nkɔ mmɛto yɛn bio*" ("Many happy returns"). Paa Koo. F. offered the groups gifts of some gem biscuits and sums of money which, it was said, were quite substantial. The applause from the happy-looking Agogo crowd was thunderous. All the Ositi dancing groups finally sang, *en masse*, their closing song:

Moma yennyae
Moma yɛnkoda O-O.
Moma yennyae O,
Moma yɛnkoda O-O.
Agoro bɛyɛ yiye a,

Efiri anɔpa tutu O-O.
Agoro bɛyɛ yiye a,
Efiri anopa tutu, tutu.
Mo ma yennyae, O,
Moma yɛnkɔda O-O...OO!

(Let's dismiss,
Oh, Let's dismiss
and go to bed,
The success of a dance
is the effect of its
early morning
good start.
Let's disperse.
Oh, let's all disperse
And retire to our beds!)

And to bed all dispersed, happy, merry and full of contentment.

The New Year's Day (*Afe Foforo Da*)

It took me some time to comprehend that Christmas and the New Year's Day celebrations marked two separate occasions. My conception (or was it misconception?) was that the New Year's Day was celebrated to round off festivities called "*Buronya*" (Christmas). The traditional Asante practice of commemorating certain events on the eighth day of their occurrences might have led me to such a conclusion. I had had the opportunity to observe, for instance, that

- a newly born child was named on the eighth day of its birth (*Yɛto akɔdaa din nnawɔtwe-da*)
- a deceased member of a family was mourned and certain rites performed on the eighth day of his/her death (*Yɛdi nea wawu nnaawɔtwe-da*)
- Some annual celebrations of non-Christians in Town were rounded off on the eighth day with certain observances or performances (*Yɛyi afahyɛ bi ano ne nnaawɔtwe-da*).

The view that Christmas day marked the start of *Buronya* and the New Year's Day, the end of *Buronya*, might have again been reinforced by the fact that only one form of greeting was heard expressing the wish of everybody anywhere during the season. It was "*Afrinhyia Pa*" all through the eight days of

Buronya festivities. One never heard of any other proper Twi equivalent of "Merry Christmas."

One other point was that the pattern of celebration of what I later learned to be the New Year's Day was almost identical with that of Christmas: an evening church service preceded a forenoon service on each of the two days. There was, however, a discernible difference in the mood of each celebration. Christmas church services were more convivial and their duration, shorter. New Year's Day church services, on the other hand, were longer and more dramatic. The attendance at the service held on the New Year's Eve to welcome the in-coming year (*Yɛkɔsare Afe*) was heavy and included many once-a-year-church goers. It started soon after nightfall and continued, non-stop, till past midnight. The programme consisted of community hymn singing, addresses by the Catechist and some church Elders, as well as prayers which were interspersed with *Mfante-nnwom* sung by some of the elderly members of the congregation. That particular item was moving, even to us as children, because the sound heard coming from the vibrant voices of men and women who had been using them for a period of sixty years and more, was fresh and melodious. Then there was the Catechist's lengthy report which touched on all important events of the year which was about to pass. He reported at length on:

• the total amount of dues collected, the total expenses made and the balance being carried forward into expected new year;
• the number of adults admitted into the church and those removed from its roll;
• people baptized, both adults and children; children born into the church during the year about to pass, and, finally,
• the Roll Call of Honour in which the names of full members who died during the year were called, one by one, and chronologically.

As part of a Memorial Service to the Dead verses from *Psalm 90* were mournfully read and a minute's silence was observed in honour of the departed. This was followed by the singing of the first verse of Twi Hymn 403:

Gyidifo trabea pa
wɔ nea wɔn Agyenkwa a,
wɔn ani da no so wɔ,
Wɔn fi pa wɔ soro hɔ

(Believers' proper dwelling place

is by the side of their Saviour
in whom their faith is placed.
Their true home is in heaven.)

A short prayer was said to commend the souls of the departed into the hands of their Maker.

The time for the arrival of the New Year was fast approaching. Members of the congregation knelt and, in silent prayer, communed individually with God in the dead silence of the cold early January night. An alarm clock standing on the Catechist's table and set to ring precisely at twelve o'clock midnight kept tick-tocking the seconds and the minutes as the Catechist, in a clear staccato voice, kept announcing at short intervals: "*Ɔ - re - kɔ, Ɔ - re - kɔ - O - O! Afe dada no, rekɔ. Ɔ - re - kɔ - O - O, Ɔ - re - kɔ - O - O - O - ...O!*" ("It is passing away. The Old Year is passing off. It is going. It is g - o - i - n - g!) Meantime four young men with flint-lock Dane guns, led by Kwasi K. (N), the freed slave and handyman of the Agogo Basel Mission community, had stationed themselves a few yards away from the church building. At exactly midnight, the alarm clock rang its shrill sound, "K - R - R - R - R - R!" signalling to the gun-men who, with guns cocked and muzzles pointed upward, shot volleys into the sky to usher in the New Year. The church bells, as if in compliance with the bidding of Lord Alfred Tennyson, simultaneously sounded to

Ring out old shapes of foul disease,
Ring out the narrowing lust of gold;
Ring out the thousand wars of old,
Ring in the thousand years of peace.

Ring in the valiant man and free,
The eager heart, the kindlier hand;
Ring out the darkness of the land,
Ring in the Christ that is to be.
           — *In Memoriam*, cvi

When the noise of the gunshot and ringing of the bells had subsided, the Catechist, in a benign tone, gave the congregation the New Year greeting: "*Mema mo nyinaa Afrinhyia pa, O - O - O! Agyanom, Ɛnanom, namfonom, mpanin, mmofra, adɔfonom, mema mo Afrinhyia pa!*" ("Happy New Year to all of you. Fathers, Mothers, Friends, Old, Young, Beloved all, I wish you a Happy New Year!") In hearty unison all in the room responded, *"Afe nkɔ mmɛto yɛn mfeɛ so."* ("Many happy returns to you.") The *Mfante-nnwom* singers whose members were all elderly men and women of the congregation, sang an impromptu, moving song:

> *Ato yɛn O - O,*
> *Ato yɛn. nne*
> *Afrinhyia pa,*
> *Ato yɛn, nnɛ*

> (It has come to meet us.
> It has come to meet us today.
> Happy New Year has come,
> It has come to meet us today.)

The long midnight church service was brought to a close with the singing of the first two verses of Twi Hymn 380:

> *Momma yɛmfa mpaebɔ*
> *ne aseda mmrɛ Nyame,*
> *afisɛ wahwɛ yɛn so*
> *afrihyia yi nyinaa mu.*

> *Mfe reba, na ɛkoɔ;*
> *yɛte sɛ akwantemfo,*
> *yefi afe dedaw mu*
> *na yesi afe fofrɔm.*

> (Let us bring our prayer
> and our thanks to God,
> for He has guarded u s
> all through the year.

> Years come and go;
> We are like travellers,
> We pass from the Old Year
> and enter the New Year.)

Hearty handshakes followed the benediction and everyone wished everybody *"Afrinhyia Pa!"* as they came out of the church building. In an atmosphere of joviality and in a feeling of warm neighbourliness, the church congregation dispersed through the chilly harmattan nights to warm beds at home.

At daybreak Mother went round and shook hands will all the inmates of the house, young and old, to wish everyone of us *"Afrinhyia Pa!"* As on Christmas Day there was a church service on the New Year's Day, but the one held on the latter day was very long and lasted most of the day. It was not only that the Catechist's sermon was lengthy, but two other events also contributed to the prolongation of the service. The first was the attendance of the Agogohene at the service. The second was the Annual Thanksgiving Harvest, which was scheduled to take place that same First Day of the year.

It was the practice that the *Ɔhene* of Agogo and his Stool Elders went to church in State on the New Year's Day to join the Christians to worship God. The admonition sternly made by the Catechist, and repeated several times, to the effect that members of the congregation should show their respect for their earthly ruler by full and punctual attendance at service that particular day, was heeded obligingly. All were seated by the time the third and last bell for the service rang that morning.

In Town, on the other hand, all was not that punctual. At the time that the Chief and his retinue were expected to arrive at the church, Stool Elders were trickling leisurely into the *Ahemfie* in ones and twos. Scarcely anybody or anything was ready in the *Ahemfie*. Drummers were then tuning their drums; horn-blowers were late; state umbrella-bearers were pulling out the giant things gingerly from their hanging places in the *Pato* room in the *Ahemfie*. The Chief himself was in his chamber where some elderly women, custodians of the Agogo customs and culture, were putting finishing touches to his dressing to ensure that he was appropriately fitted for the state function.

When all was finally ready and the procession moved from the Ahemfie, the pace was incredibly slow. That was deliberate for it was held that "*Ɔberempɔn nante berɛɛ, berɛɛ.*" ("A noble man never hurried in his walking.") It was a magnificent pageantry that moved in pomp, slowly but majestically, to the orchestrated rhythm of *atumpam* and *mpintin* drumming. The Agogohene, wearing a costly *kente* cloth with a headgear studded with gold, *Bamfina* bangles on wrists and a gold *Atweaban* chain on his neck, sat in his pallanquin borne by four strong men under a wide-brim state umbrella. The Elders also wore gorgeous *kente* cloths. The Queen-mother, a slightly short but well-built woman approaching her middle ages, was elegantly dressed in style and in attire. Her graceful carriage and royal countenance portrayed in her the ideal Asante woman! The congregation in the Basel Mission Church waited patiently, and loyally. In front of the Chief's pallanquin bearers, I saw a stool servant (*ahenkwaa*) carrying on his shoulder a pair of gold-studded sandals. He fascinated me. Some time later I asked my father to tell me why a bare-footed man should carry a pair of sandals ahead of the Chief. His explanation was "*Ɔhene nan nsi fam.*" ("A Chief's bare feet should never touch the ground.") Asked why, Father replied: "*Ɔhene nan si fam a,okɔm beba.*" ("There will be a famine on the land if the Chief trod the ground on bare feet.") He elaborated and said that it was for that reason that the spare pair of sandals I saw was carried in the procession, so that, in the event of any damage to the pair the Chief was wearing, the spare one could be used instantly to forestall the Chief's sole touching the bare ground. Father added that if the Chief willfully slipped off his sandal and touched the ground with his bare feet, he would be de-stooled immediately on the ground that he had wished the Agogo town ill by such a brazen act.

The drumming ceased on reaching the boundary between the Town and Salem (*Sukuum*), which was about a hundred and fifty yards away from the church building. The pallanquin bearers (*asoamfoɔ*) stopped and lowered it at the entrance of the building. Its occupant, the Agogohene, stepped down and walked between the rows of benches to a reserved place at the other end of the room.

Harvest Thanksgiving collections followed the sermon. It was also a function that consumed much time. Everybody in attendance — boys, girls, old and young — except the Chief and his Elders filed to the pulpit end to deposit into a big brass bowl his or her offering, small and large. The amount collected was counted and the total announced after the bulk contribution from the Chief and his Elders had been added. The church service ended, but not the service to the State. It was the practice of the congregation to see the Chief off to the *Ahemfie* whenever he attended a church service in State. That duty was done faithfully on that New Year's Day.

I stood by and watched the Agogohene's procession returning to the *Ahemfie*. Two *nkrawiri* drummers led. They beat intermittently their drums, which were decorated with some aged shin-bones said to be those of some of the victims killed in one of the many Asante wars by the Agogo warriors. Following the drummers were Stool Elders and their people in, as far as I can recollect, this order:

1. The Twafoohene
2. The Adontenhene
3. The Akwamuhene
4. The Kurontihene
5. The Atufoohene
6. The Asonahene
7. The Agonahene
8. The Aduana
9. The Gyaasehene
10. The Chief's Linguists (*Akyeame*)
11. The Agogohene himself in his pallanquin, followed by *mpintin*
    and *atumpan* drummers. It was the first time that I saw the two
    big *atumpan* drums being carried on the head of men, each
    followed closely by its drummer, thumping on it rhythmically,
    deftly, invigoratingly Each drummer's body was bared down to
    the waist where the cloth he wore had been gathered and
    tightened into *kwaha* style.

    The Chief danced as he sat in the pallaquin. As he did so,
    several of his admiring subjects raised their right hands with two
    fingers in a "V" shape to signal congratulations while others
    applauded by shouting the appellation; "Mo - a - Mu - O, O!" After
    every few steps he pulled for a brief stop and then moved on,
    raising his right hand strung with talismans and amulets of
    various sizes and shapes, to greet his appreciative subjects lining
    the streets to honour their worthy and respected Chief.
12. The Queen-mother
13. The Ankobeahene
14. The Asenehene
15. The Kyidomhene

The procession reached the *Ahemfie* in the late afternoon.
After the customary sharing of drinks, including gin, schnapps
and palm-wine, to the Stool Elders, drummers, Stool servants,
including pallanquin carriers, and all who accompanied the
Chief to the *Ahemfie*, the Catechist and his Church Elders took
leave of the Agogohene and, with them, the Agogo Basel
Mission Church members returned to Salem.

The return to Salem late that afternoon offered the members
of the Agogo Basel Mission Church the opportunity to dance
on streets in the Town in their own way. In a happy and joyful
mood they danced — openly, uninhibitedly — as they sang
their popular marching song,

Ma me gyidi ntaban
na memfa mintu;
na menhwεhwε me mu yiyi.

'bɔfo bi gyina' soro pon ano
na ɔtɔ akwaaba nnwom.
Akwaaba, Akwaaba.
'bɔfo bi gyina 'soro pon ano
na ɔtɔ akwaba nnwom.

(Give me the wings of faith to fly
to examine my inner self critically.
An angel stands at the entrance of the heavenly door
singing songs of welcome.)

All sang and danced merrily in a two-line formation. Some
elderly members of the congregation, holding handkerchiefs,
twigs, brooms and anything handy that could be waved,
danced from one end of the moving line to the other, cheering
the dancers, as they themselves dance, with

Ɔhim E!
Ogyaa-naakwa!
Awurade, Sɔre O, O, O!
Onyame mma nam O, O, O!
Ɔsaagyefoɔ, Sɔre O, O, O!
Ɔhim E!
Agyaa-naakwa!

(Triumph!
Jubilation!
Lord, arise!
The children of God are on the move.
Leader of warriors, arise!
Triumph!
Jubilation!)

Jubilantly, triumphantly, they proceeded to the house of the
Catechist at the far end of Salem. There, after a short prayer
and another benediction, the members of the church
dispersed and went home near dusk, tired, hungry and thirsty,
but with the feeling of satisfaction for a well-spent, eventful
New Year's Day.

As we reached home and started to undress and to replace
new Christmas clothes with everyday wear, Mother firmly
reminded the infatuated ones among us children: "*Buronya
asa. Buronya atwam. Buronya kɔ. Afei, ato adwuma.*"
("Christmas is ended. Christmas is past. Christmas is gone. It
is now time for work.")

10

MATRIMONIAL MEAL
(*ADUAN-KƐSEƐ*)
IN A
CHRISTMAS WEEK

"Friday in the Christmas week is the most suitable day," (*"Buronya Fiada no na ɛyɛ da pa,"*) my grandmother and her two daughters finally decided, among other things. It was at their regular fireside sit-together in the evenings that they chatted casually and intimately, or discussed seriously some domestic matters, including us, their children. At one such gathering, about a month before Christmas, suspecting that something was in the offing, I hid myself at a corner, within hearing distance, to eavesdrop. Eno Nkameraa, Mother's elder sister, had arrived at the house that evening unusually early and she appeared to have some matter on hand that needed prompt discussion. The three women took their seats at their usual places at the hearth (*mmukyia ho*). Without wasting any time she gave the other two, Mother and Grandmother, the news which had sent her posthaste to them.

Awo, [that was how the two daughters addressed their mother] Awo, a short while ago Akua Y. and her sister, Ama M., called to see me from Town. I have just seen them off. The purpose of their visits they told me, concerned Akwasua A. my daughter. Kwame D., their brother, they explained, had seen Akwasua and would like to have her for a wife. But before making a formal approach to the *abusua*, he would like to sound me and seek my consent. I have asked them to come back in three days. This, Awo, Akua, is an important matter which has to be deliberated by us all very carefully and a consensus reached before I say anything to the young man. What should I tell the two messengers when they call for my reply? This is a matter that all of us should decide.

Grandmother was the first to speak. "Who is this Kwame D.?" she asked.

Eno Nkameraa:	You must know him Awo, Kwame D., the son of Yaa A. of Etia.
Grandmother:	O, that's the one! He, I know. I thought it was the wretched Kwame D., of Bontoriase!
Eno Nkameraa:	*Tweaa, Okwasampani Kwame D. no? Asua! Tweaa* [an expression of utter contempt], that never-do-well Kwame D.? God forbid!
Mother:	Awo, You should be able to know, or must have heard, if there is any "bad" disease (yare bɔnee) running through the family of this young man. Have you, for instance, heard of any member of his family ever suffering from leprosy, epilepsy, *nkwantu* or insanity?
Grandmother:	No, not that I know.
Mother:	What about traits such as stealing, intemperance or roguery?
Grandmother:	No, I am not aware of the existence in that family of any such traits, no! Akua [she continued, turning to Mother] you know much about the young men in Agogo. Is Kwame D. an industrious young man (*osifoɔ*) or he is a wastrel (*ɔkwasampanii*) like his namesake of Bontoriase?
Mother:	Awo, of that I am pretty sure. I can say positively that Kwame D., son of Yaa A., is one of the most promising, hardworking and provident young men in this town. He is very much like Papa Nkɛtea, if a comparison were needed. Do you know? He is working a big cocoa farm at Oboakyi on the Kumawu-Agogo road. Agya Ampoma can tell you much about the young man's industry and his farm which is adjacent to his. And, Awo, you should know: Kwame D. takes fishing rights (*ahweɛ Sahene*) from the Agogohene and his Elders every year to exploit depths in the Onwan and Afram rivers in the major dry season. His fishing gang has always the heaviest catch each season and a substantial part of the fish that

flooded Agogo market last season came from his group.

That testimony scored a good point with Grandmother in the suitor's favour. Grandmother, replacing the live coal on her pipe, continued, "That's very interesting, Akua. Afua [she enquired as she turned to the direction of her elder daughter] is Akwasua aware of all these overtures?

Eno Nkameraa who had been sitting quietly all the time, replied uneasily, "What am I to say, Awo? Who can know the wiles of young men and women (*mmerantee ne mmabaawa*) of these days?

Mother: Why not find out from Akwasua herself? She is not far away. She must be sitting with her mates on the verandah outside.

Grandmother: That is a good idea, Akua. We must hear from her herself. Is that not what the Elders say? *Yon, yegye no okomfoɔ anum.* (Yes is acceptable when it is uttered from out of the priest's own mouth.)

Eno Nkameraa: I agree. Let's find out from her herself.

Mother casting her eyes about, shouted, "Yaw, Yaw! I am sure I saw Yaw loitering about here a short while ago. Where is he? Yaw!" I sneaked away quietly into the bedroom and pretended to be busy about something quite unconnected with the discussion going on in the yard

"Yaw! [persisting in her call] Yaw, where are you? Wasn't it you I saw a few moments ago? Yaw!"

"Yes, Mother, shall I come?" I responded seemingly innocently.

"Yes, of course. Do I shout for you for nothing? Would you run quickly and ask Akwasua to come home to see us?"

On hearing she was wanted at home, Akwasua rose promptly and, in a slightly quivering whisper, asked me, "Yaw, *adɛn? Mayɛ dɛn?*" ("Yaw, what's the matter? What have I done?")

"You will know, Akwasua, when you meet them."

Akwasua sat between Grandmother and Mother, feeling quite uneasy. Mother was the first to speak. "Akwasua," she asked, "Do you know Kwame D.?"

"Which of them?" enquired Akwasua in a suppressed anxiety.

"Kwame D., Yaa A.'s son. Etia." Akwasua remained silent.

That, to the mothers, was suggestive and easily understood.

"He would like to take you for a wife. Do you love him?" (*Wo pɛ no?*) Akwasua was as dumb as a stone.

"If you have no objection we, that is Awo, your mother and I, would be pleased to give you to him to marry. What do you say?" Akwasua continued to be mute.

Mother:	Shall we give our consent to the marriage? [still pressing Akwasua for a definite answer: YES or NO]
Akwasua:	[faintly and almost inaudibly] *Deɛ mobɛka biara.* (Whatever you may decide.)
Mother:	Akwasua, your answer is ambiguous. Do you agree that we give our consent to your marrying Kwame D. or you do not? Tell us precisely. Don't be evasive.
Akwasua	*Sɛ maka. Nea mobɛka biara mepene so!* (I have already told you. I agree to whatever you may decide.)
Grandmother	Akwasua, I understand you. We will, in three days' time, give our reply to Kwame D., and this is what we are to say to him. His request will be favourably considered if it is made formally through the Head of his Family. We will add further that we have your consent in saying so. If before that time you have a change of mind, let your mother know at once. We do not wish to force you in any way into a marriage that you may not favour yourself. You may leave us now.

The sprightly manner in which Akwasua went away left the parents in no doubt that she was privy to Kwame D.'s plans and that she welcomed their decision. Kwame D. was finally cleared as a fit and qualified person to be an in-law. Grandmother asked Eno Nkameraa to let Akwasua's father, Kwasi N. (K), know of the decision they had taken while she undertook to give his brother, Nana Kwadwo Bɔfoɔ, our *Ofie-Panin* a hint of what was to be expected.

A series of events followed rapidly. Three days after receiving a favourable response to his informal request, Kwame D. started making preliminary presentations, first, in cash of 10s. each to Eno Nkameraa and Akwasua; then a head of tobacco (*tawa-bon*) to Nana Kwaane which she shared with her "mothers" in town. Other gifts followed at short intervals as the number of recipients increased. On two occasions Kwame D., accompanied by three of his intimate friends, went to work in his mother-in-law to-be's farm at Kusibo, felling big trees in her new clearing (*wɔkoɔ abuo*). Formalities followed appropriately. They were:

Nkɔmmɔ-di-sa (**Conversation drink**) by which a man who has arranged to marry a woman formally introduced himself to the *Ofie-Panin* of the woman and her father. The formality is referred to variously as "*behu me nsa*" or "*aboboɔm-deɛ*". The "drink" presented by Kwame D. was *Doma* (7s.) each to our *Ofie- Panin* and Akwasua's father.

Ayɛ-yɔ (**Formal presentation of gifts**):
 i. to the Fiancée herself — *Nsoasa* (10s.)
 ii. to Fiancée's father — *Nsoasa* (10s.)
 iii. to Fiancée's mother — *Doma* (7s.)
 iv. to Fiancée *Ofie-Panin* — *Nsoasa* (10s.)
 v. to Fiancée mother's sisters (*Oni nuanom*) — (7s.)
 vi. to Fiancée brothers (*Nkontagye-sekan*) — *Browo-fa* (4s.)
 vii. to Fiancée sisters (*onua-mmaa-nom*) — *Browo-fa* (4s.)
 viii. to Fiancée father as Anyame-*dwan* (sheep for
    the father's soul) — *Asuanu* (£4.)

Ɔbaa no srɛ ne nsa-sie (**Formal request for a fiancé to be given in marriage to the fiancée and the customary registration of the marriage with the "Stamping" Drink.**) This important function was performed one morning in the house of Nana Kwadwo Bɔfoɔ, our *Ofie-Panin,* in Town. Present were close relatives of the *Ofie-Panin* and three *mmaa-mma* (children of male members of the Asona lineage). It is to be observed that at all such social functions and gatherings some *mmaa-mma* should be present to act as *akyeame* (linguists) or messengers of their "father", the *Ofie-panin*. The three *mmaa-mma* present that morning included one woman.

I saw a big palm-wine pot (*asa-hina*) in the yard topped to overflowing with whitish foam (*asa-huro*). A smaller empty pot (*akotokyiwa*) with a neat drinking calabash on top of it, was standing by the big pot of palm-wine. Five non-Asona members, two men and three women, had already arrived at the house and had been seated a few yards away opposite Nana Kwadwo Bɔfoɔ and his "family". I heard someone describing them as *Aduana-foɔ* from the *Etia Borono*. When all were seated the five visitors went round to greet the *Ofie-Panin* and his people with handshakes. Their greeting was returned after which, Nana Kwadwo Bɔfoɔ, speaking through the oldest of the "*mmaa-mma*" put the formal question: "*Ɛha deɛ, deɛ yegu ara ni, na ɔkwan so?*" ("There is nothing wrong with us here. May we know the reason for this visit?") The leader of the callers, Kofi N., addressed Nana Kwadwo Bɔfoɔ, also through his *mmaa-mma* and said something to this effect:

We have brought no bad news. We are messengers of our *Ofie-Panin* T. T. *Opanin* T.T. has sent us to you, *Opanin* Kwadwo Bɔfoɔ, with an important request which is that you agree to give your *ɔdehyeɛ* (blood relation), Akwasua A., to him, Opanin T.T., to be married to his *dehyeɛ*, Kwame D. Opanin T.T. is confident that you will not refuse his request and we, his messengers, would deem it an honour if you give your consent to the request so that we can return to give our Elder news that is pleasant. (*Yɛbenya amane pa abɔ.*)

Nana Kwadwo Bɔfoɔ looked at the direction of Akwasua and referred the matter to her, saying: "Akwasua, you have heard all that *Opanin* T.T.'s messengers have just said. Do you agree to be married to Kwame D.?" Akwasua's reply was short and straightforward: "*Nana, mepene so.*" ("Grandfather, I agree"), she said as she had been schooled to say by her mothers. Nana Kwadwo Bɔfoɔ then said to Akwasua: "*Akwasua, mo meda wo ase!*" ("Akwasua, well said, and thank you.") Then, turning to Opanin T.T.'s messengers, he said;

Kofi N., go back and tell *Opanin* T.T. that I and all members of my family agree to give our *ɔdehyeɛ*, Akwasua A., to him to be married to his nephew, Kwame D. Akwasua is, as from this day, the wife of Kwame D., but on two conditions: *nea edi kan ne sɛ sɛ Akwasua ho gu nso, gu nkra a, mibisa ɔno Opanin* T.T. (the first is that, should anything ill befall Akwasua I hold him, *Opanin* T.T. entirely responsible). *Nea etia mmienu ne sɛ: Kwame D abɛfa me dehyeɛ yi, sɛ ɔne no nam baabiara na Akwasua kotu asadeɛ biara a, ɛwɔ ɔno Akwasua ne n'abusuafoɔ. Sɛ nso, okɔfa ka biara a, Kwame D. dea. Mo pene so?* (The second condition is this: as Kwame D. has now taken away my blood relation to marry, if she happens to come to any treasure, wherever they may be, it all belongs exclusively to her and her family! On the other hand, if Akwasua, while still married to Kwame D., incurred any debt, whatever the cause might be, its defrayment is wholly the responsibility of the husband. Are the conditions acceptable to you?)

In reply, Opanin T.T.,'s senior messenger rose and said:

Ɔkyeame, let your "father," *Opanin* Kwadwo Bɔfoɔ, know that the two conditions that he has laid down are acceptable. They are not new. We are all Asante. We are not strangers and aliens (*amamfrafoɔ*). We are fully aware that the two conditions form a part of the custom (*amammerɛ*) we have grown to meet. They are applicable to all "houses." We cannot alter the custom by rejecting what our Elders have established for us (*nea mpanimfoɔ ahyɛ ato hɔ*). Therefore, on behalf of *Opanin* T.T., I affirm publicly that Kwame D. will follow our custom truly and abide by all conditions for so long as your *ɔdehyeɛ*, Akwasua A., remains his wife. May I ask *Opanin* Bɔfoɔ's permission at this stage to thank him and his family for readily consenting to our *Ofie-Panin's* request.

The messengers rose and went round to shake hands with Akwasua's *abusuafoɔ* for acceding to the request made to them. That done, the leader resumed his address and said: "*Nana Kyeame, ma Opanin Kwadwo Bɔfoɔ nte sɛ, Opanin T.T. se, ade fɛɛfɛ a ɔne n'abusuafoɔ ayɛ ama no no, ɔde nsafufuo asuhyina a esi hɔ yi da no ase.*" ("Nana's linguist, let Opanin Kwadwo Bɔfoɔ hear that in appreciation of his prompt and favourable response to his request, Opanin T.T. presents to him and his 'family' this big pot of palm-wine with his sincere thanks.") Finally, Kofi N. ended by saying: "*Ɔkyeame, ne kora kora ne sɛ, Opanin T.T. se, Obaa no tiri nsa ntakuo mmiensa ni.*" ("Nana's linguist, in conclusion, on behalf of Opanin T.T., I offer here and now, the customary marriage 'stamping drink' of 1s.6d.") The cash was handed to the senior *mmaa-mma*, who accepted it on behalf of his "father," *Opanin* Kwadwo Bɔfoɔ, the *Ofie-Panin*. All members of Akwasua's family present, led by the *mmaa-mma*, went round to shake hands with Opanin T.T.'s messengers to thank them.

I heard Nana Kwadwo Bɔfoɔ instructing the *mmaa-mma* to pour some of the wine from the big pot into the smaller pot (*akotokyiwa*) to fill it. That done, he asked the senior male *mmaa-mma* and the woman *mmaa-mma* to take the *akotokyiwa* to the *Ahemfie* to inform the Agogohene of the marriage just contracted between Kwame D. and Akwasua A. The content of the bigger pot was served in the neat calabash and passed round to all present in the yard. I saw that even those members who normally did not drink palm-wine, including my mother, did taste a wee bit of the drink to witness the contract and to wish the newly-married couple success.

At home in Salem that evening, the women members of our

family discussed and drew out a plan for the preparation of the Matrimonial Meal (*Aduan-Keseɛ*). It did not take them a long time to agree unanimously that:

- Nana Kwaane, herself, was to be responsible for the procurement of all meat that would be needed for the preparation of the meal, including fish, game, both smoked and fresh;
- Eno Nkameraa to be responsible for the procurement of all other food items, including plantains, cocoyams, yams, palmnuts, groundnuts, pepper, onions, tomatoes and okros.
- Akwasua was to go to Aduamoa in Kwawu, in company with three of her friends or sisters to purchase earthenware drinking, cooking, bathing pots and sets of dishes;
- Mother was to be responsible for all arrangements concerning supervision and preparation of the meal and, finally,
- the day for the preparation and presentation of the *Aduan-Kɛseɛ* was to be the Friday in the Christmas week.

In the evening of that day, I narrated to my father the events of the morning when I took his meal to him. He listened attentively and at the end of it commented tersely, "Kwame D. is a promising young man." As he sat in his favourite, improvised deckchair for a short rest after the meal, I went and stood at the end of the chair close to his head and asked him to tell me why some of the palm-wine which Opanin T.T. sent to thank our *Ofie-Panin* that morning was taken to the *Ahemfie*. In reply, Father said, "The drink was sent to inform the Agogohene of the marriage contracted between your sister and that young man, Kwame D."

Yaw: But why should the Agogohene know of the marriage. He is not Akwasua's father, is he?

Father: No, he is not the sister's father. You are quite right. But the Chief should know so that in case of misbehaviour while Akwasua was still married to the young man the offender could be punished.

Yaw: *Ɔyɛ bone sɛn?* (She misbehaved in which way?)

Father: If Akwasua went to sleep with another person.

Yaw: Will *Akonta* Kwame also be punished if he went to sleep with another person?

Father:	If Kwame, your brother-in-law, has sought the consent of the woman's people (*nkurofoɔ*) to marry her as was done by your people this morning, he would not be punished.
Yaw:	But how could Kwame D. know that my sister had gone to sleep with another person?
Father:	He will know, there is no doubt about that. *Woka ntam gu baye-mena mu a, efi'.* (An oath sworn into a hole of a yam mound germinated.)

The proverb confounded me. I confessed to Father that I did not understand what he was saying.

Father:	I know. *Seisei, worente aseɛ. Wunyin a, wobetɛ aseɛ.* (It should be beyond your comprehension now. You will get the meaning when you are grown.)

He ceased speaking to me in proverbs and came down to my level of understanding. In simple words he explained:

Father:	Kwame D. might himself catch Akwasua misbehaving. Or, someone might know of this misbehaviour and mention it to him. It could also happen that Kwame did not see it himself and that no one said anything to him, but Kwame's soul (*ne kraa*) will know. The misdeed would blemish his *soul (Ɛde efii aka ne kraa)* and Kwame would fall ill. If he could not get a cure in the normal way by a herbalist and continued to be very ill, what Kwame would do would be to consult a fetish (*Ɔbɛkɔ abisa*) where the secret would be revealed by an *Ɔbosom* (fetish). Kwame would confront his wife who might confess or deny.
Yaw:	What happened if his wife did not confess and said she was innocent?
Father:	Yaw, *wo ho yɛ ahodwan.* (Yaw, you are too inquisitive.) [He complained casually, but tolerated me. Calmly he answered.] Kwame D. will inform his *Ofie-Panin*, T.T., who will send his messengers to Opanin Kwadwo Bɔfoɔ to let

him know of the revelation made by the *Ɔbosom*
to Akwasua's husband. At the same time the
messengers would notify Akwasua's *Ofie-Panin*
of his intention to take his wife to the Fetish
Afram to swear (*di nse*) to declare her innocence,
and request formally that *Opanin* Kwadwo Bɔfoɔ
should arrange for his messenger to take
Akwasua to Afram-*fie* on a specified day,
generally on a Saturday which was the Fetish
Afram's day of worship. Early in the morning of
that day of fetish-swearing (*nsedie*), Kwame
would take with him two eggs and, in company
of his uncle's messengers, go to the fetish
house. His wife, also with the messengers of her
Ofie-Panin, would arrive at the house at the same
time.

The linguist of the Fetish Afram (*Afram
Kyeame*) would call upon the wife to swear by
Afram (*frɛ Afram di nse*) to declare her
innocence. The wife would be given one of the
eggs. Holding it in the right hand and facing the
entrance of the room in which the fetish is kept
(*abosonnan*) she would swear and say: "*Nana
Afram, sɛ efiri sɛ Kwame D. bewaree me yi, sɛ
mahu ɔbarima biara da ka ne ho, na mese
merenda nkyerɛ no a, ku me.*" ("Nana Afram, if
any man has 'seen' me other than Kwame D.
since he took me for a wife, and I would not
divulge it to him, you may kill me.")

On the pronouncement "kill me" (*ku me*), she
throws the egg to hit the wall of the fetish room.
The linguist of the fetish would then call upon
the husband to endorse the curse. He would do
so by holding the second egg in his right hand
and swear, saying: "*Nana Afram, sɛ efiri sɛ
Akwasua bɛwaree me yi, sɛ wahu ɔbarima biara
ka me ho na ɔmpɛ se oka kyere me a, ku no!*"
("Nana Afram, if Akwasua has been 'seen' by
another man since she became my wife and
should would hide this from me, kill her.") He
would also throw the other egg to hit the wall at
the side of the door to the fetish room. All
parties would disperse and leave the fetish
house. The matter would be left entirely with the
fetish to deal with it. Kwame and Akwasua would
continue to live their normal life as husband and
wife, no one bearing the other any grudge.

If Akwasua were truly innocent, nothing ill would happen to her and there the matter would end. If, on the other hand, she had something to hide, she would either become critically ill or some misfortune would befall her suddenly. If such a thing happened she would be taken back to the fetish where, in almost all cases, the wife would confess her infidelity in order to save her life.

Yaw:

But they forbid swearing in Salem. Would our Mother permit Akwasua, my sister, to go to any fetish to swear?

Father:

Akwasua is a very well-behaved girl, I have no doubt about that. Her character is beyond reproach. I am confident that she would never permit any unfortunate situation to arise. But in the very unlikely chance of her being unable to resist a temptation, it would be up to her husband to decide what action to take. You wanted to know, Yaw, why some of the *tiri nsa* (palm-wine brought to stamp your sister's marriage to Kwame D.) was sent to the *Ahemfie*. If you would cease digressing I would be able to explain that to you immediately.

Feeling repentant, I entreated, "Yes, Papa, do explain it to me."

Father:

Akwasua, I must repeat again and again, is a self-respecting young woman of sound common sense. I am not suggesting that she would ever lose her head and do something silly. I am sure she will not do anything that would bring shame to herself and a disgrace to her family. No, not her! What I am saying is supposition: *mede me susa babadua a, ɛpɔ nni mu!* (if the impossible became possible). If she misbehaved herself and she confessed to her husband, she would mention the name of the bad man who tempted her to sleep with him. *Opanin* T.T. would then send his messengers to inform the Agogohene of the affair of the wife of his nephew with the other man. The Agogohene would dispatch an *ahenkwaa* (Stool messenger) to the bad man to enact the appropriate penalty (*ɔkɔgu no ayefarɛ*).

The bad man would pay to the Stool messenger a charging fee (*nte-hoo*) which he would take as his Service Charge, and then the *ayefarɛ* which was the penalty paid for having sexual intercourse with someone's lawfully married wife. The *ayefarɛ* penalty varies according to the status of the offended husband. It ranges from *Osua ne doma* (£2.7s.) for an ordinary man like Kwame D to *mpredwan-mmiɛnsa* (thrice £8—) for the Chief. The *Ahenkwaa* would claim from the bad man an amount of £2.7s. and hand it to *Opanin* T.T. to be given to Kwame D.

Yaw:

But if the bad man was a stranger and ran away from Agogo? [I couldn't resist interrupting Father.]

Father:

In that case *Opaanin* Kwadwo Bɔfoɔ, the *Ofie-Panin* of Akwasua, would be held responsible for the payment in full of the *Ahenkwaa*'s *nte-ho* and the *ayefarɛ*.

Yaw:

Would *Akonta* Kwame D. send my sister away after he had received the *ayefare*?

Father:

That would be a matter entirely for the husband to decide. He might decide to keep your sister as his wife, or he might decide to divorce her (*ɔgyae no awareɛ*) and send her back to Opanin Kwadwo Bɔfoɔ on the grounds of infidelity. Divorce is purely a matter which must be left entirely to the husband or the wife to initiate, except in very glaring cases where the continuation of a marriage would, it was genuinely felt, seriously affect the health or reputation of the husband or the wife. And now you understand why some of the palm-wine was sent to the *Ahemfie*. The Agogohene is the sole authority in the town to order the execution of an *Ayefare* penalty. If the drink was not sent to the *Ahemfie*, it would mean that the *Ɔhene* was not aware of the marriage contracted between Kwame D. and your sister Akwasua A. and he would, in that case, not dispatch any *ahenkwaa* to demand the payment of the *Ayefarɛ* compensation from the bad man.

Plans carefully drawn by the mothers for the preparation of Akwasua's traditional Matrimonial Meal (*Aduan-Kɛseɛ*) were carried out promptly. Three days after the decision on the suitable day for the presentation of the meal had been taken, Akwasua, accompanied by two young unmarried women of her age, travelled on foot to Kwawu-Aduamoa to purchase needed earthenware pots and dishes to begin her marriage life. They were given an amount estimated to be sufficient to pay for the following items with a little extra for contingencies:

> Two large size water drinking pots (*ahina*) with lids.
> One bathing pot (dware-sɛn) with lid.
> Two sets of food dishes complete with lids, each comprising:
> > one large size food dish to take 4 *fufu* balls (*ntoa nan ayowa*).
> > one medium size food dish to take 3 *fufu* falls (*ntoa mmiensa ayowa*).
> > one small size food dish to take 2 *fufu* balls (*ntoa mmienu ayowa*).
> Two sets stew dishes (*abomu-yowa*) complete with lids.
> One set cooking stoves (*mmukyia*).
> Two vegetable grinding dishes (*apotɔ-yowa*).

The account of the journey to Aduamoa and back given by Akwasua herself was, as far as I can recollect, as follows.

Aduamoa had its weekly market on Wednesdays. Leaving Agogo early one Monday morning the three gay and lively "sisters" reached Onyemso village shortly after midday and stopped at the Agogo side on the bank of River Onyem for a meal and a short rest. The river was fordable, being in dry season, and, without any difficulty, the travellers crossed into Kwawu land. At Abetim, a few miles from the Onyem river, the Kwawu-Agogo boundary, they stopped for the first night. At dawn the following morning they left in order to cross *Ɛserɛ-kɛseɛ*, a wide open grassland country through which the footpath passed, before it became hot in the day. Following a short-cut which by-passed the Hwee-hwee village, the three sisters arrived at Abene, the seat of the *Ɔmanhene* of Kwawu Traditional area, earlier than was expected. At the outskirts of that Kwawu capital town was a gloomy cemetery on the right as one entered from Abetim. On most of the graves were earthenware busts of persons, men and women, who must have been especially prominent one way or another during their lifetime and in whose memory the busts had been erected when they passed into the Land of the Dead.

The three young travellers merely turned their eyes to catch a glimpse of what appeared to be, to them, beautiful dolls, a few of which they would have wished to own. But fear pushed them on fast — fear of the ghosts of the dead men and women that might be hovering about in the hideous Abene burial ground, and fear of their parents' anger if it was heard in Agogo that their daughters, faithful Agogo Christians, became interested at Abene in something connected with idol worship (*abosomsom*). They had to move on hurriedly passed the graveyard. Soon they were in the Kwawu *Ahenkuro*, the seat of the *Ɔmanhene*, and continued to the Subiri River, lying quite close to the town at the other end of it. On its bank they stopped and had a snack of mashed plantain mixed with palm-oil which was prepared the previous evening and preserved in packed *anwonomoo* leaves left on the hearth overnight. It was a long and leisurely rest. Much of their time there was spent sitting on some dry rocks jutting out of the river, with their legs suspended in its current to cool. In frolic they leapt from one rock to the other, across, up and down the stream. After a while they left the Subiri and the Abene women doing their washing in the fast bubbling river. A gradual climb led them to a point where the footpath forked: one going straight ahead to Albetifi and the other, turning slightly right, led to Aduamoa. Parting with two women travelling companions at the junction, the Agogo girls did their last lap alone and reached their destination about the time farmers were returning home from their farms in the afternoon.

The three strangers were led to the house of Mena Ama M. who had just then returned home from the farm and was sorting out her head-load of cocoyams, *nkontomire*, pepper and a few sticks of firewood. On hearing who her guests were she hurried to embrace Akwasua tightly, hugged her warmly and, as she did so, said affectionately: "*Awaaa ... Awaaa ... Awaaa, Atuu - u - u - u, Akumaa.*" ("I embrace you cordially. You are warmly welcome, my sister-in-law.") Mena Ama M. confirmed to Akwasua that she was the elder sister of Kwaku O., an Aduamoa man who had been living in Agogo for quite a time and who was the husband of two women there, the younger one of whom was Akwasua's husband's sister. At Agogo, Kwaku O. of Aduamoa, was popularly called *"Ntwa-kayɛ"* (Left-over pieces). He had earned that name as a cloth peddler who, like the *mpepefoɔ* from the North, took cut-pieces of cloth to sell

during the few weeks preceding Christmas. But unlike the
mpepefoɔ, whose cry was *"Pe! Pe!,"* the man Kwaku O. from
Aduamoa, cried: *"Ntwa-ka yɛ ni O – O! Ntwa-ka-yɛ papa aba.
Ntwa-ka-yɛ, Ntwa-ka-yɛ, Ntwa-ka-yɛ!"* ("Cut-cloth pieces for
sale. Quality cut-cloth pieces available here. Cut-cloth pieces,
cut-cloth pieces, cut-cloth pieces!") In course of time, the
proper name of the Kwawu peddler, Kwaku O., was completely
discarded and replaced with *"Ntwa-ka-yɛ."* It was in the
Aduamoa house of the sister of Agogo *Ntwa-ka-yɛ* that Akwasua
and her sisters lodged.

Mena Ama M. took Akwasua round to meet some of the close
relatives of Kwaku O. who were all delighted to know her and
her sisters from Agogo. Wherever Akwasua went in Aduamoa,
the women of the town addressed her, *"Akumaa"* ("Sister-in-
law"). That was Tuesday. Wednesday, the following day, was
Aduamoa's weekly market day. All roads in Kwahu led to the
town that special day. In the market was a concourse of people
from almost all the towns and villages in Kwawu. They had
travelled from Abetifi, Nkwatia, Bepɔn, Mpraeso, Atibue,
Ɔbɔmen, Asakraka, Bukuruwa, Kwahu-Tafo, Akwasiho,
Hweehwee, and from far away places in the Afram Plains such
as Adɔwso, Mankron and Worobɔn. From some non-Kwawu
towns in Asante and Akyem also had come a few traders.
Included in the crowd were some people who were there, not
for the purpose of buying or selling, but merely to while away
the time and to "feast their eyes" (*"bɔ wɔn ani akɔnhama"*).

Sellers were early in their arrival at the market-place that
Wednesday morning. They arranged their wares attractively in
sections, commodity by commodity, with lanes in-between for
free movement for hagglers, serious buyers, as well as loafers.
There were sections for yams, cocoyams, plantains, vegetables,
smoked fish and game meat (*mpunam*), smoked herrings from
the coast, earthenware pots and dishes; various farming
implements, such as cutting and digging hoes, earth-chisels
(*sɔsɔ*), cocoa plucking chisels (*nsɔsɔwa*) and locally made axes
(*mmo-nnua*). Imported goods included buckets, chamber pots,
cutlasses, cheap cut-pieces of cloths, headkerchiefs, pomade,
talcum powder, felling axes, felt hats and caps, singlets and
bath towels.

In the shade of a big tree close to the market place was a
section of open-air restaurants where prepared meals could be
bought and eaten. Ready for sale or in course of preparation
there were *apra-pra-wonsa*, *ɔfam*, boiled yams, cocoyams,

plantains with various stews such as *nkontommire*, beans and garden-eggs. Available too from very early that morning were *fufu* meals with the popular palm-soup, groundnut soup or plain soup. Aduamoa market was full that Wednesday morning in every sense of the word.

Mena Ama M. took Akwasua and her sisters straight through to the pottery section of the market and helped her make a selection out of a wide range of pots and dishes of various sizes put on display. Herself an expert potter, Mena Ama M. could tell off-hand a good quality pot or dish from an inferior, cheap and shoddy one. Knowing exactly what to look for in quality earthenware pots, she put every single article which Akwasua wished to buy to a critical test by knocking at the bottom part of it with the knuckle of the middle finger of her right had, held it close to the ear to hear the sound it made. She then passed her hand round the rim to detect minute cracks that might be there. Satisfied with its soundness, she bargained hard for it. By her so doing Akwasua could collect first rate pieces at costs far below what an unwary buyer would have paid.

Mena Ama M. was, however, not satisfied with the quality on display of one of the items that Akwasua needed urgently. It was a bathing pot (*dware-sɛn*) which she had to have at all costs. The expert hostess did not think much of any of the stock on market that morning and said so to Akwasua who became somewhat upset. Sensing her feeling, Mena Ama M. put her at ease by giving her the assurance that she would take her to a specialist *dware-sɛn* maker — the best in all Kwawu land — for one pot which she, Akwasua, would be proud to own. She was led to a two-roomed house at the far end of Aduamoa town. The owner was a busy-looking, past-middle age, but strong woman who looked much younger than her age. She specialized in *dware-sɛn* pot making. Her pots were, however, never sent to the open market for sale. They were all made to order and she had a long waiting list, including wives of Elders and fiancées of prominent men of all walks of life. On Mena Ama M.'s prompting, the specialist agreed to release for sale to Akwasua at cost a deluxe bathing pot just completed for delivery to a beloved junior wife of a wealthy man who wished to express her gratefulness and reciprocate her husband's many kindnesses and affection. Akwasua had obtained a V.I.P. *dware-sɛn* for her Kwame!

Through the sharp bargaining ability of Mena Ama M., Akwasua had, by the close of that Wednesday market, succeeded in buying more pots and dishes of good quality than had been estimated for by her parents. And more besides. Mena Ama M.'s sisters to whom Akwasua was introduced as her *akumaa* (sister-in-law) who had gone to Aduamoa to buy her matrimonial earthenware pots and dishes, presented her with generous gifts of quality Kwawu-made pots and dishes to take back home.

Observing that Akwasua had more than could be conveniently head-loaded by the three sisters, Mena Ama M.'s two unmarried daughters of the Agogo buyers' age, volunteered to help them carry the whole lot to Asante to save a second journey to Aduamoa and back. That welcome gesture firmly cemented the bond of friendship that had started and which continued for many years later.

The return journey to Agogo should have started the following day, but Mena Ama M. persuaded Akwasua and her sisters to stay a day longer to enable her to smoke-polish expertly the pots and dishes purchased or presented to her as gifts. It was a splendid job that was done that Thursday by the specialist Kwawu potter. All who saw the completed lustre-black pots and dishes acclaimed them of being the best that ever went outside Aduamoa, and, for that matter, outside Kwawu land.

Early on Friday morning, Mena Ama M. saw the young women off at the outskirts of Aduamoa town, and wished them safe journey and to Akwasua, in particular, good luck. Scarcely had the good Mena Ama M. turned her back to the five happy-go-lucky young travellers than they started singing love-songs in praise and admiration of the beauty of their lovers whose real names were suppressed but referred to as *"ɔdo-yɛ-wu"* ("love-is-death") — their be-all and end-all they were either leaving behind at Aduamoa that night or were expecting to meet at Agogo the night that was to come. Similes were gratuitously used and every part of a lover's body, from head to toe, received its appropriate, explicit comparison to some valued or admired thing of beauty or worthy attribute:

- the hair on the head which was as black as the soot under a new cooking pot (*Ne tiri nhwi tumm te sɛ Owisia-pun*);
- the forehead which was as broad and flat as that of fish (*Ne titi tadwaa to sɛ opitire*);
- the eyes which were as red and sparkling as those of ɔpanben (bird) (*N'ani son-son te sɛ ɔpaben*);

- the neck which was as straight and slender as a forest land reed (*Ne kɔn srɔ-srɔm te sɛ ɔdoroben*);
- the nose which was as slender and sleek as that of the carved fertility doll (*Ne hwene tea-tea te sɛ aba-dua*);
- the teeth which were neat, firm and neatly-spaced like those of a crocodile (*Ne se nhweawa-nkweawa te sɛ ɔdɛnkyɛm*);
- the hair on the chest which was bunched as the mane of a lion (*Ne kokom nhwi te sɛ gyata*);
- the buttocks which were as firm as Buruku Hill (*Ne to pirim-m-m te sɛ Buruku*);
- the thighs which were wholly and comforting as a well-filled velvet pillow (*Ne srɛ dofoo, pintin-n-n sɛ ago sumiyɛ*);
- the shanks which were as stout and proportionately shaped as an *atumpan* drum (*Nanantu kutu-kutu-u-u te sɛ atumpan*);
- the fingers which were as straight as the fruit of *aheneba-Nsateaa* pepper (*Ne nsateaa nteawa-nteawa te sɛ aheneba-nsaduaa*);
- the body-build which was proportionate, fresh-looking and chic as an *asɔbayerɛ* (yam) in bloom (*Ne honam bromm-m te sɛ asɔbayerɛ dɔtɔɔ*).

Some of the similes which the uninhibited young women used to compare other parts of their lover's bodies as they romped on excitedly along the lonesome Agogo/Kwawu footpath might have been unbearably tantalizing to some hunters who were within hearing distance, lying in wait for game to kill. But those unprintable similes immensely helped keep the spirits of the infatuated young lovers high, making the long journey less of a drudge and more of a pleasure. With hearts made so gay by thoughts of their lovers, loads made light by sharing, and feet, nimble by rapturous love-songs, the descent to Abene was completed in a matter of a few minutes and the low-lying patches of grassland and the bordering deciduous forest that stretched to the outskirts of Abetim village were covered with a surprisingly fast speed. It was possible for the travellers to continue to Onyemso, the first Agogo village from Kwawu, where they stopped for the last night of the journey.

By noon the following Saturday the five young women with their bulky loads of pots and dishes were back in Agogo hale, lively and full of news. They received hearty handshakes and were congratulated for a successful journey. As their head-loads were unpacked and their contents displayed in the open-front *pato* room, all items purchased, the *dwaresɛn* (bathing pot) in particular, were highly praised by those who examined them carefully, as well as those who chanced to glance at them briefly. The gift items were similarly admired and gratefully received. The two kind-hearted Aduamoa girls who rendered yeoman service to the three Agogo Asona pot buyers were treated with all the hospitality that they deserved. They were taken to Town to greet their uncle, Kwadwo O. of Aduamoa, alias "Ntwa-kayɛ" of Agogo. More exciting was the opportunity they had to meet Akwasua's husband of whom much had been heard and who, they both agreed, was a handsome young man, indeed. The Sunday was spent meeting friends of their friends, both boys and girls. On Monday that followed, they parted company, all hearts heavy and eyes in tears, but with the consolation that they would be eating again soon when they returned to Agogo to help in the preparation of Akwasua's *aduankɛseɛ* planned for presentation on Friday of the Christmas week that was soon to come.

Our house, the first on the left as one entered Salem from Town, was a hive of busy women and girls from dawn to about midday of that memorable Friday in that Christmas week. Under the general direction and supervision of Mother, work on the preparations of Akwasua's Matrimonial Meal (*Aduan-Keseɛ*) was organised well and carried out smoothly. Grandmother, sitting by a short table in the *pato*, distributed choicest meat including smoked fish, game meat, broiled snails and smoked mushrooms. Her younger sister, Nana Yaa Kuma, kept her company all the time. Eno Nkameraa stationed herself in the kitchen store and distributed expeditiously other food items, as were required. One of her sisters from Town remained to assist her in the assignment.

At one end of the yard were set six separate traditional cooking stoves in sets of three earthenware pots (*mmukyia*), each of which was in the charge of an elderly woman with two young women to assist her. All Akwasua's young brothers and sisters were there in the yard in force. They did odd jobs such as fetching water needed from the Aboabo stream for washing utensils or for cooking and to run on errands. Each of the six *mmukyia* groups concentrated on the preparation of a specific dish as follows:

Bukyia Group 1: cooked groundnut soup (*kate-nkwan*) with mixed smoked fish, game meat and broiled snails.

Bukyia Group 2: cooked palm-soup (*abe-nkwan*) with mixed smoked fish, game meat, smoked mushroom and broiled snails.

Bukyia Group 3: cooked plain/pepper Soup (*nkrawa*) with mutton, some smoked fish and game meat.

Bukyia Group 4: boiled and pounded cocoyams into twenty *fufu* balls (*ntoa aduenu*).

Bukyia Group 5: boiled and pounded into twenty *fufu* balls (*ntoa aduenu*) plantains mixed with some cassava.

Bukyia Group 6: boiled and pounded yams into twenty *fufu* Balls (*ntoa aduenu*).

The two young Aduamoa women, daughters of Mena Ama M. who helped Akwasua carry some of her pots and dishes to Agogo, honoured their promise. In the afternoon of the Thursday preceding the Great Day, they arrived in Agogo, accompanied by a third Kwahu young unmarried woman who was introduced as one of the nieces of Kwaku O., alia "Ntwakayɛ". They brought with them a package containing three pieces of *Aduan-Kɛseɛ* dishes of exquisite design and finish, complete with lids. They were presented to Akwasua as a joint gift from her *nkumaa* (sisters-in-law) in Aduamoa The three visitors readily attached themselves to the cooking groups and, in no time, proved to be good mixers and jolly young fellows.

Each of the three *fufu* pounding groups had three exuberant, cheerful pounders. The pestles they used were fresh, straight *esa* saplings which Father had cut from the forest adjacent to his Apampramasu farm and carried home himself in three instalments of three sticks in a bundle. It was, as he told me, his contribution to the preparation of the *Aduan-kɛseɛ*. The simultaneous heavy pounding of boiled plantains, cocoyams and yams into *fufu* balls, shook the ground of the yard. All that could be heard in and around the house was the rousing, thumping sound, "*Ti-tim ... Ti-tim! Ti-tim ... Ti-tim!*" made by the pestles operated by nine maidens from whose backs and bared, heaving virgin breasts trickled bits of sweet and gentle sweat. The co-mingled pleasant smell of groundnut soup, palm-soup and plain fatty mutton soup induced irresistibly the flow of saliva from under the tongues of many a passer-by.

By about midday all was ready. The old women were all satisfied that the dishes had been well prepared *à la Asante* and the high standard of what they knew their mothers maintained had been attained. The dishes were ready and so were the accompanying articles which, by then, had been assembled together in the *pato* room. The smart, neatly dressed girls carefully selected to carry the articles were ready with smiles on sweet dimple cheeks. The two leaders were ready. They were both uniformly attired. Their down-piece cloth was green wax print. The top-piece was a white *kente* cloth worn by passing the piece under the right armpit and flung onto the left shoulder in the proper Asante fashion. The forehead (*momaso*), polished smooth and liberally besmeared with specially treated shea butter, was sleek and shone brilliantly. On the neck was a set of three long, jade-green necklaces. To match, on the right wrist, was a set of costly *nhuuwa* beads. The application of some locally prepared cosmetic gave the skin its natural, beautiful complexion whose tender, youthful look could put to irrepressible shame the so-called modern women with nauseatingly bleached skin in modern Agogo and elsewhere in Asante.

The procession was ready to move. At the head was Nana Adwoa B., a vivacious, witty, eloquent, plump elderly woman. When all loads of dishes and accompanying articles were on heads, she stood at the entrance to the yard, and, holding a white handkerchief in a raised right hand, exhorted:

Yaa-nom, Mo mmɛsen ma yɛnkoɔ.
Yɛbɛkyerɛ Aduanafoɔ nnɛ, sɛ:
Asonafoɔ wɔ hɔ.
Yɛbɛkyerɛ won sɛ
Yefiri Tete.
Yefiri Tete, Tete, Tete ... Te ... T-e-e-e-e ... T E!

(Come along, Folk,
Let's be on the move.
The Aduana people will be made to know today
The stuff the Asona people are made of.
They will be taught today,
We are a people of Old.
We have existed for a very, very, very long time!)

With a sprightly jump she turned about, adjusted her up-piece cloth and moved briskly out of the house into the street. Following her, in order, were young girls and maidens carrying:

1. Akwasua's prized *dwaresɛn* (bathing pot) full of warm water;
2. A flat plate containing three local sponges (*sapɔ*) and a packet of native black soap (*samina tuntum*);
3. A flat plate containing pomade, talc powder and a bottle of lavender water;
4. A very large dish (*ayowa*) of twenty plantain/cassava mixed fufu balls carried by one of the Aduamoa maidens;
5. A second very large dish containing twenty cocoyams fufu balls

carried by the second Aduamoa maiden;

6. A third very large dish containing twenty yam fufu balls carried by the third Aduamoa maiden;
7. A large soup pot containing groundnut soup;
8. A second large soup pot containing additional groundnut soup;
9. A third large soup pot containing palm-soup;
10. A fourth large soup pot containing additional palm-soup;
11. A fifth large soup pot containing plain soup;
12. A sixth large soup pot containing additional plain soup;
13. A large pot of fresh palm-wine;
14. A flat plate containing finely split *tweapea* chewing sticks.

At the rear was a gentle, sober, elderly woman, who was followed by three other women.

The procession made its way from Salem through Apetenyinase, the *bɔrɔnoo* of Akwasua's people, *Asonafoɔ*. It reached Pampaso, the center of the *bɔrɔnoo* amid a crowd of cheering kinsfolk. Instead of moving on straight ahead for only two hundred yards to reach Kwame D.'s house in the Atowaase *Bɔrɔnoo*, the leader caused a detour. It turned to the left and followed a street that led to Bontoriase *Bɔrɔnoo*. Half-way, it turned again to the right and reached the Agogo High Street (*Abɔnten Kɛseɛm*) at a point opposite the Fetish Afram house (*Afram Fie*). By then the news of the procession had spread throughout the town. Hailed by a crowd of admiring onlookers, the leader, followed by a train of carriers of polished pots and dishes, strutted confidently the length of the street to the entrance of Kwame D.'s "family" house at the top end of it near the spot where a few days earlier the various Agogo *Ositi* dance groups entertained Paa Koo F., the wealthy quest of the Agogohene.

Previously notified of the presentation of the *Aduan-Kɛseɛ* that day, *Obaa-Panin* Yaa A., Kwame D.'s mother, with her sisters and daughters had assembled in the house waiting. To a loud door-knocking cry, "A - G - 0 - 0 - 0!" ("Shall we come in, please?"), came an instantaneous response, "A - G - O - 0, B-A." ("Yes, please, Do."). At long last the procession entered Kwame D.'s house, carriers were off-loaded and all were seated. After observing briefly the normal formalities, Nana Adoa B., the leader, in a short but gesticulatory address said,

Ɔbaa Panin, Yaa A., Woase Akwasua A. se, yɛmfa kakra yi mmerɛ ne kunu, Kwame D., nsɔ ne bo. Ne nsuo, ne sapɔ, ne samina ne bɔɔdoba a, ɔmfa nnuare ni. Ne 'pawoda, ne sradeɛ ne n'ahuanhuanneɛ nso ni. N'aduane kakra a, ɛyɛ Nkate-kwan, Abɛ-kwan, Nkrawa nso ni. Ne Nsa,

Ɔfrantaa a, ɔmfa mpia n'aduane a obedi no nso, ni; Ne tweapea duaa a, odidi wie a, onwe nso, ni. Yebae a, na yeammaneɛ tiawa a yɛde nam abedu ha anɔpa-wia yi ne no.

(Nana Yaa A., Head woman of the house, your daughter-in-law, Akwasua A., has asked us to bring to her husband Kwame D. a humble meal to still his hunger. She presents this pot of water, together with a sponge, soap and towel for his bath before meal. She presents this talc powder, lavender water and pomade for his toilet; this dish of groundnut soup; this dish of palm-soup; this dish of plain/pepper soup; the big pot of palm-wine over there to wash down the meal, and the *tweapea* chewing sticks for use after meal. That, in short, is what has brought us here this forenoon.)

The eloquent, short address was greeted with a spontaneous applause. Nana Yaa A. and all her sisters and daughters assembled in the yard rose up and expressively chanted the commendatory praise:

Akwasua A. ayɛ, na mompene no! (Soloist)
Heh - e - e - e - eh! (Chorus)
Wayɛ ade, na mompene no, (Soloist)
Heh - e - e - e - eh! (Chorus)
Asonafoɔ ayɛ ade, na mompene wɔn. (Soloist)
Heh - e - e - e - eh! (Chorus)

(Akwasua A. has excelled. Let her be commended,
Yes, we concur.
She has excelled, and deserves commendation.
Yes, we concur.
The Asonafo have excelled and should be commended,
Yes, we concur.)

Members of our family who remained behind in the house in Salem continued to work, cleaning cooking pots, pans, dishes, utensils, mortars and pestles. The yard was swept clean and things were put in order. By design, Nana Kwaane and Mother saw to it that substantial left-overs were kept for both the young and the old, and for all who assisted in the preparation of the *Aduan-Kɛseɛ*. The elderly women received a generous share of reserved fish and meat for a take-away-home. The young women had packets of meat and some uncooked yams, plantains and cocoyams. Those who needed them collected left-over tomatoes, pepper, onions or okro. Much of the pounded *fufu* was left for all to enjoy. We, the children, ate to our fill and felt that we had been amply rewarded for the

countless number of times we had run to the stream to fetch
water for cooking, washing and other purposes.

I was too busy at home to follow the procession to town and
to *Akonta* Kwame D.'s house. I recollect, however, the following
account which a playmate who lived in the *boronoɔ* and
witnessed all that took place in the house, gave me a day after
the presentation of the "Big" meal. According to him:

The food and all that was presented were distributed in such a way
that everyone who mattered in Kwame D.'s family received a share,
more as a token than for satiation. Distribution, by two elderly women
of the family, was made in order of seniority in the house as follows:

1. To the *Ofie-Panin* (Head of the House), *Opanin* T.: three balls of
    plantain *fufu* with groundnut soup and a pot of palm-wine
    (*akotokyiwa ma*);
2. To the elderly men and women of the family: two balls of *fufu*
    each with soup to taste;
3. To other men and women of the family: one ball of *fufu* with soup
    to taste;
4. To Kwame D.'s male friends who were not members of the family:
    one ball of *fufu* with soup to taste;
5. To any member of the public who took a receptacle to the house: a
    share of a lump of *fufu* ball with soup to taste
6. To children who followed the procession into the house: lumps of
    fufu balls served in a big enamel basin which they scrambled for
    wildly in the yard.

Nana Yaa A. reserved a respectable share of all the dishes for Kwame
D. who was all the time absent from the house, and his intimate
friends.

The dishes returned to our Salem house in the evening with
an amount of *osuaa ne doma* (£2.7s.) placed in one of the
dishes. It was said to be *ayowamto-deε* (a gift placed in a dish
meant for the carriers of the food and other items presented).
Curious enough to me, Akwasua was nowhere to be seen all
that day. The question that I kept asking myself was: "*Na
Akwasua wɔ ɔhe koraa?*" ("Where at all is Akwasua?") I learned
later that the elders intentionally did not want us to know her
whereabouts. She was, in fact, taken into a house in Town and
kept in a room alone with two elderly women experienced in
marriage matters. There, it was said, Akwasua was given her
final grooming in wifely duties, including good bed manners.
She was polished meticulously, toiletted and dressed for the
task ahead of her that night and the nights that were to follow.

When she was brought back to Salem near dusk, our Akwasua was a completely changed woman — in mind, in bearing and in look. Dressed in a new *daano* (wax print) up-piece, down-piece with a smartly cut cover-shoulder dress (*osoro ne fam ne kaba*); a gold necklace with a neat, simple locket adorning the sleek neck; *abonko* earrings in the ears and, freshened with a locally prepared *krobɔ* perfume whose mild, alluring scent, cosmetic manufacturers in Paris would find difficult to beat, our sister Akwasua was, that evening, simply charming. So charming was she that were a slight adaptation made in the first line of "The Lass with a Delicate Air," the first verse of the popular lyric could have been aptly applicable to her, and sung:

Akwasua who live in Agogo Salem,
Whose fame every maiden with envy doth fill.
Of beauty she's blessed with so amply a share,
Men call her the lass with a delicate air.

She did not have to wait a long time. Soon Kwame's messengers arrived to take her away. I saw they were the same two sisters who were sent to make a preliminary approach on the marriage. They bought to Eno Nkameraa the traditional gift to be presented to a mother of a newly married wife on the removal of the daughter from her bedside to that of the husband's (*afa-yi-deɛ*). Akwasua left the house with the sisters-in-law, one leading her with a new, brightly shining hurricane lamp and the other following the shy young wife.

What happened in Kwame's house that evening or what actually did take place in his bedroom that night, was scarcely a matter of any interest to me. My mind was filled with the bright prospect of substantial left-overs (*nka-nii*) expected out of the early morning *fufu* meal to be prepared for our brother-in-law (*nkun-nuane*) when Akwasua returned home from her husband's bedside (*nkun-kyire*).

11

MY FIRST BRUSH WITH DEATH

Our parents were almost all cocoa farmers whose routine of work was more or less set. Whether, for the sake of convenience and time-saving, they stayed in their farm cottages for a spell of time, or they went from town in the morning to work on the farm and returned in the evening, the routine remained the same. Hard concentrated work was done on three days each week on cash crop farms that were situated in the forest areas some distance away from town. Known broadly as *Afuom-da* (Farming Day), the heavy farming days were Mondays, Wednesdays and Saturdays, except when, for the non-Christians, any of those three days fell on the forty-day *Da-bɔneɛ* [1] (Bad Day) sacred day cycle.

Tuesdays, Thursdays and Fridays were generally days of "light" work which, for want of a better term I would refer to as "*Afoofi-di-da.*" "Light" is used in the sense that the vast majority of the people engaged themselves on odd jobs other than heavy farmwork, in and near the town or in farm cottages. It was, for instance, the practice of the womenfolk to work on their foodcrop farms (*mfikyi-fuo*) which were not far away from town. On those days, too, women did environmental cleaning individually, by clearing weeds around compound houses (*mfikyi-dodɔ*) or communally, by cleaning the surroundings of water supply places (*nsuom-tee*) and places of convenience. Young women and girls might go to collect floor-dubbing red-ochre clay (*ntwama*). In the harmattan season, some women and girls went group fishing (*ahweɛ*) on an *Afoofi-di* day.

Men similarly engaged themselves in "light" work on those *Afoo-fi-da* days. They might work communally on brushing weeds round the town (*nsɔsɔɔ-bɔ*), or work in their quarters (*aborɔnoo*) digging pit-latrines (*tiafi-bɔ*) for both men and

---

[1] See Appendix 1.

women. Damaged houses, including leaking roofs, broken fences and walls, were repaired or some work on the construction of new houses done. Cocoa bean drying-mats (*asrɛnɛ*), sleeping-mats (*kɛtɛ*) with different materials, such as "Goa" (made of *anwonomoo* stalks), *nton-kɛtɛ* (made of Pandamus tree) and *sibre-kɛtɛ* (made from the hard bark of *sibre* plant) as well as fishing traps (*adwokuo*) were woven on *Afoofi-di* days. Some men, on those light farmwork days, accompanied their wives to foodcrop farms to give a helping hand. During cocoa harvesting season the splitting of cocoa pods for fermentation of the beans was an operation which was generally carried out on an *Afoofi-di* day.

Sunday was, of course, a day of rest and divine worship for the Christians. For most of the non-Christians it was generally another day of "light" work in the week. For those of us children in Salem who had not grown old enough to be kept in school, the three "light" work days of the week afforded us an opportunity for hearty play of games. We played in daytime and we played at night, particularly on moonlit nights. Our games followed a general pattern. When a sufficient number of playmates had arrived at an open space opposite the church building on the right as one entered Salem from town, the leader called out: "*Me mma - E!* (My children!) *Me mma - E!* (My children!)" The players responded: "*Ye - e - e,* (Yes, Mother dear.) *Eno-waa!*" He ran about zigzagly, repeating the call, "*Me mma - E!*, *Me mma - E!*" We responded, "*Yaa - e - e, Eno-waa*" and followed him wherever he went till he stopped mid-field. We surrounded him with both arms stretched forward to touch him. On his order, "*Yaa - a - a - a!*," we moved backwards and stood in a circle formed round him. He then got us into a formation for a particular game he might decide. The popular ones of our games were:

Ahunta-hunta (Hide and Seek)

At a signal, Group A members disappeared and hid themselves at odd places. Group B members followed after a short interval to locate a hider who was to be chased and touched before he had reached a fixed point and had shouted, "*Wo - sie - e - e!*" (I am untouchable!). A hider touched before reaching the fixed point was eliminated. Group B, in turn, became hiders and Group A, the seekers. The game continued, the role of hiders and seekers alternating until the two groups had the same number of chances of hiding and seeking. The winner was the group with fewer eliminated players.

Ane-naam (Passing the Ball Through)

Members squatted in a circle formation with cloths worn in such a way that they covered all the body, leaving a passage clear between the thighs and the legs of the players sitting to the right and left. Through the passage a piece of cloth folded into a handy ball was passed. One player stood in the centre of the circle and tried to intercept and seize the ball as it was being pushed fast from left to right of one player to the other, as all sang: "A - ne -n - a - a - a - m (It is running through). *Yaa - a - a -a - m.* (Yes, through and through)." The game was made exciting as a smart player sitting hit the player standing in the circle with the ball of cloth at the back and quickly returned it into the passage before it could be intercepted. A player in whose area the ball was seized replaced the searcher and the game continued till the leader called for a change.

Anwe-nwee (Fun-Cracking)

Players sat in rows, shortest in front, tallest at the back. The leader called one member to play the part of the jester. He stood in front of the group and told funny stories with gesticulations to induce laughter. Other members tried to suppress laughing, but he who could not resist and was identified, replaced the jester and made jokes until he too succeeded in getting another player to laugh and to replace him.

Nkɔtɔfan (Wrestling)

Our leaders were careful in pairing competitors who matched in years and hardiness. Bouts were organized on a knock-out basis and a wrestler who succeeded in throwing down the most number of competitors was declared champion for the night. His prize was a ride on the shoulders of the vanquished to a point at the end of the field and back. My mother did not object to my taking part in the rigorous *Nkɔtɔfan* game, provided I did not cry back home if I was knocked down hard or suffered a bruise or a cut. She asked us always to bear in mind that,"*Ɔbarima nsu.*" (Any brave man does not cry). The other condition was that she should know of any injury we might sustain in the course of a bout as soon as we returned home.

Koturomua agyekum (Thumb on Clenched Fingers)

Players were lined up. The first in the line stretched one arm with the thumb folded in a fist. The player standing next after him in the queue placed his fist, one after the other, on those of the player immediately ahead of him. The third player moved on to add his fists, and so on, player after player. As the fists mounted up and up players sang repeatedly: "*Koturomua Agyekum - m - m! Yaa - a - a, Agyekum - m - m!*" The catch was that thumbs must not be exposed. He was the odd-man who forgot himself and exposed a thumb.

Whoever slipped was given heavy beatings on the back of his trunk
as he ran to touch a fixed point at the other end of the playground.

There were several other games which, for time and space,
cannot all be described now. They include, for instance,
Abahyɛ, Kokompe (Hopping) and, of course, the ever-popular
Ananse-sɛm.

Occasionally an inter-quarter "cloth-fighting" (*Ntɔmaa*) was
organized. It was a miniature soldierly engagement which
called for tactics, strategy and required very good stamina. Our
"arms" were cloths (*ntama*) which were folded and twisted.
Holding the ends firmly, we hit at the "enemy" with the looped
end as hard as we could until he was "conquered." An
opponent who ceased fighting and yielded was deemed to have
succumbed. The team with a fewer number of "casualties" after
a period of fighting was declared the winner of the contest. It
did often happen that the unscrupulous members of some
teams from *aborɔnoo* in Town did not observe the rules of the
game and put sand or, in some cases, stones at the looped
ends of their cloths to hit an opponent. Or they aimed hits at
the head and in the belly causing, at times, serious injuries
during a fight. Such unruly teams were shunned and boycotted
till their misbehaved player had been excluded from members
selected to play in future competitions.

A game which was quite popular in Town in our childhood
days was *Ahen-ahen* (Husband-and-Wife). Our parents, as could
be expected, unreservedly disapproved of its being played in
Salem. Their contention was that marriage matters were
delicate matters for grown-ups. Children therefore, ought not
to be permitted to toy with them however innocently they were
conducted.

Afoofi-di da, a day of respite from heavy farmwork, was a
day of certainty of two square meals with the possibility of the
unusual but much relished forenoon *fufu* meal (*anɔpa-fufuo*).
They were, therefore, to us children, days of pleasure: less
strenuous work, more time to play and food galore. Our
daytime games included marble playing (*ntɛ-sie*), *ɔsɔɔma* and
mpuri. And we played football, too — "football" because we
used our feet to kick a round thing. The thing was the fruit of a
bɔnowa tree. It was a hard fruit but it became soft and puffy if
left in a flaming fire for a few moments. We collected the fruits
by the dozen and took all trouble to treat them well for our
game of "football." It was, for a long time, used in place of

rubber balls, which became a common plaything for children of later generations.

On *afoo-fi-di* days, too, we engaged ourselves at bird-snaring. Some birds were caught all the year round by bow and chord traps (*nnomaa-firie*) baited and hung on trees bearing their favourite fruits, notably *ogyama*. In the harmattan season (*ɔpɛ-brɛ*) bird-catching became, to all intents, a profitable pastime for us children in an operation called *amantoɔ* (rubber trap laying). The crude rubber, *aman*, used for trapping birds, was some latex tapped from a forest climber. *Agyaamaa* was its name. The grey liquid, mixed with the juice of lime fruits (*ankaa dweaa*), thickened into a semi-solid mass which was kneaded into resinous balls. When boiled in water in an earthenware pot (*aman-senawa*) the balls became flexible and tenacious. The substance was then used very effectively for catching wild birds in large numbers. An *amantoɔ* operation was carried out in the afternoon during the major dry season around Christmas. Most streams were then almost dry, leaving their beds shallow pools of water to which birds flew to bathe.

Boys of Salem, as those from Town, went to *amantoɔ* in groups of threes and fours under their leaders. Each group decided when and where to go for the operation. I was a member of four in a group whose leader was Kwame O., a son of my mother's father's brother, Agya A. whom we met in his cottage at Oboakyi the day we were returning to Agogo from Kwaaman. He was Mother's brother and so I called him "*Wɔfa*" Kwame. The other two members of the group were related but not closely. A section of the lower end of Apampramasu stream up to a point where it met the Ntɔn stream was our favourite place of operation. On a section of the left bank of the former stream was my father's new cocoa farm. With our parents' consent we left home about mid-day. Being the youngest member of the group, I always carried the pot containing crude rubber (*aman-senawa*). The second member held a piece of firewood (*gyentia*) and the third, an enamel basin containing some uncooked food, some salt packed in *anwonomoo* leaf, a cooking pot and a drinking calabash (*koraa*). At a convenient spot about twenty yards away from the stream we stopped and cleared a space for use as our operation base. Fire was set to boil, the *aman*, cut into lumps to render it pliant and flexible. Meantime a number of sticks of about four feet long, together with some lengths of a special climber called "*amanhama*" were gathered by our leader. They were packed into bundles and, together with the boiled *aman* in pot, were carried to the stream. The traps were set by fixing the sticks slanting over pools and covered all over with a layer of *aman*. Lengths of the strings similarly covered with *aman* were stretched across pools from bank to bank. Care was taken to have the setting completed before mid-afternoon by which time the feathered creatures of the forest went down for their day's bath. We repaired to our operational base to wait. Meantime a meal of boiled cocoyam or plantain sprinkled with salt was prepared and eaten. At reasonable intervals *Wɔfa* Kwame together with one or two of us went round of watch to see what luck had brought to us. Silence — absolute silence — was one of the cardinal rules of the game of *amantoɔ*. A leader of any group insisted on its strict compliance, lest the birds, the cunning ones in particular, were scared away. Punishment for disobeying the rule was harsh, including birching and possible exclusion from taking part in any future operations.

The rule of observation of strict silence at *amantoɔ* suited me very well. Left on the bank at the fireside when the others had gone to the stream to bring in the catch, I took the opportunity to philosophize. I loved being in the forest and felt at home there especially when alone and in silence. The obsession might have been caused by my ever-longing to see or meet something that I could not very well describe. Could it have been *Sasabonsam*, The Forest Monster, about whom much had been heard in our *Ananse-sɛm* telling, but, disappointingly, I did not meet in the dense Bomfun Forest when we traversed it on our journey from Kumawu to Agogo? Was not the possibility there that I might chance to meet in other forests one of the relatives of the Monster (*Sasabonsam busuani*), say, his wife's brother (*n'akontagye*), his stepson (*n'abanoma*) or his uncle? Or was it *Mmoatia*, the Mischievous Dwarfs, that I was going to see? SOMETHING, I felt was there in the forest. I knew not what, but I had no doubt whatsoever that THE THING was there in the forest. How then could I easily give up expecting to see IT there?

Possessed with such gnawing longing, all talks by other children of fear of being alone in the forest were hardly credible. They were often heard telling glibly grisly tales of man-eating animals such as the leopard, King of the Dense Forest (*Kuretwiamansa, Kwae-bibrem-hene*); about biting, hissing snakes and about eye-pecking birds such as eagle, the King of Birds, (*Anomaa Kɔdeɛ*). I did not at all share their views.

The conviction I held was that, in general, any creature, be it a dweller in a city, in a town, in a village or a denizen of the wild, lived and let live if left unmolested and unprovoked. There were, of course, a few exceptions, I would not delude myself. Some individuals among all creatures, including the so-called highly developed *Homo Sapiens*, did attack unprovoked at times. As in men, so it could be, even more so, in other animals said to be inferior. I was firmly convinced of that. Did not, the other day as I was returning to Salem from Father's house, a bully ragamuffin, unprovoked, run and hit me hard in the stomach causing me to fall down in the street as I felt so giddy? Would anyone be justified in condemning a beast if it acted in a similar manner? Did not men, including my grandmother's father, a celebrated big game hunter of his day, not kill animals by the thousand every day for their meal and, even, for the pleasure of taking away life? Have such slaughterers any right to complain when a hungry leopard (ɔsebɔ) caught only one man for his meal? Had not many boys at *amantoɔ* (bird-trapping) caught and wrung off heads of harmless birds such as *ɔpɔreɛ, apatupre, abuburo* or *asrewa-sika-nsuo*? Must men be suffered in their self-righteousness in showing all that revulsion against an eagle should it, by any chance, peck off an eye of any one such naughty boy? Did not the red-eyed green mamba (ɔkyereben) I saw curled round a young tree when I was out in the bush collecting snails leave me alone to run away hurriedly because it was left unprovoked?

I honestly disagreed with my mates who, through groundless fear, were biased against any and every creature not of their kind, thereby condemning them for whatever they did while such mates ignored or even commended those of their species for any atrocity they committed against dumb creatures. Instances were not wanting. Were some unruly, blood-thirsty boys about the town not, with careless abandon, killing red-headed lizards (*mpomponii*) by their rubber tyre shots, not for the purpose of eating their meat, but to satisfy a cruel desire to see an innocent creature die? It puzzled me for a long time — that inhuman bias of men against other animals. My disgust worsened each time our Catechist, at our Sunday School class, joined in swollen neck-veins to sing:

All things bright and beautiful,
All things great and small,

All things wise and wonderful,
The Lord God made them all.

He gave us eyes to see them,
And lips that we might tell
How great is God Almighty,
Who has made all things well.

"*All* things great and small...?" Indeed! "The Lord God made them *all*...?" Indeed! Indeed! Abhoring senseless cruelty to animals, the lowly ones in particular, I found solace in a verse of a short poem:

Turn, turn thy hasty foot aside,
Nor crush the helpless worm.
The fame thy wayward looks deride,
None but our God could form.

My intense pleasure at *amantoɔ* operation in the Apampramasu stream was further heightened as I followed *Wɔfa* Kwame on a round of snare watch. There it was: the stream I had become so familiar with. The stream from which I had, on countless occasions, collected cool, fresh water for my parents to drink as they suffered thirst while working hard on their farm lying on its bank. The stream in which I had seen Father wading knee-deep in the rainy season to pull out his fishing traps (*adwokuo*) which were carried to the bank where I waited, to be emptied of their contents of live crabs. The stream in which I had followed Mother and her friends on group-fishing (*ahweɛ*) wherein crabs, prawns and small fishes such as *nkawa*, and *mmɔbɔnse* were caught by the wooden-bowlfuls. The stream at whose head-waters we drew our daily supply of water for our farm cottage use. As I walked in the cool sand of its dry bed in the wake of *Wɔfa* Kwame, my sentimental attachment to Apampramasu deepened, and confirmed my justification for referring to it as "our stream" (*yɛ 'asuo*).

All birds we trapped were killed instantly. There was no difficulty in finishing a helpless bird. It was very simple: twist the little neck around sharply and the poor creature was gone! Those captured were plucked at the fire site and their entrails removed by pressing hard at the upper part of the abdomen. They were skewered through the lower jaw and hung on a forked stick kept standing by the fire to preserve and prevent

foraging ants from getting at them. Late afternoon was the
birds' bathing peak period. It was at that time the worthies,
notably, *ɔpaben, abrunsumabɛn, otuabire, kɔtɔkɔsaben* and
mmuburo went for their day's bath. *Nkɔwerɛ*, too, descended in
flocks of twenties, thirties or more to bathe at that time. We
waited patiently and silently to the end when the fortunate
ones had bathed, drunk and flown away safe into their nests on
tree tops and the unfortunate ones captured and plucked for
meals at home the following day. The *aman* was withdrawn
near dusk when late bathers had satisfied themselves and were
gone. The lumps retrieved from trap sticks and string were all
kneaded into a ball and stored in the *aman-senawa* (pot) half-
full of water. We returned home. *Wɔfa* Kwame led, holding a
brand of palm branch torch (*tɛnee*) if it was a dark night. Our
parents were aware that we would not be back home before
nightfall and so it did not worry them unduly if our arrival was
late. Beside, they had confidence in the ability of *Wɔfa* Kwame
to take appropriate action to deal with any eventuality should
one happen.

It was one day at *amantoɔ* operation that I fell ill — really
very ill. I remember the day quite well: it was a Friday, an
afoofi-di day. I remember that we set out from home just in
time that Mother and her colleagues had returned from some
communal work at the cemetery. From very early that morning
and, in fact, all through that week, I had felt out of sorts and
not quite myself. Because I did not wish to miss the excitement
of an *amantoɔ*, I forced myself to go, hoping I would get over
that unusual gripping, crippling seizure in the course of the
day, more so, when I was back in the forest. But things did not
happen the way I expected. I did my best to hide the sharp
pangs I was feeling between my chest and the abdomen as we
walked to our operational base. *Wɔfa* Kwame noticed my
unusual behaviour and suggested tactfully that I stay behind at
the fire site to prepare our afternoon meal. I was left behind,
alone. Try as hard as I could, I was unable to control some
irresistible urge to lie down to sleep. As if pushed by some
strong force, I fell on the bare ground by the fire, restless,
breathless, helpless. All was void. When the others returned
from the snare-setting, they found me lying prostrate, eyes
blank and unable to answer any of their many questions. My
two young mates panicked. *Wɔfa* Kwame, our leader, did not.
He was as cool as a cucumber, calm and collected. He acted
promptly. He decided that I was to be carried home at once on

his back while the other two boys went back to the stream to undo the traps and follow with all possible speed. Fortunately, on reaching the main footpath, he met a couple who were our Apampramasu cottage neighbours returning from town where they had gone on a day trip to buy some salt, kerosene and a few other cottage needs. Promptly they relieved *Wɔfa* Kwame of his heavy burden and brought home to Mother her panting, gasping, near-death son. My father was sent for at once. Another person in the house was dispatched to tell her brother Kwaku A., a reputed herbalist who lived not far away in the Apetenyinase quarter, the critical condition of his nephew and to ask him to come speedily, prepared to treat him.

Up to that morning and ever since we returned home from Kwaaman, I had been as strong and healthy a child as any mother would wish to have. There were occasional touches of fever now and some slight stomach upsets then, a cut here and some bruises there, but by and large I had, under the conditions as then existed, enjoyed a life which could be said to be above normal. My near perfect condition of health was not by chance. In a large measure, it could be attributed to the stringent care exercised by my mother over the observance of some basic personal hygiene. Even more insistent on neatness and care of the body was our grandmother who, in all matters of personal cleanliness, as well as environmental sanitation, was meticulous to a fault. Among other things, we, the children of the house, were enjoined to obey eight simple rules of early morning personal hygiene, namely:

1. **Hohoro woanim**
   Collect water in a calabash and wash the face first thing in the morning, taking care to remove dried over-flow saliva (*ntotro*) at the corners of the mouth and scales in the corners of the eyes (*aniase-nkyene*).

2. **Ho woanum**
   Fill the mouth several times with water and puff it to clean it before conversing with another person.

3. **Twitwiri wo se**
   Brush the teeth thoroughly with a piece of beaten cut-end of the unripe plantain fruit (*borɔde-tire*), dusted with ground charcoal (*gyebirie*).

4. **Ko tiafi**
   Attend to "Nature's Call" to clear your bowels in the morning.

5. **Nom nunum-dudo**
   Before taking any meal in the morning, drink an appropriate measure of a decoction of *nunum* leaves and some pieces of barks of trees boiled in a small earthenware pot (*asenawa*) to which was added a pinch of salt and a squeeze of *nhyeraa* pepper.

6. **Pra wo dabere (boys); Pra adiwo (girls)**
   Sweep your sleeping place clean (boys); sweep the yard clean (girls).

7. **Hohoro didi-pon so (boys); Hohoro nkukuom (girls)**
   Wash Father's Eating Table (boys); wash household utensils (girls).

8. **Dware**
   Take a bath at least once a day, preferably before going to bed, but twice on an *afoofi-di* day.

Every effort was made to keep our bodies, our rooms and our compound and all surroundings clean. And yet, I became ill that fateful Friday!

My herbalist, *Wɔfa* Kwadu A., hurried to Salem. Much was at stake. His sprightly nephew was in the throes of death and must be saved. No chances were to be taken. His healing ability was on crucial test. He must work hard. On seeing my condition he dashed out of the house frantically and was back in a brief space of time with some leaves and herbs. Nervously he pressed them together with the palms of his hands in a calabash of water. The mixture was forced through my almost blocked throat. I vomited. An enema was applied without any response. Some black powder was blown into my nose, but my condition grew worse and worse. It was agreed that an urgent message of appeal for help be made to the leading medicine-man of the town.

Meantime the Catechist and some Church Elders had arrived at the house. They prayed hard and sincerely, but I sank lower and lower. The medicine-man arrived posthaste. He, too, worked very fast. A decoction of some leaves and barks hurriedly prepared was forced into my mouth. I gulped a mouthful. That was all I could remember. I fell into a deep coma. For how long I remained in that state, I could not say. It must, however, have been a long time, for, when I came to, there was quite a large crowd of people in the yard. The first words that I heard when I opened my eyes were: "Akua, *gyae su. Onwui, Wanyane.*" ("Akua, cease wailing, He isn't dead. He is back to life.")

As I turned my weary, benumbed head, I saw my mother lying flat on the dusty ground of the yard, rolling her body all over the place in a fit of violent, uncontrollable grief, hair dishevelled and wailing pathetically:

Yaw e-e-e, Yaw e-e-e, Yaw!
Agya, Mawie O - O
Agya, Mawie O - O!
Buei... Buei... Buei!
Ɛde aye me O,
Mɛnyɛ dɛn ni... O?
Mɛnyɛ dɛn ni... O?
Owuo, Mayɛ wo dɛn O?
Owuo, bɛfa me O - O... O!
Agya..i, Agya..i, Agya..i!
Mensono mu O!
Mensono mu O!
Yaw e-e-e. Yaw e-e-e, O... Yaw!
Me na mini O..O!
Agya, Mawie..O-O!
Buei... Buei... Buei!

(O-O-O, Yaw, O-O-O Yaw! Yaw No, No, No!
O-O, Father, Woe is me, Father!
Woe betides me!
Alas! Alas! Alas!
Cruelly cursed am I!
What shall I do?
What have I done, Cruel Death?
What have I done to merit such a heartless cruelty?
Cruel Death, away with me too!
O-O, Father, woe betides me!
My stricken bowels!
O-O-O, Yaw, My Yaw. NO, NO, NO, Yaw!
O Fate! What painful a decree!
O-O-O, Father, I am done — miserably done!
I am finished — inconsolably finished!)

It was in the cool morning before the sun had risen high in the sky. I saw myself lying on a mat spread on the ground in the yard surrounded by many grief-stricken relatives and some friends of Mother's. By my side at the pillow end sat an elderly woman, Nana Adwoa Akwaa. It was her voice I heard giving the cheerful, comforting news of my return to life to Mother. Nana Adwoa was holding my left wrist in the palm of her left hand with the palm of the right hand on my chest feeling my feeble pulse calmly but with some suppressed anxiety writ large on her wrinkled face. She was a kindly, soft spoken, self-possessed old woman with a cataract on the left eye. She was the wife of Opanin Kofi Asadu, on of the Church Elders. Because he was so handsome in spite of his age and had such a deep round bass voice for singing *Mfante-nnwom* (Fante traditional church songs), he was nick-named "*Osoowa*" (the Charming) Kofi Asadu.

Amid grief turned rejoicing, I heard someone being told to run fast to call back a messenger who had been sent to give the news of my death to my father. Nana Yaw Nkroma, Grandmother's uncle and an Elder of the Church who was among those gathered in the yard, was heard ordering complete silence, saying: "*Obiara nyɛ kom-m-m-m! Monsɔre ma yɛmmɔ mpae!*" ("Let everyone be silent! Shall we all pray, standing!") He led in a prayer in which thanks were offered to God for bringing His little child back to life. Then he prayed that the revival might not relapse, but that it continue to improve speedily. At the end of the moving prayer, all in the yard joined in saying *The Lord's Prayer* thankfully, in a mood of deepest solemnity. The sympathisers' prayer was answered. I recovered steadily and regained my normal health, my boyish strength and vivacity in a few weeks. I had survived my first brush with death!

About thirty years after what was said to be my miraculous escape from death, I had to take a medical examination at the Korle Bu Hospital, in Accra, to qualify for an award of a scholarship from the Colonial Welfare Development Fund to do a course of professional study overseas. A series of exhaustive tests including a chest X-ray were made at my first appearance, after which I was requested to report again in two weeks for a further X-ray examination of the chest. I did. At the end of the second appearance, the Medical Officer who conducted the examination asked me to see him in his office. I did. He offered me a seat there. I sat. Looking me hard in the face and tapping the end of his pen on the table, the examiner enquired: "Tell me, Mr. er, er..." finding some difficulty in pronouncing what might have been to him, a queer name with an awkward spelling, "K-Y-E-I". I helped by pronouncing the name myself and explained to him the "k-y" in Twi was pronounced as "ch" in English. "Thank you. Yes, Mr. Chee, tell me," he repeated, looking somewhat puzzled, "when was it that you were last admitted at a hospital for the treatment of lung disease?"

"My lung disease? I have never had any lung disease, Doctor," I replied confidently.

"You don't mean it?"

"As far as I am aware! I should have added," I said, qualifying my first statement.

"You are not aware, yourself, but have you been told or have you heard from any source that you have ever been treated for a lung disease?"

Suddenly, from the inner recess of my sub-conscious mind the fact emerged, enabling me to answer promptly: "Yes, Doctor, I can very well remember that I fell critically ill when I was quite young. I am unable to say however what the disease was."

"We are getting somewhere. How long ago this was, do you remember?"

"Quite some time now. About thirty years, I am sure," I replied.

The Medical Officer bent down his head and started scribbling something on a form lying in front of him on the neatly polished writing desk. As he did so I heard him mumbling, "It has been with him, or he has been with it all these years. He can continue to be with it more years."

He raised his head and, in a friendly mood, said: "Good luck, Mr. Chee. I wish you a successful course in Britain." I shook his outstretched hand, said "Thank you" to him and left his office and Korle Bu.

At Oxford about a year later, I mentioned my interview with the Korle Bu doctor to a medical doctor friend of mine. Out of interest he arranged for my chest X-ray, which revealed unmistakably deep scars on both lungs, caused by some acute inflammation. It was at that time that I knew the first messenger whom Death, the Leveller, the Absolute Controller of Life (*Odomankama Wuo*), sent to summon me so early in life was no less an agent than PNEUMONIA.

12

WHERE I BELONGED

People will not look forward to posterity who never looked
backward to the ancestors.

— Edmund Burke

Central to Ghana's social institutions is the "family," but it is
important to first define what the Ghanaian concept of the
"family" means. While in the non-Ghanaian sense of the word the
family includes only the parent and the children of the house, in
Ghanaian society it embraces a whole lineage. Among the Akans,
the family includes all the maternal relatives...[1]

I was fortunate enough to meet my grandmother, Nana Yaa
Kwaane, my great-grandmother, Nana Afua Adem (also called
Gyaa) and her younger sister, Nana Akua Adwapa. The two
great-grandmothers were inseparable. They lived together in
one house in Apetenyinase, the Asona *borɔnoo*, in Town. They
shared one room, each sleeping on one of two swish-built
platforms (*esɛ*) raised to about a foot from the floor level on
the opposite sides of a room whose door was a palm-branch
mat (*asrɛne*). Between the two platforms was a three-piece *esa*
tree wood fire which remained burning all night, all seasons, to
keep the aged bodies warm.

Many times a week they went together to their Oboase
foodcrop farm (*mfikyi-fuo*) which was about half a mile away.
Leaving home in no haste, and with the support of their
faithful, time-worn walking sticks, the two sisters covered the
accustomed distance with incredible speed. They stayed long
in the farms, struggling with their sapped energy to do the
work which they were able to accomplish with ease in their
youthful, vigorous days.

---

[1] F.K. Buah, *A History of Ghana* (London: Macmillan, 1980), 43.

The two grand old women lived in sisterly and complete harmony in spite of some noticeable dissimilarities in temperament and outlook. Both of medium height, the elder sister was plumper, reticent, tolerant and liberal in outlook. Nana Akua, the younger sister, on the other hand, was lighter in build, stooped slightly, was a ready talker, and deeply conservative. I recollect vividly an embarrassment that Nana Akua Adwapa caused me one day by her outspokenness. It was one Sunday after church service. Mother had sent me with a dish of prepared food to her grandmothers in Town, wearing my light-brown suit. The elder sister, Nana Afua, who was the first to see me enter the house, met me at the entrance (*ntwoonoo mu*) and took the dish off my head, relieving me of my load. Gratefully and affectionately, she said to me: "*Baafoɔ, Yɛma wo adware. Woabɛdom yɛn. Mo! Mo! Mo! Baafoɔ, Kyei, Ɔkɔkɔɔ Nana, Yaw.*" ("*Baafoɔ*, we thank you for the food. You have come just at the right time. Well done, *Baafoɔ* Kyei, grandson of he who was rich in gold.") Nana Akua's reaction was quite different. Standing askance and looking at me from head to toe in surprise tinged with disgust she addressed me in a mood of contempt, saying: "*Adɛn, Yaw, Woyɛ efun na yɛahyɛhyɛ wo sɛɛ yi? Hm - m - m, Boe. Ɛnnɛɛmafoɔ de biribi aba wiase!*" ("Why, Yaw, are you dead to be so copiously attired? Forsooth! The moderns have brought wonders into the world.") It was the body of a dead person lying-in-state which was covered with an assortment of cloths. My wearing a suit of a pair of trousers and a coat over a shirt and underwear was, to her conservative mind, a novelty which could only be understood as appropriate to a corpse.

My memorable impression of Akua Adwapa was her unbounded pride in her Asona *abusua* (lineage). To her, everything about the *abusua* was the best and so she took every opportunity to talk with us seriously and enthusiastically about the lineage. She was particularly boastful of Ɔpemkɔkɔ, the settlement of the Asona immigrants who, she said, were the very first people to reach, and settle at, the place now known as "Agogo." She punctuated her frequent affectionate references to the place as "*yɛamanfoo-so*" (our former homestead), reciting each time the sounding of the combined Asona horn and drum language which she interpreted authoritatively as: "*Asona, Kɔtɔkɔ!* (for the horn sound) *Yefri Tete..., Tete..., Tete-e-e...Te!* (for the drum sound)." ("Asona, Kɔtɔkɔ, we have existed from time long past.") One other thing I noted about Nana Akua was that, whenever she mentioned the name of some of her departed relatives, the old woman raised herself slightly up her wooden stool and said, "*Asomasi,*[2] *mete ne so a, masɔre!*" ("So-and-so, I rise in his/her honour!") Many years passed before I understood that Nana's action was in veneration of those distinguished Asona people who contributed in one way or another to the progress of the lineage and to the welfare and happiness of its individual members. The understanding dawned on me at a church service of a denomination which I attended. In the course of the worship a hymn was called. All stood up and sang,

> When morning gilds the skies,
> My heart awakening cries:
> May Jesus Christ be praised,
> Alike at work and prayer
> To him I would repair,
> May Jesus Christ be praised.

I observed that each time the name, "Jesus Christ," was mentioned every member of the congregation bowed low in honour of his/her Saviour.

Nana Akua spoke to us frequently about deceased and living members of the *abusua*. At the same time she spoke untiringly about notable events connected with the *abusua* which occurred in the past. Our interest in her narrations encouraged her to talk more and at length. We listened with due respect, my brothers and I, but, to be quite frank, much of what she said was, at times, outside the range of my particular interest. In the end, I was left with bits and pieces of incoherent information about my lineage. Nonetheless, Nana Akua succeeded in implanting firmly in my tender mind one very important piece of knowledge which was the hallmark of a noble Akan-born, unto whom a disgrace was ill-befitted (*Ɔkannii ba a, animguase mfata no*). I knew from my own grandmother at that tender age that I was an Akan-born (*Ɔkannii ba*). I could say proudly, "*Meyɛ Ɔsonani ba*" ("I am a member of the Asona lineage") with some indefinable inner feeling of elation no less high than that which prompted Paul of Tarsus to proclaim: "*Civis romanus sum*" ("I am a Roman citizen"). Above all, I had learned that I was one of a group of

---

[2] *Asomasi* is the name used to refer to a person whose name is suppressed.

distinguished people who, through their mothers, have all descended from a common ancestor. With that feeling I grew up, ever confident that in whatever difficult situation I might find myself anywhere, anytime, I could count on someone of my relatives for help. At the other end, I felt I had an obligation to go to the aid of anyone of the members of my *abusua* who was in genuine need because that person was someone related to me through my mother.

My knowledge about my lineage at that time was, as a whole, hazy and skeletal. It remained so till many years later when an opportunity for its study in some depth offered itself. It happened in 1944 when I was seconded to a team of researchers from Oxford in Britain, who arrived to carry out in Ashanti a "Social Survey." Under the direction of its leader, the erudite late Professor (at that time Doctor) Meyer Fortes, I worked on the preparation of a genealogical tree of the Agogo Asona cognate lineage, my own *abusua*. The moment was opportune, for there were alive at the time quite a few elderly members of the lineage knowledgeable in its history who were willing to co-operate and give me whatever information I needed and which they had in their possession. It was possible in the circumstances to complete for the Survey a chart showing eleven generations up to the known common ancestor, mine being the tenth.

The work deepened my interest considerably and my appetite was whetted for a further study on the subject. Once again luck was on my side. My own uncle, Kofi Donko, whose other name is Thomas Bonsu, who was one of my most obliging informants in the 1944/45 research was still alive and his willingness to co-operate had not diminished. "Uncle Thomas," as I call him, is a very remarkable old man now in his eighties. Physically infirm as a result of some protracted illness said to be a malignant tumor, he is still mentally alert with keen eyesight and manages to hobble about wearily dragging his full masculine stature by the support of an imported walking stick. The third of three sons born of Eno Henewaa, herself the only daughter of great grandmother Akua Adwapa, Uncle Thomas, named "*Donko*" (Slave), followed the Akan practice of giving a derogatory name to a child which survived after death in infancy of the immediately preceding sibling or siblings. Eno Henewaa died when her son Kofi was an infant child, leaving him in the care of his grandmother, Akua Adwapa. Living and growing among elderly people of the lineage, Kofi listened and stored up in his extraordinarily retentive memory all that he could imbibe from his grandparents who were well-versed in the lores, history and tradition of the Asona *Abusua.*

Uncle Thomas was not sent to school, but with the exception that he is unable to read and write, he is more than a match, in every respect, for any of his companions or compatriots who were fortunate to receive formal classroom education. In manliness and courage, both physical and moral, he is hard to beat. His first career as a gold and silversmith in Agogo brought him into contact not only with fashionable women of his age, but also with men of means and influence who placed substantial orders with him for trinkets. His travels round, to peddle gold and silver earrings, finger-rings, bracelets and bangles took him to several places in the whole country where he had an opportunity to meet and know other people and their different ways of life. Later, as a cocoa farmer, he settled in the Nso-Nyame Yɛ farm village which he founded and became its first *odekuro,* sharing in the experience of farm life in all its ups and downs.

In local, as well in national political affairs, Uncle Thomas has played his full part. Starting as a member of the erstwhile Agogo Local Council, he became, in his heyday a constituency chairman of the political party which held power in the country for some fifteen years. In religious affairs he was one of the founders of the Roman Catholic Church in Agogo, but backslided when he took unto himself three wives. It was therefore not unexpected when our late head of the "house" (*Ofie-Panin*), Nana Kwadwo Bɔfoɔ (Nkansa), willed that, even though the youngest of his surviving "nephews," he, Uncle Thomas, was to succeed him on his death. By this succession, Kofi automatically became our *Ofie-Panin.* Later he was enstooled *Akyeamehene* (Chief Linguist) of Agogo, a post once held by his deceased uncle from whom he had inherited. In the course of the past ten years Uncle Thomas has discharged his traditional *Ofie-Panin* functions creditably and has proved to be a fit *Opanin* in terms of the criteria which an eminent Ghanaian philosopher has outlined:

What made him (*Opanin*) a man of importance, outstanding in the eyes of his fellow men, was the fact that he had lived his life as an ordinary citizen and had not lost in dignity or honour and not suffered any disgrace.... This absence of disgrace, this attainment and maintenance of dignity, makes the moral subject an excellent person. He had married and been given in marriage with honour. He had bought or sold in open or private market with honour, brought up children with honour, worshipped at shrines with honour, suffered bereavement with honour, and, above all, had joined with others, or acted by himself, to settle family and other disputes, bringing peace and increase to the family, with honour. He had done all these and come up on top without disgrace, without debasement to the dignity of a man of the Akan. This, they say, is surely an *Opanin*, one fit to rule the family, tribe, clan or state, anointed head of the people, revelation of God in man, discovered by man.[3]

I have relied mainly on my eminent *Ofie-Panin*, Uncle Thomas, for the bulk of information which has helped me trace my ancestry and record on a Genealogical Chart, the relevant branch of which is produced as Appendix 3 to this Memoir. Given below is a record of one of my frequent informal discourses with this walking encyclopaedia of the Agogo Asona lineage and, indeed, of the past and contemporary events of the Agogo Traditional area. From the particular conversation it has been possible for me to fill in much of the blanks in my knowledge on the origin and other relevant historical facts and events concerning my forebears.

A RECORD OF A CONVERSATION WITH MY UNCLE ON OUR ANCESTRY

Uncle: Kofi Donko (Thomas Bonsu)
Nephew: Yaw Kyei (Thomas)

Nephew: *Wɔfa*, you grew under the care of Nana Panin Akua Adwapa, and must have heard quite a lot from her concerning our Asona Abusua *mpaninsɛm* (history, tradition and customs of lineage).

Uncle: Yes, indeed, I did. No one would stay a day with that old lady without learning some Asona *mpaninsɛm*. But there were other sources, too.

Nephew: Such as?

Uncle: The Asonahene, Nana Kwaku Agyei. His house was next to ours at Apetenyinase. In fact, we shared a common *odwuma* board party wall. Whenever there was a gathering in the house —

---

[3] J.B. Danquah, *The Akan Doctrine of God* (London: Lutterworth Press, 1944), 121-22.

and there were several of them in a week — I often stood by and listened to the Elders of the lineage deliberating on some family matters. Many a time, too, I had to hold myself in readiness and be about the house, to run on errands. The other principal source of my information was through my uncle, *Wɔfa* Kwadwo Bɔfoɔ, who was, for a long time, the *Akyeamehene* of Agogo. I was the carrier of his skin covered-seat chair to the *Ahemfie* where I sat behind him. There, too, I listened to the discussions and debates by the Chief and his Elders on some important issues affecting the town. Then again, when *Wɔfa* travelled outside the town, generally to Kumasi and Juaso, on some state business, I accompanied him, carrying his pack (*n'abɔtɔwa*). Much of what was said in all those places were *mpaninsɛm* which interested me immensely.

Nephew:	*Wɔfa*, if I may refer back to Nana Akua who impressed me as an old woman of considerable knowledge of our Asona *mpaninsɛm*, could you say what was her main source of information?
Uncle:	Nana grew and stayed for some time with her grandmother, Ama Pɔnkɔ. I heard from Nana that at the time of her grandmother, Ama Pɔnkɔ, all the *Asonafoɔ* lived together in Gyedua-Yaa-ase, from where the quarter extended to Apetenyinase. The new extension was a place where there stood a big silk-cotton tree (*onyina*) on top of which flocks of crop-eating vultures congregated, hence the name: *Apete* (vultures), *Nyina* (silk-cotton tree), *Apete-nyinase* (Under the silk-cotton tree of vultures).
Nephew:	Had Gyedua-Yaa-ase been our ancestral dwelling place from time immemorial?
Uncle:	No, certainly not. They moved from the former place called Ɔpemkɔkɔ to Gyedua-Yaa-ase.
Nephew:	Oh, I see. Ɔpemkɔkɔ, the name we often heard! Where exactly was that historic place, the mere mention of whose name enamoured Nana Akua?

Uncle:	The area lying right off the Agogo-Hwidiem road, extending from the present site of the Magistrate's Court building to the Akogya stream, roughly, was Ɔpemkɔkɔ.
Nephew:	Mother's Nkwatam foodcrop farm (*mfikyi-fuo*) was on a part of the old place (*amanfooso*), then?
Uncle:	That's right. And so were foodcrop farms of some other Asona old women, including Eno Adwoa Pɔ and Eno Asantewaa, both sisters.
Nephew:	For how long did our ancestors stay at Ɔpemkɔkɔ before they moved to Gyedua-Yaa-ase?
Uncle:	Three years, I was told.[4]
Nephew:	Before then, where were they? I mean, from which place did our noble ancestors move to settle at Ɔpemkɔkɔ, if they had not been living there all the time?
Uncle:	It's a very long story.
Nephew:	That makes it all the more interesting. I would very much like to hear it all, or as much of it as you can recollect and tell me.
Uncle:	It's a very long story, I have said, but briefly it is this: Our ancestors lived together with their brothers and sisters, mothers and grandmothers, uncles and children at Nsodua, a town near Akrokyerɛ in Adanse.
Nephew:	Nsodua near Akrokyerɛ. Did you, in one of your many travels about the country peddling trinkets, have the opportunity to visit Nsodua?
Uncle:	Yes, I did. It has now shrunk into a small village not bigger than Hwidiem. I was told when I was there that many years ago, it was a large town bustling with vigorous inhabitants, mostly of the Asona lineage. In course of time, so I was told, the *abusua* grew and extended. As it increased more and more in numbers, it became necessary

---

[4] Between *circa* 1700-2 and 1706-8.

for one reason or the other, for sections to leave the town from time to time, in groups of varying sizes, to settle in other places far, far away. From Nana I heard that one of the groups moved (northward) to Ofenso; another moved (northwestward) to Edweso and a third group moved (southwestward) to Akyem Abuakwa. Our ancestors, according to Nana, were among the Akyem Abuakwa stream, but at a point on their journey, somewhere near the Prah, they decided to leave their kinsfolk and moved (northward) to Ɔpemkɔkɔ where they settled.[5]

Nephew:

From Nsodua to Ɔpemkɔkɔ via Praso! I understand now why Nana Akua used to say boastfully that it was our ancestors who first settled in the area we now know and call Agogo. Who were the nearest neighbours of the Ɔpemkɔkɔ immigrants? Did you hear about that, *Wɔfa*?

Uncle:

Yes. I was told that Nana Fempɔn Manso had established his Kotoku Kingdom in the neighbourhood of the present day Juansa and Kurofa (south) area. From there he moved to Dampɔn where he lived with his people for a time before continuing to a place they called Nsuaem, later Ɔdaa, in Akyem Kotoku.[6] The other kingdom which was near Ɔpemkɔkɔ at that time was said to be one far east in the Afram Plains. The ruler of the kingdom was a powerful king called Atara Finam.[7]

---

[5] *circa* 1700-1702.

[6] F.K. Buah writes: "During their dispersion from somewhere in the present-day Asante, the Kotoku are said to have first settled for a time in the area of present-day Edweso, about twenty kilometres east of Kumasi. Their next sojourn was in the present-day Asante Akyem, where their principal town was old Kotoku. From here they finally settled in the present territory, with new Kotoku as their capital. In due course, Ɔdaa replaced Kotoku as capital." Buah, *A History of Ghana*, 28.

[7] On the kingdom in the east, W.E.F. Ward writes: "And more than this. The people of Agogo in Ashanti-Akim say that when their first chief went to settle there he found all the Afram plains, and the whole districts of what we now call Kwahu and Ashanti Akim, ruled by a

Nephew:	Did you hear something about our ancestors who were said to be the first to arrive and settle at Ɔpemkokɔ, for instance, their names, number and how they related one to the other?
Uncle:	Oh, yes. Nana spoke about them as if they were alive and were living next door. She said there were five of them: two men and three women, all from the same womb (*yafun koro mma*). The two brothers were Adwapo Koramoo (the elder) and Frempɔn Ako the younger. The three sisters were Baduaa Asɔ (the eldest), who had no child, Amene Kɔkɔ, and Akwiamaa (the youngest).
Nephew:	Did Nana or anyone tell you the name of the mother of the five brothers and sisters?
Uncle:	I am afraid not. All she said about their mother was that she lived, died and was buried in Nsodua before her children left the place. Her name, however, was never mentioned to me.
Nephew:	Our ancestors from Nsodua arrived and settled at Ɔpemkokɔ alone. Were they some time later followed by a group of another *abusua*?
Uncle:	Yes, by a group of a larger number, the *Aduanafoɔ*.
Nephew:	From where?
Uncle:	That also is a very, very long story, but again, I will try to be brief. The first group of the Aduana people who arrived at Ɔpemkokɔ came all the way from Akwamu. I was told that Akwamu was a powerful warlike state whose capital town was Anyanawase in the neighbourhood of the present day Nsawam. They fought several battles against their neighbours who were the Akyem, the Accras and the Akwapims, and many others. In one of their battles the Akwamus were heavily defeated and so they fled eastward,

great and strong chief, whose people did not speak Twi. His name was Atara Finam or Atara Fuom." W.E.F. Ward, *A Short History of Ghana* (London: Allen and Unwin, 1958), 13.

crossed the Volta and settled at a place they named Akwamufie. A subchief of the Akamu Aduana lineage decided not to settle with his people at Akwamufie and so moved on northward with his close relatives and subjects in search of a better land.[8]

Nephew:

As you know, *Wɔfa*, a locality in Agogo is named "Nyanawase." Has the name any connection with the vanquished Akwamu capital?

Uncle:

No one has told me anything about that, but there appears to be a strong suggestion that the two names have some historical link. Be that as it may, the story I heard was that the bulk of the Akwamu state settled at Akwamufie. A small section of the Akwamu Aduana which kept roving on finally settled on the Afram Plains at a place called Satenso.

Nephew:

What was the name of the Akwamu sub-chief who led his break-away people to settle at Satenso?

Uncle:

Nana Ofori Sasraku was his name. His sister, Nana Mansa Ntim, was the Queen-mother. As I have already told you, the whole of the Afram Plains area then formed a part of the territory of the powerful Atara Finam. Nana Ofori Sasraku entered into an alliance with Kumawuhene and Kwaamanhene, both of the Asante Aduana lineage, and so were his brothers, to fight Atara Finam. They fought him for about three years. In a fierce battle the joint army, under the supreme command of Nana Ofori, the enemy was decisively beaten. Atara Finam, the monarch of the plains, was driven away. He fled east across the Volta. Nana Ofori Sasraku earned the title (*abɔdin*) "*Kɔbɔn*" ("The Leopard") after the battle

---

[8] Ward has recorded the movement as follows: "These people were the Akwamus ... they built themselves a town on the slopes of Nyanao and called it Nyanawase ... about the year 1600. ...The Akwamus lost the battle, and fled along the ridge of the Akwapim hills to the Volta.... Some of Ansa Sasraku's people fled from Nyanawase to Agogo...." *Ibid.*, 14, 20 and 83.

for some tactics employed through a leopard, conjured by the Fetish Dɛntɛ of Krakye whose aid the Commander in Chief of the Allied Army had sought to win the war.

Nephew:

Why didn't Ofori Kɔbɔn settle in peace at Satenso in his conquered territory, but had to move farther on?

Uncle:

The break-away Akwamu-Aduanas were forced to vacate. Satenso was under a very strange and pathetic circumstance.

Nephew:

How?

Uncle:

Before going to the attack, Ofori Kɔbɔn, as was the practice in those days and has continued even up to now, consulted the Fetish Krakye Dɛntɛ (*Ɔkɔɔ abisa*). He pledged to the *Ɔbosom* an offer of a sum of money, some number of sheep and slaves if he helped the allies to defeat Atara Finam. The war lasted a long time but they won in the end. Ofori Kɔbɔn ignored his pledge (*aboadeɛ*) and failed to honour it. Some time later, so the story went, Krakye Dɛntɛ changed himself into a little beragged, weeping yaw-sore-covered, dirty child, and went to the *Ahemfie*. When he saw the child, Ofori ordered that the filthy, ugly thing be cleared out of the house at once. The loyal attendants dragged the child away. From the Chief's house he crawled to the house of the Queen-mother. Nana Mansa Ntim felt pity for the child and showed a deep concern for the hapless little visitor. She gave him some food to eat and water to drink and took it upon herself to dress the child's weeping wounds, soothing them with a mixture of some ground leaves and shea butter. She laid him on a mat to sleep in a cool, airy, room and sat by him to drive away flies that attempted to settle on the sores.

When the child awoke he revealed to the kind and gentle Queen-mother that something dreadful was going to happen to the town and to all that dwell in it. As a small reward for her kindness and concern shown to him, the child said he would advise her to besmear some parts of her exposed body with powdered white clay (*hyire*). She was to instruct all members of her household to take similar precaution. When the ugly child had got the Queen-mother to promise solemnly to act promptly on his advice, he changed suddenly into a plump, clean, neatly dressed child and revealed his identity, saying: "*Me ne Krakye Dɛntɛ* ("I am Krakye Dɛntɛ") and vanished. The awe stricken Nana Mansa Ntim did as she was bidden by the strange child. Meantime, some of the townsmen who saw her acting frantically, suspected that the old lady had taken leave of her senses and mocked her and all the other followers who, on an ordinary weekday, had besmeared their bodies with powdered white clay. But their jeering was short-lived.

In no time, the whole past-midday, bright and sunny Satenso sky suddenly became dark with a thick swarm of angry bees. They swooped down and stung hard every living thing in that fateful Satenso town. Men and animals — domestic birds and beasts — were attacked until individuals succumbed pitifully and died the painful death of stings of myriad bees. Nana Ofori Kɔbɔn, his Elders, court servants and several of his followers, driven to desperation by the violent bees, ran helter-skelter to the bank of the Onwam River at Bun-Febi Waterfall where, the *atumpan* drums beating and throbbing, they tumbled precipitately into the depths of the bubbling waters of the river and were swallowed up. The Queen-mother and all her people who identified themselves with the *hyire* were left unscathed.

Nephew: That must have been a very sad and dreadful experience.

Uncle: It was. Shocking and terrifying to the old lady in particular. She decided therefore that Satenso be abandoned at once. The badly-shaken Queen-mother and her few remaining followers of the Akwamu Aduana royals headed for Abɔyɛ, the nearest settlement which was situated at the meeting place of the Afram and the Onwam Rivers. At Abɔyɛ she made known to the inhabitants of the village why she had fled from

Satenso to find a fruitful place, far away from the land of bees, where she and her followers could settle in peace. Ɔpemkokɔ, lying west in a fertile forest land, was recommended as an ideal place and she was advised to proceed there.[9] An Asubɔyɛ man called Asante, on whom the appellation, "*Ɔde-bae*," was later conferred by the Agogohene, was chosen to lead the Satenso remnants to Ɔpemkokɔ where the few Nsodua Asona emigrants had settled.

Nephew: It must have been to the Akwamu-Aduana people a long, adventurous journey from Nyanawase to a happy ending at Ɔpemkɔkɔ.[10]

Uncle: Yes, indeed, it was. Their hosts received them with warm hearts in open arms. A short while later, the two groups — the earlier Asona settlers and the new Aduana immigrants — decided together to move to a more open place where a new town, Agogo, as we grew to meet, was developed.[11]

Nephew: What was the original layout of the new town they named Agogo?

Uncle: It was a very carefully planned layout.[12] The early planners must have foreseen the future growth of their new town, and made adequate provision for its extension. In outline, the layout plan was this: a very wide street they named "Abɔnten-kɛsee" ran straight through the whole length of the town. On the left and right of the main street were blocks of plots for *aborɔnoo* (quarters) which were separated by wide (at the time) streets which ran into the *Abɔnten-kɛsee* at right angles. Each *abusua* developed a particular block to house its members. And so, as we came to meet the town, at the top end of the Abɔnten-kɛsɛ, on the left, was the Aduana *Borɔnoo*. A little down on the right was the Asona *Borɔnoo*.

---

[9] *circa* 1703-1705.

[10] *circa* 1703-1705.

[11] *circa* 1706-1708

[12] See Figure 2, p. 9.

Nephew:	Did each *abusua* do something to mark and distinguish its section?
Uncle:	Yes, they did. A shade tree, as was the practice of the period, was planted, after which a particular *borɔnoo* was named.
Nephew:	What tree was planted by the *Asonafoɔ* and which, by the *Aduanafoɔ*, to mark their respective *borɔnoo*?
Uncle:	*Gyedua* tree by the Asonafoɔ. It was planted by Nana Frempɔn Ako on a Thursday, hence the name "*Gyedua-Yaa.*" The *Aduanafoɔ* planted *atowaa* tree.
Nephew:	Oh, I can now understand. It was from those trees that the Asonafoɔ were referred to as "*Gyedua-Yaa-Asefoɔ*" and the Aduanafoɔ, "*Atowaa-Asefoɔ.*"
Uncle:	Exactly so.
Nephew:	Was any ritual involved in the planting of the *abusua* shade tree?
Uncle:	Certainly so. In all *abusua* tree-planting certain rituals were performed. Some things known only to the Elders of the *abusua*, including a few ounces of gold dust, were put into the hole and a libation poured before the tree was planted.
Nephew:	But why was all that done?
Uncle:	An *abusua* tree was planted to stabilize the lineage and to symbolize its existence. It was therefore regarded a sacred thing and had to be treated so. A harm done to it, in any way, was taken as wishing the particular lineage ill and the perpetrator was dealt with accordingly. In the case of *Gyedua-Yaa*, for instance, any person who struck it and caused its latex to flow was made to slaughter a sheep at once.
Nephew:	I can now understand why *Gyedua-Yaa* was so highly revered even though a tree. It was to the

	abusua, what a flag meant to other nations: "A small bit of bunting...an old coloured rag, but..."
Uncle:	*Gyedua* as a tree, yes. But *Gyedua-Yaa* was not an ordinary woody perennial plant. It was the embodiment of the Agogo Asona *abusua*. Consequently it deserved respect, not only from it own members but also from any other person who has the least regard for the entity of the lineage.
Nephew:	I appreciate that. And now Uncle, there is one other thing I have observed. At an annual *Akwasidεε-kεsεε* celebration, the Agogohene going in-State to perform a ritual at the Akogya Shrine stops at a point near the present-day Magistrate's Court building and alights from his palanquin. From there he walks to the Shrine and back before he is carried back home to the *Ahemfie*. Could you tell me what the significance of the particular custom is?
Uncle:	The point at which the Agogohene alights from his palanquin marks what were the outskirts (*nkwantia*) of the old Ɔpemkɔkɔ town. Even though the town ceased to exist long ago when its inhabitants moved to settle at the new site which was named Agogo, the memory of the deserted town (*Amanfoɔ*) has been preserved. Hence, by tradition, a reigning Agogohene crossing that point in-State is regarded as entering the town of the people he came to meet. He therefore shows his respect by so doing and in remembrance of the first dwellers of the ancient place (*Ɔde kae Nananom*).
Nephew:	Is any other custom observed at that particular spot — the point which you say marks what were the outskirts of Ɔpemkɔkɔ?
Uncle:	Yes. When the Agogohene has alighted, the Akyeamehene pours a libation to the *nsamanfoɔ* (the ghosts) of the Asona people who lived in the town which was deserted.
Nephew:	You are the present Akyeamehene. Could you tell me exactly what you say when pouring a libation at the time-honoured spot?

Uncle:	I pour down at the spot gin or schnapps drink and say:

"Nana Adwapo Koramoo, bɛgye nsa nom. Asonafoɔ nsamanfoɔ a, mo wɔ ha, mommɛgye nsa nom. Nana Agogohene (...Asimasi...), na ɛnnɛ ɔretwam akɔ Akogyaso akoma Akogya biribi adie; Mommɛgye nsa nom. Yɛrekɔ, momma bone bi nka obiara, na yɛnkɔ nsan mmɛsen nkodu ofie asomdweyem."

("Nana Adwapo Koramoo, here is a drink. All ye Ghosts of the Asona ineage present here, accept a drink. Nana Agogohene [...So-an-So...] is passing through today to give Akogya something to eat. Accept a drink. We are on our way to the place. Let not evil befall anyone, so that we reach the place and return home safely.")

Nephew:	All that Nana Akua Adwapa was telling us is becoming clear now. I suppose, Uncle, that there was inter-marriage among the two lineages, the Asona and the Aduana, as they lived in the opposite quarters of their new town.
Uncle:	Of course, there was, but not immediately. There were not yet many Asona women, but the few available were so comely, so handsome and so well-mannered and industrious that they were quickly snatched by the most influential among the Aduana men, including the Chiefs. Such "nobility marriage" (*adehye-wareɛ*) continued and reached the highest dimension when one of our ancestors was married to no less a potentiate than the Asantehene, Nana Osei Yaw. Kwaatemaa Animen, whose other name was Kwaane and who earned the appellation "Ɔhyeaka" (Liquidator of indebtedness). As you may have heard from Nana Akua, Kwaatemaa was the first of our ancestors, but not the least, to qualify for that high honour.
Nephew:	Yes, I remember the name quite well. Nana Akua, many a time, mentioned it but it was one of the many names I heard from her. They were all mere names to me at the time. Could you help me piece them together now? I wish very much

to know how you and I, for instance, fit into the long string of names.

Uncle:
The tracing of her ancestry was a daily song that Nana sang. I have told you many a time that the two brothers and their three sisters, who left the main stream moving from Akyem Abuakwa, settled at Ɔpemkɔkɔ. Their names, I repeat again, were: [the brothers] Adwapo Koramoo, the elder brother and the *Opanin* of the family who, consequently, was the first Agogo Asonahene, and Frempɔn Ako, the younger brother and the second Agogo Asonahene. He planted *Gyedua-Yaa*. And [the sisters]: Baduaa Asɔ, the eldest sister who had no child, Amena Kɔkɔ, the second sister, who bore Gyankɔmaa, Akwiamaa, the youngest sister, and...

Nephew:
Oh, yes. I remember. Gyankomaa's descendants, Nana said, came into possession of the famed *Ɔdomankama* Fetish and her descendants, from that time, have been referred to as "*Ɔdomankama Fie.*"

Uncle:
Exactly so. I was saying that the youngest sister, Akwiamaa, was the mother from whom all the other members of the Agogo Asona, not in the *Ɔdomankama Fie*, have descended. She bore two sons and one daughter. The sons were Yaw Dɛkyerɛ, the third Asonahene, and Akoayɛna, the fourth Asonahene. Her only daughter was Foriwaa Du. Foriwaa was her proper name but because she bore ten children she earned the other name "Du."

Nephew:
And who were her ten illustrious children?

Uncle:
The eldest child was Dansoaa Panin. After her came, in the following order of seniority: Oponwaa Akwasua, Agyɛpomaa Dapaa, Akwarimaa, Kwaaemaa Animen, also called Kwaame, Ofosuaa Nsia, Obiri Adaakwaa, and the only son who survived, Atwereboanna. Two of her children died young. Her fifth daughter, Kwaatemaa Animen, the name you have just heard, did not have any child. The other six did, and their descendants now form the remaining six sections of the Agogo Asona cognate lineage,

the seventh being the offspring of Gyankɔmaa or *Ɔdomankama-Fie.*

Nephew: From which of the six daughters did you and I descend?

Uncle: From the third, Nana Agypomaa Dapaa. She had only one daughter, Atewa Afua, who bore five children: three men — Obeng Panin, the sixth Asonahene, Kwasi Duro, and Kwaa-Kuwa (Ponamon) — and two daughters — Ama Pɔnkɔ and Awisi.

Nephew: Oh, Ama Pɔnkɔ. Was she who Nana Akua mentioned was her grandmother?

Uncle: Exactly so. Awisi had only one daughter, Amankwaa, and her sister, Ama Pɔnkɔ, had two daughters whose names were Ɔbema and Awuaa. Awuaa was childless, but Ɔbema bore five children, three sons — Yaw Kɔdaa (also called Amponsa Panin), Kwaku Dwira, and Kwaku Kuma (Amponsa II) — and two daughters — Afua Adɛm also called Gyaa, the elder one, and Akua Adwapa. The rest of the story, you should know.

Nephew: Yes, I am sure I know, but I must tell it to you for correction in case I am wrong. Nana Akua Adwapa bore two children — one son, Kwaku Amponsa, and one daughter, Adwoa Henewaa, your mother. I know that she bore you. You were her youngest son. Your other elder brothers were *Wɔfa* Kwaku Apea and *Wɔfa* Kwasi Agyare. Nana Afua Adɛm (Gyaa), I know, was the mother of five. Two sons, Kwadwo Bɔfoɔ (Nkansa) — he was our *Ofie-panin* for a long time and was also the Akyeamehene of Agogo many years — and Kwabene-Atɔbra, the younger son. Also three daughters: Yaa Kwaane, my grandmother, Yaa Kuma, and Adwoa Bruku (Tanewa), who had no child. I know that Nana Yaa Kuma bore four sons: *Wɔfa* Kwasi Sei, *Wɔfa* Osei Yaw Panin, *Wɔfa* Osei Yaw Kuma, and *Wɔfa* Yaw Nyame. She also bore a set of twin daughters, Ataa Pokuaa, the younger of whom died young. My grandmother, Nana Yaa Kwaane, was the mother of five daughters: Afua Nkameraa, Akua Agyei (Hannah, my mother), Yaa Asotu (also called Yaa Konadu Kyerewaa, who, I heard, died tragically when a maiden), and Adwoa Bona, also called Agyakoma. She also bore on son, Kwasi Opong (Christian).

Uncle: Eno Kwaane, you may not know, bore two other sons with her second husband. Their names were Kwadwo Anin and Kwaku Apea, but they both died in infancy.

Nephew: No, I did not know about that. What was the name of Nana's second husband?

Uncle: Kwabena Owusu. He was an Akyem man.

Nephew: And so this is how I descended:

Yaw Kyei (Thomas)
First son of Akua Agyei (Hannah), mother of five children, two of whom are living, namely Kwabena Kyei (Benjamin) and Ama Nkoso (Sophia) and two who died young, namely Kwame Kyei, Ama Afra and Akya Kyeiwaa
Hannah Akua Agyei
Daughter of Yaa Kwaane
Yaa Kwane
Daughter of Akua Adɛm (Gyaa)
Afia Adɛm (Gyaa)
Daughter of Ɔbema
Adwoa Ɔbema
Daughter of Ama Pɔnkɔ
Ama Pɔnkɔ
Daughter of Atewa Afua
Atewa Afua
Daughter of Agyepɔmaa Dapaa
Agyepɔmaa Dapaa
Daughter of Foriwaa Du
Foriwaa Du
Daughter of Akwiamaa
Akwiamaa
Daughter of an Asona woman who lived, died and was buried at Nsodua near Akrokyerɛ in Adanse, but whose name is unknown.

Uncle: You have done quite well. It is already a long line, but it continues to get longer and longer to infinity (*pɛ a enhun ano*).

Nephew:	Nana Akua often mentioned the names of some past Asona people with deepest affection and regards. Three such persons I very well remember were Ɔbɔfoɔ Duku, Kwaatemaa Animen and Obeng Panin. She did not explain to us why. Perhaps you know.
Uncle:	Ɔbɔfoɔ Duku was the son of Ɔhenewaa, daughter of Obiri Adaakwaa, the seventh child of Foriwaa Du. He took to hunting, the principal profession of his day, and became a brave, skillful hunter. His exploits in hunting won for him the recognition of the Agogohene Nana Toku, who honoured him by conferring on him the title, Atufoɔhene of Agogo.
Nephew:	Oh, that explains why there were two separate Black Stools in our lineage.
Uncle:	You are quite right. The other person you mentioned was Nana Kwaatemaa Animen. Her other name, as you have heard, was Kwaane. I have already told you, she married the Asantehene, Nana Osei Yaw. She was childless but a very wealthy woman. She did not keep her wealth to herself, but spent it generously on the needy members of the lineage. Her generosity won for her the appellation, "*Ɔhye-aka,*" (Liquidator of indebtedness), appropriately, because she was unsparing in bailing out her relatives who were in debt and in desperate need of help. Kind-hearted, industrious, highly intelligent and tactful, Kwaatemaa Animen, was a beloved wife. When she died, her husband, the Asantehene, caused a Black Stool to be consecrated to perpetuate her memory.
Nephew:	And where is the Black Stool now?
Uncle:	The Stool is in the custody of Kwabena Asadu, son of Adwoa Pɔ, a descendant of Akwarimaa, the fifth daughter of Foriwaa Du, and an elder sister of Kwaatemaa.
Nephew:	It must have been lying vacant for a long time now. Why has no one been appointed to occupy the Stool?

Uncle:	That, I am afraid, is a matter for all Asona people to decide.
Nephew:	And Nana Obeng Panin?
Uncle:	A great man. Nana Obeng Panin was the first son of Nana Atewa Afua and the Agogohene, Nana Amoako. Nana Akua Adwapa was her grandniece. He was enstooled the sixth Asonahene. An amiable, kind-hearted and wise leader, he was much loved and highly respected. In one of the several wars of the Asantehene against some people on the Coast, Nana Obeng Panin served in the *Gyaase* contingent of the Asante army and fought gallantly in the battle of Akantamansu.[13] He was wounded and brought home. His bravery in action was brought to the notice of Asantehene who sent to him a gift of *ntaa-nu* (twice £8—) to help pay the cost of his treatment (*n'ayaresa ka*). Such a gracious recognition of the exploits of a brave warrior, was a pride, not only to the person of Nana Obeng Panin, but to all the members of our *abusua*, past, present all those coming after him.

Inspired by the impressive record of the lineage to which I belonged, I could not help congratulating myself as I soliloquized:

---

[13] Ward has recorded the following account in his *A Short History of Ghana*: "One division of the Ashanti army was led by Opoku Frɛfrɛ, the brave, old gyasehene, and another by the Akwamuhene of Kumasi.... A British army was formed to meet the Ashantis, and on August 7th, 1826, the met by the little stream called Akantamansu, ten miles south of Dodowa...."(116) "...the British commander sent messages to the Denkyeras and the Akwamus to come back and help the centre. They came; but the battle stretched over four miles of country, and it took them some time to reach the place where they were wanted. Before they reached the place, some of the Christianborg people and some of the Accras had been driven back, and the Ashantis pressed farther forward still.... Then the British commander called up the white men. They came up with some cannon, and with a new weapon which the Ashantis had never seen before. This was the machine for shooting rockets — the same sort as those fireworks that we shoot into the sky — only to shoot them straight forward instead of upward. The rockets rushed among the Ashantis with long tails of fire, and exploded and burst into pieces, killing several men at once. The Ashantis could not stand this long. They broke and fled...."(118)

A worthy ancestor, Nana Obeng Panin, an Asonahene of Agogo in the past, fought bravely and distinguished himself at Akantamansu. Fearlessly, he faced a new British weapon, the *Asraman-tuo*. He was wounded fighting, but he survived.

Appendix 1: A 1983 Calendar of Some Asante Sacred Days

A 1983 CALENDAR (ASRANNA) of "NNA-BONEE" (SACRED DAYS)

Date	ƆPEPƆN January	OGYEFUYE February	ƆBENEM March	OFORISUO April	KOTONIMA May	AYEWOHOMUMU June	KITAWONSA July	ƆSANAA August	EBO September	AHINIME October	OBUBUO November	ƆPENIMA December
1	Sat	Tues	Tues	Fri	Sun	Wed	Fri	Mon	Thur	Sat	Tues	Thur
2	Sun	Wed	Wed	Sat	Mon	Thur	Sat	Tues	Fri	Sun	Wed	Fri
3	Mon	Thur	Thur	Sun	Tues	Fri	Sun	Wed	Sat	Mon	Thur	Sat
4	Tues	Fri	Fri	Mon	Wed	Sat	Mon	Thur	Sun	Tues	Fri	Sun
5	Wed	Sat	Sat	Tues	Thur	Sun	Tues	Fri	Mon	Wed	Sat	Mon
6	Thur	Sun	Sun	Wed	Fri	Mon	Wed	Sat	Tues	Thur	Sun	Tues
7	Fri	Mon	Mon	Thur	Sat	Tues	Thur	Sun	Wed	Fri	Mon	Wed
8	Sat	Tues	Tues	Fri	Sun	Wed	Fri	Mon	Thur	Sat	Tues	Thur
9	Sun	Wed	Wed	Sat	Mon	Thur	Sat	Tues	Fri	Sun	Wed	Fri
10	Mon	Thur	Thur	Sun	Tues	Fri	Sun	Wed	Sat	Mon	Thur	Sat
11	Tues	Fri	Fri	Mon	Wed	Sat	Mon	Thur	Sun	Tues	Fri	Sun
12	Wed	Sat	Sat	Tues	Thur	Sun	Tues	Fri	Mon	Wed	Sat	Mon
13	Thur	Sun	Sun	Wed	Fri	Mon	Wed	Sat	Tues	Thur	Sun	Tues
14	Fri	Mon	Mon	Thur	Sat	Tues	Thur	Sun	Wed	Fri	Mon	Wed
15	Sat	Tues	Tues	Fri	Sun	Wed	Fri	Mon	Thur	Sat	Tues	Thur
16	Sun	Wed	Wed	Sat	Mon	Thur	Sat	Tues	Fri	Sun	Wed	Fri
17	Mon	Thur	Thur	Sun	Tues	Fri	Sun	Wed	Sat	Mon	Thur	Sat
18	Tues	Fri	Fri	Mon	Wed	Sat	Mon	Thur	Sun	Tues	Fri	Sun
19	Wed	Sat	Sat	Tues	Thur	Sun	Tues	Fri	Mon	Wed	Sat	Mon
20	Thur	Sun	Sun	Wed	Fri	Mon	Wed	Sat	Tues	Thur	Sun	Tues
21	Fri	Mon	Mon	Thur	Sat	Tues	Thur	Sun	Wed	Fri	Mon	Wed
22	Sat	Tues	Tues	Fri	Sun	Wed	Fri	Mon	Thur	Sat	Tues	Thur
23	Sun	Wed	Wed	Sat	Mon	Thur	Sat	Tues	Fri	Sun	Wed	Fri
24	Mon	Thur	Thur	Sun	Tues	Fri	Sun	Wed	Sat	Mon	Thur	Sat
25	Tues	Fri	Fri	Mon	Wed	Sat	Mon	Thur	Sun	Tues	Fri	Sun
26	Wed	Sat	Sat	Tues	Thur	Sun	Tues	Fri	Mon	Wed	Sat	Mon
27	Thur	Sun	Sun	Wed	Fri	Mon	Wed	Sat	Tues	Thurs	Sun	Tues
28	Fri	Mon	Mon	Thur	Sat	Tues	Thur	Sun	Wed	Fri	Mon	Wed
29	Sat	–	Tues	Fri	Sun	Wed	Fri	Mon	Thur	Sat	Tues	Thur
30	Sun	–	Wed	Sat	Mon	Thur	Sat	Tues	Fri	Sun	Wed	Fri
31	Mon	–	Thur	–	Tues	–	Sun	Wed	–	Mon	–	Sat

Reference:
- XXXX — Memeneda-Dapaa
- ..... — Akwasidee
- Fɔdwoo
- Kwabena
- ♭♭♭ — Awukudee (Kwukupaakuo)
- Fofie

— ASANTE — NNABƆNEE (Sacred Days) Reckoning Chart

Reference:
- □ No of days after Akwasidee
- ○ No of days to Akwasidee

Appendix 2: Father's Family Tree

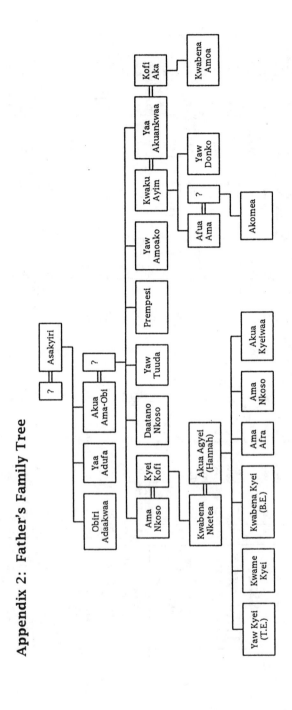

Appendix 3: Mother's Family Tree

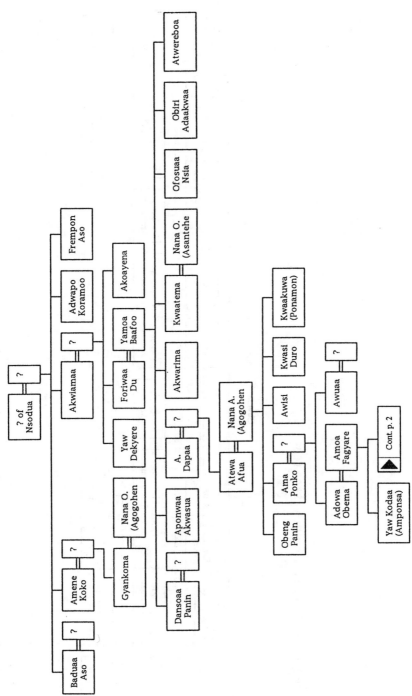

Appendix 3: Mother's Family Tree (cont'd.)

218

Appendix 3: Mother's Family Tree (cont'd.)

APPENDIX 4:   CROPS I SAW GROWN IN MY GRANDMOTHER'S AND MY MOTHER'S *MFIKYI-FUO* (FOODCROP FARMS) IN MY CHILDHOOD DAYS

A.   ASAASE-DUANE (Tuberous Crops)

     A.1   BAYERE (YAMS)

         A.1.1   -   AFASEE (Water Yams)
- Afase-pa
- Akwaati-bire
- Apoka
- Ko-ase-kɔhwe

         A.1.2.   -   BAYERE-PA
- Aso-bayere
- Baye-dee
- Dabreko
- Eyere
- Krukrupa
- Kuntuo
- Mensa
- Mpakyiwa
- Nana-nto
- Pasadwo*

         A.1.3   -   NKAMFOO

     A.2   AMAMKANI (Cocoyams)
- Amankani-pa
- Amankani-atwibo
- Amankani-kooko*

     A.3   BANKYE (Cassava)
- Bankye-pa*
- Bede-kofi**
- Bankye-Kalabaa**

     A.4   ABORO-DWOBAA - Sweet Potato*

B.   ASI-DUANE (Grains)
- Aburoo (Maize or Corn)
- Adaduanan-mmuroo**
- Emoo*

C.   ESORO ADUANE (Plantains)

     C.1   BORODEE (Plantains)
- Apantun
- Apem
- Nwiritia

     C.2.   KWADU (Bananas)
- Asante-kwadu*
- Borofo-kwadu
- Alata-Kwadu*

D.   ATOSO-DEε (Vegetables)

     D.1   ADUA (Beans)
- Adua-apea**
- Adua-apatram
- Adua-pa
- Adua-asontem

                       Akyii - (Bambara beans)
                       Ase-due
                       Nkate-pa - (Groundnuts)
                       Osaman-nkatee**

D.2   AMAKO (Peppers)
                       Ama-akati
                       Amako-pa
                       Amako-huam
                       Ahenemma-nsatee
                       Ntonkom

D.3   NNUADEWA (Garden-eggs or Egg Plant)
                       Atropo
                       Nnuadewa-pa
                       Nsusuwa*

D.4   OTHER VEGETABLES
                       Gyeene - (Onions)
                       Nkruma - (Okro)
             Tomatoes** - (Tomatoes)

E.   OTHER CROPS
            Aborobe - (Pine-apples)
            Ahwereε**
            Akaka-duro-pa**
            Akakaduro-kɔkɔ*
            Akam*
            Akatewa
            Boofere - (Pawpaw)
            Efere* - (pumkin)

NOTE :

* Crops seen grown only by my grandmother.
** Crops seen grown only by my mother.

APPENDIX 5:   NOTES AND GLOSSARY OF SOME AKAN WORDS USED IN THE TEXT

ababaawa	(pl. *mmabaawa*), a young woman, married or unmarried.
aberantɛɛ	(pl. *mmerantɛ*), a young man, married or unmarried.
abɛkwan	oilpalm soup, (see *nkwan*).
aberɛbeɛ	a wild animal of the cat's family (see *mmoa*).
aberewa	(pl. *mmerewa*), an old woman.
aboadeɛ	a thing or things, including money, promised as payment or reward to a fetish, a medicineman, a healer or an occultist, when a cure or other request sought brought through him was effected successfully.
abɔfo-nnwom	(a compound word: *ɔbɔfoɔ*, hunter and *dwom*, a song). Hunters' dirge, sung generally on occasions connected with the killing of a big game, such as an elephant.
abusua	(pl. *mmusua-kuo*), lineage. A group of persons who trace their descent through the mother to a common ancestor. I grew to know the following eight *mmusuakuo* living together in their separate *aborɔnoo* (quarters). (see Fig. 2)
adaduanan	fortieth day, roughly, from the occurrence of some notable event, such as the death of a person, when certain customary rites have to be performed. (see *nna-bɔnee*)
adowa	an antelope, (see *mmoa*).
aduan-kɛseɛ	(a compound word from *aduane*, food or a meal and *kɛseɛ*, big, grand.) *Aduan-kɛseɛ* was therefore a special, grand meal prepared by a bride and formally presented to the groom soon after the marriage formalities had been completed and the couple became traditionally recognized husband and wife.
aduro	medicine, for healing sickness and diseases, for killing or for success in some enterprise to be undertaken.
adwokuo	a fish-trap woven with palm- or raffia-branches or cane.
adwen	a generic name for all fishes in rivers, (see *nsuom-nam*).
afena	a state sword, hence - *afena-soanii*: a state sword bearer.
afoofi-di-da	the word has, for lack of a better one, been used in the text for days of the week during which some light work was done in and around the house, generally on Tuesdays, Thursdays and Fridays. Sunday, the Sabbath for Christians, was a light work day for some non-Christians. *Afoofi-di-da* has been used in contradistinction to *afuom-da*. (see below)

afrinhyia-pa an uninterrupted run of time for 365/366 days from a particular date, hence: *Afrinhyia-Pa*, a wish in the form of greeting for a happy return of the year.

afuo a farm, a clearing in which some crops were under cultivation.

afuom-da one of the three days in the week on which, generally, hard concentrated farm-work was done in cashcrop farms some distance away from town. The days were Mondays, Wednesdays, and Saturdays, except when any of the days happened to be a *da-boneɛ*, a sacred day, for non-Christians. (see *da-boneɛ*)

ahenkwaa a stool servant who might either run on errands with a state sword; collect a Chief's fees in cash or in kind, or arrest litigants who swore the Chief's oath.

ahweɛ a method of fishing by which water of pools in streams was scooped with pans and wooden basins (*koroɔ*) to expose fishes and crabs to be caught with large raffia-spine sieves (*sɔne-yɛ*) and nets. *Ahweɛ* was a harmattan season engagement.

akɔm a fetish dance, hence - *akɔm-ase*: a fetish dancing place.

akranteɛ a grass-cutter. (see *mmoa*)

akokonin-kan first crow of the cock, which was used by long distance travellers as a signal for the very early morning start of a journey done on foot, before the alarm clock became available. The first crow was said to be heard around three o'clock in the morning.

akuaba a doll carved out of an *ɔsɛsɛ* or *ofruntum* tree.

akumaa a husband's sister, or a woman's brother's wife.

akwanso-sa a customary drink offered to welcome a visitor/guest.

amam-merɛ tradition, belief, custom, law, etc., orally transmitted from one generation to another.

amane latex from *agyaamaa* tree, called *ɔpɔweɛ*, was tapped and co-agulated for sale for export. *Ɔpɔweɛ-bɔ* was a flourishing business in some parts of Asante in the latter part of the last century and continued into the first decade of the present one. *Amane-mmɔ* drew many young men of Agogo to distant places north in the Bono (Brong) area and in the adjacent areas in the Ivory Coast. One such place whose name was commonly known in the town was Bahuren. It was a favourite *aman-mmɔ* centre where many young men of the town drifted, in search of fortune. Many returned with cash and property, but a few others died and were buried there.

amaneɛ a message or purpose of a visit, hence - *amane-bɔ*: delivering a message or stating the purpose of a call or visit.

amanfrafoɔ (sing. *omanfrani*), a non-native of a place; an alien.

aman-nɛ   (lit. things of the state), ways or usages of a people.

anohyira   (lit. mouth-blessing), a ritual performed by a man on the weekday of his birth to purify, cleanse or sanctify his soul (*ne kra*). It was generally carried out after an escape from some misfortune, a disgrace or disaster. It was also performed to incite the Soul to jubilate on a man's unexpected triumph or success in some daunting venture, or to propitiate an aggrieved soul within him.

anuu   a method of fishing by drugging the leaves of *ɛhweɛ* shrub; or with the latex of an *akane* tree.

anwenhema   a monkey (see *mmoa*).

anwonomoo   a plant which bore a single broad leaf which was commonly used as wrapper. The stalk of the plant was used in making mats (see *kɛtɛ*).

apaafoɔ   (sing. *ɔpaanii*), hired labourers for any service, hence - *kookoo apaafoɔ*: persons, generally women and young men, hired to carry cocoa purchased in Agogo and its cottages to the buying centre at Asokore.
- *kookoo-paa*: hired cocoa load carrying business.

apakan   (pl. *mpakan*), a cane basket for carrying goods, such as smoked fish and game meat, pots of palmwine and palmoil, salt and other articles. *Apakan* was also the name of a long cane basket in which a Chief was carried on State functions.

aprapra-wonsan   a meal prepared with ground fried corn, palmoil, onions and some smoked herrings (*ɛman*), spiced with *prɛkɛsɛ* fruit.

asamando   the dwelling place of the Dead (cf: Hades of the Greek mythology); the abode of the departed spirits.

asoɛ-yɛ   a rest-stop on a footpath, cleared and "furnished" with seats of pieces of logs and wooden racks for holding headloads.

Asomasi   So-and-So. A name used in referring to a person whose name was suppressed.

asratoa   a tree which bore fruits whose dried husk was used for storing snuff, hence - Asratoa: a snuff box.

asrɛnɛ   a cocoa-drying mat made from raffia palm, oilpalm tree branches or by cane. Asrɛnɛ was also commonly used as a screen at the entrance of doors, hence the saying: - "Asrɛnɛ-dan mu yɛ na." (It is difficult to see the inside of a room with an *asrɛnɛ*- screened entrance.)

atifii   the top end, hence
- *asu-tifii*: toward the source of a river.
- *asu-naafoo*: toward the lower end of a river.

atɔdwɛɛ   direct planting of seeds into the soil on the farm without first nursing them for transplanting.

atuduro	gunpowder.
atuntuma	an outhouse with a small yard complete with a bathplace, a kitchen and storage places all attached to a compound house of an elderly man.
awareɛ	marriage, recognized as such when customary formalities had been performed and the union "stamped" by the giving of head-drink (*tiri-nsa*) to the woman's head of "Family" (*Ofie-Panin*). *Mpena-wareɛ* was the cohabitation of a man and a woman when the head drink (*tiri-nsa*) had not been formally given.
aye-fa-deɛ/ aye-farɛ	an amount of money paid as customary compensation to a husband by another man who had an illicit sexual dealing with the husband's properly married wife. The *ayefarɛ* rates chargeable in Agogo were fixed and graduated according to the husband's status in the community
bruka	localised form of the word "Broker," an agent employed or contracted to purchase cocoa direct from farmers for expatriate produce buying firms whose offices and "yards" were established at various urban centres in the cocoa growing areas.
buronya	Christmas.
daa-noo	a name given to good quality Dutch or Manchester wax print cloths (see *ntama*).
da-boneɛ	(lit. a bad day, pl. *nna-bɔneɛ*), a sacred day. Sacred days occurred once in a period called *Ada-duanan* (fortieth day). Precisely, the cycle is a forty-two-day one. On *nna-bɔneɛ* the living Chief and Stool Elders, as well as fetish priests/priestesses, through libation pouring and the offer of ritual meals, communed with the spirits of departed Chiefs, Elders and the *Abosom* (fetishes) in the town. Six *nna-bɔneɛ* were observable in Agogo. Two of these, devoted to the service of Stools, were: *Akwadidɛɛ* (on a Sunday) and *Awukudɛɛ* (on a Wednesday).
dadaso	a farm cleared and cultivated in a previous year. Its extension for the current year is *foforom*, the prefix "*afu*" is often omitted.
dua	(pl. *nna*), a tree.
dudo	a decoction of bark(s), root(s), leaves, herbs, for medicinal use.
dufa	a traditional healer's pill, made of some ground herbs, barks and/or roots, moistened with water and formed into small balls of various sizes.
dware-sɛn	an earthenware bath pot for men. A wife who lived with her mother in a separate house boiled and sent warm water in a *dware-sɛn* to her husband's house for his bath.
dwem-tae-deɛ	an amount of money which was to be deposited at a Chief's court before an oath case was heard. Pre-payment of the fixed amount was binding on both the swearer and the respondent of

the oath. A litigant who lost his case forfeited his *dwem-tae-dɛ*.

di bem   to be found not guilty, or to have one's case decided in one's favour.

didi-pon   a small short table on which meals for men in a household were served. It was one of the early morning duties of boys in the house to wash their elders' *didi-pon*.

di nse   to swear by a fetish (*ɔbosom*),
a. to testify one's innocence, or
b. to commit one's self to the faithful discharge of an obligation or undertaking. It was held that a swearer invoked unto himself or herself a curse if the oath was violated or was sworn in vain.

ɛman   smoked herring brought from the coast to sell at local markets. It was a popular food item for the preparation of soup in Agogo, especially in our farm villages.

Eno-waa   an affectionate address to a mother (i.e., Mother Dear!).

esa   a hardwood tree popular for its sharp, hard burning fire.

ɛsɛ   a swish-built platform raised in a room, about 6 to 12 inches high, on top of which mats were spread for sleeping.

ɛsɛn   a court-crier at *Ahemfie* who cried: "*Yenti! Tie-e-o-o...A, Yentie!*" (Oyez, Oyez! Let all present listen!).

funuma   the navel; the umbilical cord.

gye-birie   charcoal.

gyedua   a shade tree. Different trees were used for planting as shade trees at convenient places in the town. Under their shades people in the neighbourhood rested during the day. The most popular tree was the one itself called "*Gyedua.*"

gyentia   a short piece of wood with live-fire at one end. Handy ones were carried in place of match box to make fire on the farm.

hyire   a white clay dug and used for white-washing walls of buildings before quick-lime was introduced. *Hyire* was also refined into powder which was used on several ceremonial, ritual and other occasions.

kɛtɛ   a sleeping mat. Mats locally woven in Agogo were named after the materials with which they were made.

kookoo   a cash crop grown in forest areas. It was introduced into Agogo by the pioneer Basel Mission Church Elders in the late 1890s.

kra   the soul or spirit of a person.

kunkuma	*kunkuma* was said to be the greatest *suman* (charm) in Asante and the father of all asuman.[1] A fetish priest/priestess initiated into its cult was believed to have become immuned to all counter-attacks by any other *ɔbosom*.
kuse!	an exclamatory word expressing pleasure, uttered after the last gulp of a drink, as the dredge was rolled on the ground.
kwae-bibrem-hene	The Monarch of the Deep Dense Forest: a title applied to the leopard.
kwae-fuo	a farm in a forest area, generally one for cash crop such as cocoa.
mfikyi-fuo	foodcrop or vegetable farm on fallow land not far away from town or village, generally worked by women. Listed under Appendix 4 are foodcrops I saw being grown in my mother's and grandmother's *mfikyi-fuo* in my childhood days.
mma	(sing. *ɔba*), off-spring; children.
mmaa-mma	children of male members of an *abusua* are, individually or as a group *mmaa-mma* to the lineage. To any such child, male or female, a male member of the *abusua*, be he a grown-up or a young person, is *Agya* (father), and a female member of the *abusua* is a *sewaa* (father's sister).
mmoa	(sing. *aboa*), living creatures possessing sensation and power of voluntary motion. In this context, Man is excluded from mmoa.
Mmoadoma-kurom	an imaginary township of Birds and Beasts we heard spoken about in our *Ananse*-story telling time (*Ananse-sɛm to berɛ*).
mmoatia	*mmoatia* were said to be some short creatures in the shape of man, but with their heels pointing forward and toes backward. They were said to be cave-dwellers in dense forests; had magical powers; were invisible; communicated with one another by whistling, and were fond of bananas, their chief food. They were regarded, in the main, as mischievous creatures who abducted young children and carried them into their caves where they were fed with boiled eggs and mashed yam mixed with rich palm-oil (*ɛtɔ-kɔkɔɔ*).
mmukyia	traditional fire cooking stove which was a set of either three earthenware pots specially made for purpose, or supports of some three conically-shaped mounds, moulded by mothers themselves and were fixed at a convenient place in the yard (*adiwo*) or at a spot in a room set aside for use as a kitchen (*egya-ase*).
mmusuo	a calamity; disaster; misfortune; misery.
ɛnam	meat.

---

[1] Christaller, *Dictionary of the Asante and Fante Language*, (Basel: Basel Evangelical Missionary Society, 1933), 271.

nku	shea-butter; pomade.
nkuraa-tena	cottage to cottage round of visits.
nkwan	soup. The common ones in our childhood days were: - *abεkwan*: palm soup - *abε-duro*: medicinal palm soup - *nkatekwan*: groundnut soup - *nkrawa*: plain (pepper) soup - *ntohuro*: meatless soup (on rare occasions when there was no meat of any kind in the house)
nkyεmfe-hena	potsherd.
nkyereε	a primitive men's latrine erected with wood in the form of inclined platform.
nnaawɔtwe	eight days; a week, hence: - *nnaawɔtwe-da*: eighth day celebration or observance of an important event, such as the death or birth of a person.
nna-bɔnee	bad days, "bad" in the sense that they were sacred (see *da boneε*).
nnanso	hunting camp.
nno	oil (understood to be all vegetable in our childhood days) hence, - *abε-nno*: palmoil - *adwe-nno*: palm-kernel oil - *kube-nno*: coconut oil - *nkate-nno*: groundnut oil.
nnomaa	(sing. *anomaa*), birds.
nnuadwea	fruits of egg-plant commonly called garden-eggs.
nnuane	(sing. *aduane*), a meal; foodstuffs, either harvested or growing on farm (see Appendix 4).
nsamanfɔ	(sing. *ɔsaman*), spirits of dead person; ghosts, hence: - Nsamampom: a burial grove; a small wood in which dead persons were buried before modern cemeteries (*asie-yε*) were planned.
nsennerε	shingles; thin pieces of wood prepared mainly from logs of *amire* tree, used for roofing buildings in Agogo prior to the introduction of corrugated iron sheets in the 1910s.
nsεnia	a portable weighing scale which "brokers" carried with them to cottages, or from house to house, in Agogo for the purchase of cocoa beans direct from farmers.
nsɔsɔɔ-bɔ	brushing-off of weeds around the town, generally done communally by men in Agogo before the introduction of the Local Government system (in the modern sense of the word) into the country.

nsuom-nam   (lit. meat from rivers), meat of fish and other creatures which lived in water.

ntama   cloth worn in one-piece by men or in 3-piece by women, known as *ɔsoro ne fan ne kaba*. *Ntama* could also mean an uncut piece by the unit of *ɛpo*, of twelve yards. The unit of 24 inches wide was a short piece, *mpotrawa* and the long-piece unit of 36 inches was *apo-kɛsɛ*. Quality uncut piece of wax print cloth was called *daa-noo*

ntama-go   a worn-out piece of cloth; rag.

nte-hoo   money paid to a Stool Servant (*ahenkwaa*) by parties on oath-swearing case as a sort of summons fee.

nto-asɛ   a deposit for purchase of goods or service to be rendered. In the text the word has been used in the sense of payment made in advance to a herbalist or a medicine-man, before treatment was started.

ntonkom   a species of pepper.

ntwoma   red-ochre clay collected from pits at particular spots called *atwoma-mena*. It was kneaded into balls and preserved for daubing (*kwa*) floors of a swish-built platform (*ɛsɛ*) in bed rooms or of plant *pato* (open-end) rooms.

ntwoonoo   a roofed entrance to a yard of a compound house.

nufusu   milk.

nwa   a snail.

ɔbaatan   a woman nursing a baby; a mother.

ɔberempɔn   a great, powerful man of wealth and noble birth.

ɔbosom   It was, and still is, a belief held by some people that *ɔbosom* is a spirit which is less powerful than God, *Onyame Tweaduampɔn, Tete Kwakoramoa*. These lesser spirits, held to be a creation of *Ɔdomankama a Ɔbɔɔ Adeɛ*, the Creater of All Things, are believed to dwell in inanimate objects, such as rivers, mountains, rocks and in some particular trees — all phenomenal objects in a locality. They, the lesser spirits, the *abosom*, are worshipped at, or near the place of their abode. This might have given the erroneous impression to many foreigners that it was the inanimate object which was worshipped. Such inanimate objects, believed to be the dwelling place of an *ɔbosom* are regarded sacred by its followers and worshippers in the same way that the Israelites, for instance, in compliance with God's warning through Moses, their leader, held Mount Sinai, the mountain on whose top Yahweh, the God of Israel, was said to have dwelt, sacred.

oburonii   a generic word for pink-skin persons from overseas commonly called the "White-man".

oburumuu	a wild big game.
ɔdɔsɔ	a raffia fibre skirt worn by fetish carriers at fetish dances.
pato	an all-purpose room in a compound house with the side to the yard open. In it visitors were received, family members discussed and meals taken when the weather was inclement. Deceased members of the house were laid in-state (*deda efun*) in the *pato*. In time of need, it was used as a sleeping place, generally by boys of the house who were too old to share a bedroom with the parents. It was also used for the storage of harvested cocoa before the beans were sold to brokers.
pieto	a man's short underwear of cotton prints sewn by local tailors.
piren	a load of cocoa beans weighing 60 lbs., hence, - *piren-fa*: half a load of cocoa weighing 30 lbs.
Praso	The Agogohene's oath. It was consecrated by the Asantehene for Agogo and other Stools whose occupants suffered tragic death at Praso in one of the many Asante wars with the people at the other side of River Prah.
saawa	a small silver spoon made specifically for feeding a newly-born child (*asukɔnomaa*). It was made by a local silver-smith to the order of the father who presented it, together with other articles, to the child on the day it was named, generally on the eighth day of its birth (*nnawɔtwe-da*).
sa-koraa	a calabash for drinking palm-wine.
samina	soap. The soap in use, *samina-tuntum*, was made locally by women from the ashes of dried husks of plantains mixed with palm-oil.
sasa-boa	an animal said to possess powerful haunting spirit, *sasa*, such as *ɛkoɔ*.
Sasabonsam	a fabled, tall monster in human form whose abode was said to be on top of trees in dense forests. It was said to have extraordinarily long legs which could be shortened or lengthened telescopically at the monster's will.
suminaso	dunghill; a rubbish dumping place.
tawa	imported leaf-tobacco.
tɛnee	a torch made of dry palm branch-stalks.
tiafi	a place of convenience (latrine), hence - *kɔ tiafi*: off to toilet. - *bɔ tiafi*: dig a pit for use as latrine.
tiri-nsa	(lit. "head-money"), a drink, then worth 1s. 6d (*ntakuo-mmiensa*) given by a man to the head of a woman's "family" (*Ofie-panin*) to "stamp" a marriage contracted. Returning the amount to the husband by the wife's *Ofie-panin* registered the effective dissolution, by consensus, of the marriage.

toa	a calabash for carrying water, palmwine and other liquid.
wawa-abena	a split-bark of an ɔwawa (tree) log.
wɔntɔn	a tree which was easy to propagate and was used in several places for growing as a shade tree (*gyedua*).
yare-dɔm	plague; epidemic disease
yareɛ	(pl. *nyarewa*), sickness, illness; ailment; disease; malady.
Ye'amanfoo-so	the ruins of our former town or settlement abandoned.
Yefiri tete	The Agogo Asona drum and horn language. Interpreted, it means "Our existence is primeval."
Yɛma wo adware	an expression of gratitude for a meal received: "Thank you for a nice and welcome meal."
Yentie! Tie O-O- A!	a cry for silence made intermittently by a court-crier at an assembly whenever the Chief was addressing the people.
yi no dwem	to honour a friend, a relative or a lover in public by bestowing on him/her a token gift in cash or some petty gifts while dancing. To follow or face a dancer on floor with the index and second fingers of the right hand raised in a "V" shape, is another way of congratulating and honouring a beloved dancer publicly.

APPENDIX 6: "In Sum"

A Humble Contribution to the Development and Progress of the Gold Coast (Later, Ghana) in General, and of Asante and Agogo, My Home Town in Particular

THOMAS ERNEST (YAW) KYEI
Born in November, 1908

	Formal Education
1915-1917	Infant Classes 1 to 3 in the Agogo Basel Mission (later, Scottish Mission) Infant School.
1918	Pioneer pupil of the first Standard 1 Class at Agogo when the Local Infant School was extended to Standard 1 with effect from January 1, 1918.
1919-1920	Standards 2 to 3: Bompata Scottish Mission Central School.
1921-1923	Standards 4 to 6: Abetifi Pioneer Scottish Mission Senior School.
1924-January to May	Standard 7: In the Kumasi Scottish Mission Senior School.
August to December	Continued at the Juaso Government School — One of the pioneer Standard 7 pupils presented by the School for its first Standard 7 Examination.
	Professional Training
1925-1927	At Accra in the Government Teacher Training College (among the first batch of students to do the extended four-year Teacher Training course).
1928	Continued in the Prince of Wales' College, Achimota, (one of the Achimota pioneer students when the Government Training College in Accra was absorbed and removed to Achimota).
	Educator of the Nation's Children in Asante for 15 Years
1929-1943	Taught pupils in every class, from Infant Class 1 to Standard 7, in all Government Schools then in existence in Asante (including Brong/Ahafo at the time) as follows:
1929-1930	Mampong Junior Trade School (Literary Instructor)
1931-1935	Sunyani Government School (Mixed)
1936-1938	Juaso Government School (Mixed)
1939-1943	Kumasi Government Boys' School.

Planner of Primary and Middle School Education Development in Asante, 1944:

A member (later, leader) of an Education Survey Team assigned the task of carrying out a survey of all existing facilities for Primary as well as Middle School education in Asante (including Bono-Ahafo) and submitted recommendations to the Chief Commissioner of Ashanti, for expansion, new openings and absorption of existing "non-designated" primary schools and "permitted/private" middle schools, into the public system.

Ashanti Social Survey, 1945/46:

Was seconded to the ASHANTI SOCIAL SURVEY in 1945 as Principal Research Assistant. A Survey undertaken at the instance of the West African Institute, had as its aim: "to get a broad, general picture of the social and political structure of Asante (as in the 1940's) and investigate aspects in which ecological and economic factors play a bigger part."

The members of the team were: Dr. (later, Professor) Meyer Fortes, Anthropologist, Leader; Mr. (later, Professor) Robert W. Steel, Geographer; Miss Peter Ady, Economist.

Based in Kumasi, the team carried out its field-work in various towns and villages in Asante, with the support and co-operation of the Chief Commissioner, Asantehene, President of the Asante Confederacy Council, *Amanhene* (Chiefs), Missionary bodies and people of Asante.

Further Education and Professional Studies Overseas, 1946-1948:

Was awarded a scholarship under the Colonial Welfare and Development Fund for further professional training at Oxford in the University Department of Education, in the course of which, I was granted a special dispensation by the Hebdomadal Council of the University to be entered in 1947 for the post-graduate Examination in Theory, History and Practice of Education for a Diploma in Education.

Took a special six months' course in Social Anthropology at the Oxford Institute of Social Anthropology.

In the Senior Service of the Gold Coast (Later Ghana) Government, 1949-1960:

Assistant Education Officer attached to the office of the Asante Regional Education, Kumasi with the task of assisting teachers in primary and middle schools in the Region to teach effectively.

Was posted to Sunyani for a sort period to take charge of a District Office that had been opened there.

On Secondment to Social Welfare and Community Department, 1951:

Was attached to the Mass Education team of the Department set up to undertake mass adult literacy drive started in the Volta Region and to be continued in Asante.

Was assigned the task of Field Organizer for operation in the following places: Booyem (now in the Brong-Ahafo Region), Achinakrom and Sekyedomase.

Promoted Education Officer, 1952-1956:

Put in charge of newly created, separate Kumasi District, which included Juaso and Goaso sub-districts, 1952-1956. Principal task: to ensure maintenance of high standard of teaching and discipline in primary and middle schools in the district.

- Assistant Education Officers were stationed at the following convenient centres to assist teachers in their work: Ahenkro (near Offinso), Achinakrom, Bechem, Goaso, Juaso, Kuntanase, Nkawie, Ntonso, Teppa.

- An Emergency Training Centre for 6 weeks' concentrated training of pupil teachers, was opened at Antoa and removed later to Offinso.

Service in the Volta Region (then, Trans-Volta Togoland):
Promoted Senior Equation Officer and transferred to the T.V.T. where my service to the nation continued as District Education Officer in charge of Ho District, later removed to Kpandu.

Regional Education Officer:
For a few months, District sub-offices, manned by Assistant Education Officers, were opened at Anfoega, Dzolokputa, Jasikan, Ho, Hohoe, Peki, Nkonya-Wuropon.

On relieving duty:
Tamale: Regional Education Officer, Northern Territories (including the present Upper East and Upper West), for six months; Kumasi: Regional Office (then including Brong/Ahafo); Koforidua: Eastern Region (including the present Greater Accra region).

Posted back to Ho:
Volta Region, as substantive officer in charge of the Region in the year of Ghana's Independence (1957).

Promoted Principal Education Officer, 1958:
Posted to Headquarters to hold the schedule of Principal Education Officer/General Duty.

On two months' relieving:
Cape Coast, then Western Region, comprising the present Western Region.

Posted back to Koforidua:
As substantive Regional Education Officer, from where I retired from Ghana Civil Service in November, 1960.

Post-retirement contribution to the course of education in the country:

A representative of two major U.K. educational publishers for ten years:
Messrs Evans Brothers Limited, London, and Messrs Edward Arnold (Publishers) Ltd., London. Had the opportunity of advising on suitability of books to be published for use in the country.

Voluntary service on Board of Governors of several higher institutions in Asante, including the following:
- Agogo Presbyterian Women's Training College
- Agogo State Secondary School (Chairman)
- Akrokerri Training College (Chairman)
- Bompata Training College (later Secondary School) (Chairman)
- Konongo/Odumase Secondary School
- Kumasi Academy (Chairman)
- New Edubiase Training College (later Secondary School) (Chairman)
- Osei Tutu Training College (later Secondary School) (Chairman)
- Osei Kyeretwie Secondary School
- Toase Training College (later Secondary School)
- Yaa Asantewaa Girls' Secondary School (Chairman)

On an Important National Assignment, 1972:
Appointed a member of Commission of Inquiry — Duffor Traditional Area, set up by the President of the Second Republic of Ghana with the following terms of reference:

The Commission shall inquire into the claim that the towns of Finte and Frankadua and the villages of Ahovikope and Norvekope and their surrounding lands are part and parcel of the Duffor Traditional Area and consequently should form part of the Volta Region. In determining whether the said towns and villages are part and parcel of Duffor Traditional Area the Commission should consider the following matters:

(a) whether or not the people in the said towns and villages are Ewes;
(b) whether or not the people in the said towns and villages have any cultural and linguistic affinity with the people in the Duffor Traditional Area;
(c) whether or not the people in the said towns and villages owe allegiance to the ancestral stool of the Duffor Traditional Area.

The Commission shall report its finding to the President stating whether in the light of its findings the said towns and villages are part and parcel of the Duffor Traditional Area and consequently should form part of the Volta Region.
The Commission had as its members:
• Mr. Justice F. K. Apaloo, Chairman
• Nana Wiafe Akenten II, Omanhene, Offinso Traditional Area, member
• Dr. A.K.P. Kludze, University of Ghana, Legon, member,
• Mr. J.K. Essiem, Barrister-at-Law, Sekondi, member
• Mr. T.E. Kyei, Retired Civil Servant, member
• Mr. E. Tetteh, Secretary

Humble Contribution to the Progress and Development of Agogo, My Home Town
"Self-help," now a common place word and a cliché in the air every day heard from places all over the country, is not new to the people of Agogo. They have practiced it, not merely in words, but truly and realistically for many decades.
It has been a source of pride to me to have been given the opportunity and the trust to play a humble role in many self-help projects planned, executed and properly completed for the improvement of our town in the fifties, sixties and seventies of this century.
That humble role was played through:
• full and prompt payment of my share of monetary contributions;
• careful supervision and diligent direction and control of expenditure on all projects undertaken by direct labour;
• accounting properly to the people at regular intervals for all money they had paid toward a particular project, and;
• intensive education in the purpose and usefulness of the project, and the need for contributing willingly for its execution.

Of the many self-help projects undertaken and completed during the period of our stewardship, the following are, for the purpose of this exercise, considered worth mentioning:
• the construction of Fifire River bridge (grant from the central government received for payment of part of cost);
• construction of Kurowire River bridge (cocoa tax);
• a temporary shed (corrugated Iron sheet) for the Agogo State secondary school at the old site (voluntary contributions);
• the Agogo Post Office building (graded contributions from members of the Agogo Improvement Society and Central government grant of £200);

- construction of the Agogo Local Council Hall and offices (housing Ghana Commercial Bank (by direct labour paid for from central government grant);
- Agogo State Secondary School: A two-story block of building at the permanent site, and one single-story structure, furnished and equipped (cocoa tax);
- schools housed in buildings constructed at new permanent sites:
    i. Methodist primary and middle schools on the other bank of Kurowire;
    ii. Roman Catholic Primary and Middle School on a permanent site along the Resthouse road;
    iii. L.A. Primary 2 — a double stream school; L.A. 6 — Middle School on the abandoned State Farm; L.A. 7 — Middle School along Anane-krom road.

Honoured by Asanteman in 1991:

Awarded a certificate signed by Asantehene, Otumfuo Opoku Ware II "in recognition of his outstanding contribution towards the welfare of the people and development of Asanteman in particular and Ghana in general on the occasion of the *Adae Keseε* held in February, 1991.

INDEX

About the Author and Editor

T. E. KYEI (1908–1999) was educated at the Agogo Basel Mission School and the Scottish Mission Schools in Bompata, Abetifi and Kumasi. He completed teacher training at the Accra Government Teacher Training College and Achimot College. Kyei spent his life as a teacher, civil servant, and an ardent student and recorder of Asante culture and history.

JEAN ALLMAN is a member of the Department of History at the University of Illinois. She is also co-editor for Heinemann's Social History of Africa series.